Using PC-File®

Trudi Reisner

Using PC-File®

Library of Congress Catalog No.: 90-64397

ISBN: 0-88022-695-1

93 92 91   4 3 2 1

Interpretation of the printing code: the rightmost double-digit number is the year of the book's printing; the rightmost single-digit number, the number of the book's printing. For example, a printing code of 91-1 shows that the first printing of the book occurred in 1991.

Screens reproduced in this book were created using Collage Plus from Inner Media, Inc., Hollis, NH.

This book is based on PC-File, Version 6.0

Publisher: Lloyd J. Short

Associate Publisher: Karen A. Bluestein

Acquisitions Manager: Rick Ranucci

Product Development Manager: Thomas H. Bennett

Managing Editor: Paul Boger

Book Designer: Scott Cook

Production Team: Michelle Cleary, Mark Enochs, Brook Farling, Sandy Grieshop, Audra Hershman, Betty Kish, Phil Kitchel, Bob LaRoche, Laurie Lee, Tad Ringo, Linda Seifert, Louise Shinault, John Sleeva, Bruce Steed, Lisa Wilson, Phil Worthington

To Meryl Heller Yoffa

In appreciation of her encouragement and support

Product Director
Shelley O'Hara

Senior Editor
Jeannine Freudenberger

Production Editor
Betty A. White

Editor
Vickie West

Technical Editor
Andrew Young

Composed in Garamond
by Que Corporation

Trudi Reisner

Trudi Reisner is a computer consultant specializing in training users of IBM PCs and compatibles in the use of applications software. She is president of Computer Training Solutions, a Boston, MA, PC training and writing services company that provides training, writing, and consulting services.

Ms. Reisner was the first Marketing Support Representative in the country for Apple Computer in the National Accounts division. She wrote and illustrated the *Bitstream FaceLift for WordPerfect* software documentation manual for Bitstream Inc.

In addition to training hundreds of users in business applications through hands-on computer classes, Ms. Reisner also has trained the staffs of large corporations in the use of microcomputers and developed the written training materials used. Her books integrate both text and graphics to provide practical applications for new and experienced users.

Ms. Reisner is also the author of Que's *Allways Quick Reference, Quattro Pro Quick Reference, Using PC-Write,* and Sybex's *The ABC's of Q&A 4.*

TRADEMARK
ACKNOWLEDGMENTS

Que Corporation has made every effort to supply trademark information about company names, products, and services mentioned in this book. Trademarks indicated below were derived from various sources. Que Corporation cannot attest to the accuracy of this information.

CompuServe is a registered trade mark of CompuServe Incorporated and H&R Block, Inc.

dBASE is a registered trademark of Ashton-Tate Corporation

Epson is a registered trademark of Epson Corporation.

Hayes is a registered trademark of Hayes Microcomputer Products, Inc.

Hewlett-Packard and Laserjet are registered trademarks of Hewlett-Packard Co.

IBM is a registered trademark of International Business Machines Corporation.

Lotus and 1-2-3 are registered trademarks of Lotus Development Corporation.

Microsoft, Microsoft Excel, Microsoft Word, and Microsoft Windows are registered trademarks of Microsoft Corporation.

Okidata is a registered trademark of Oki America, Inc.

PC-File is a registered trademark of Buttonware, Inc., and is also a trademark of Jim Button.

Peachtext is a registered trademark of Peachtree Software, Inc.

PostScript is a registered trademark of Adobe Systems, Inc.

Snapshot is a trademark of Design Software.

The Source is a service mark of Source Telecomputing Corporation, a subsidiary of the Reader's Digest Association, Inc.

WordPerfect is a registered trademark of WordPerfect Corporation.

WordStar is a registered trademark of MicroPro International Corporation.

Trademarks of other products mentioned in this book are held by the companies producing them.

ACKNOWLEDGMENTS

I owe thanks to many others who helped complete this book. Foremost are Shelley O'Hara, who edited the manuscript and gave suggestions and support throughout the life of this project; Betty White, production editor; Vickie West, copy editor; and Karen Bluestein, publishing director, who suggested the project.

Special recognition must also go to: Lloyd Short, Publisher; Terri Solomon, Acquisitions Editor; Mary Bednarek, Product Development Manager; Jerry Ellis, technical advisor, and the entire production staff for their support.

Thanks to Dee Dee Walsh, Marketing Communications Manager at Buttonware, for providing helpful information on the history of PC-File and for supplying the copies of the documentation and software that I needed to write this book. Thanks also to Eric Teutsch, Technical Support Manager at Buttonware, for his technical support.

CONVENTIONS USED
IN THIS BOOK

The following conventions used in this book have been established to help you learn to use the program quickly and easily. As much as possible, the conventions correspond with those used in the PC-file documentation.

1. Text the user should enter from the keyboard appears in italics. Both DOS commands and PC-File commands that the user enters are shown in lowercase italics because it is not necessary to type them in uppercase.

2. Throughout the text, Enter is used instead of Return to refer to the Return key on the keyboard.

CONTENTS AT A GLANCE

TABLE OF CONTENTS ▼

III   Working with PC-File Records

IV Working with Other PC-File Features

Introduction

PC-File, by ButtonWare, is a fast and powerful, full-featured database manager program used to track and monitor, edit, query, and print any kind of information. It also has graphing, report writing, letter writing, label generation capabilities, and complete compatibility with dBASE files.

The first version of PC-File was released in 1983 for IBM-PCs and IBM-compatibles. Several upgrades that include PC-File III, PC-File/R, PC-File+, and PC-Filedb followed the first release, making major milestones for PC-File. Each upgrade contains new features and enhancements that improve the database manager program. PC-File 5.0 was released in January 1990 and contains major enhancements including mouse support, telephone dialing, improved dBASE index compatibility, multiple input screens, a maximum of 128 fields, PostScript printer support for graphs, and multiple subtotal levels.

The latest version, PC-File 6.0 was released in January 1991 and offers a windows-like interface as well as many improvements that make the program friendlier and easier to use.

Where Can You Get PC-File

Earlier versions of PC-File have been available through Shareware, which is a distribution method for selling software through an information network such as CompuServe and The Source. PC-File has been one of the most popular Shareware database manager programs around. You can still purchase earlier versions of PC-File through the shareware system, but version 6.0 is not being offered through Shareware or any other shareware system.

PC-File version 6.0 is available from Egghead Discount Software, PC Connection, CompuAdd, Soft Warehouse, Walden Software and Electronics Boutique, and most other software vendors.

You also can buy PC-file directly from Buttonware. Buttonware's address is P.O. Box 96058, Bellevue, Washington, 98009.

PC-File 6.0 currently is available for $149.95. The complete package consists of PC-File disks, a Getting Started book, a User's Manual, a Tutorial manual, and a discount on the next release of PC-File, as well as discounts on the purchase of other ButtonWare products. The products include PC-Type, a word processor program or PC-Calc+, a spreadsheet program. If you register by phone through Buttonware, call 1-800-JBUTTON and in addition to the PC-File software, you will receive a free PC-File application. You can choose from either Business Contacts, Accounts Payable, or Home Inventory software.

Registered users can call for help with technical questions anytime by dialing ButtonWare technical support at 1-900-454-8000. The first minute of the call is free, and every minute thereafter you are charged $1.00 per minute. You also can call for technical support through CompuServe, Canada Remote, and Button-Net, Buttonware's in-house assistance. Currently, there are 700,000 copies of PC-File used by business professionals, non-programmers, and other computer users both domestically and internationally.

What Makes PC-File Unique?

PC-File became popular so quickly because it is easy to learn, simple to use, very powerful, and inexpensive to buy. Its versatility lets you use it in business, corporate, and home, as well as educational environments, and the program makes it fun so that you might not even realize you're actually working.

PC-File has all the usual database manager features you would expect to find in a flat file database program—that is, a simple data storage program. For example, the program offers you standard database commands such as search, retrieve, modify, index, sort, and print. The standard report generation features let you design and print your own reports in various formats such as page, row, mail label, and free form. There are advanced report commands for creating a custom tailored report.

Advanced database manager features are linking multiple databases, mail-merge for producing form letters and labels, and graphing for creating line, bar, and scatter graphs, and pie charts. PC-File lets you access your dBASE databases to create customized reports, graphs, and mailing labels without leaving the PC-File program. Another powerful feature lets you import and export data between PC-File and other programs such as Lotus 1-2-3, WordPerfect, Wordstar, Microsoft Word, and many more. Some unique features such as mouse support, network support, auto dialer, macros, a calculator, password protection, and Drop to DOS make PC-File 6.0 a flexible and sophisticated flat file database program.

What's New In Version 6.0

In PC-File 6.0, you can select commands from pull-down menus with the keys or the mouse. With the new menu structure, you save hundreds of keystrokes. In earlier versions, PC-File might have required six or seven steps to perform a task. Now you can perform a task in one step. You can find a database, reports, letters, and graph files on any drive and directory at any time by selecting the file from a list displayed in a File Selection dialog box. In addition, Buttonware has improved the Help screens so that you can scroll through them to see more detailed information on specific features.

Now you can define a database in one step, whereas previous releases of PC-File would take six steps. In earlier versions of PC-File, you entered a dBASE command string to create indexes. Now in PC-File 6.0, you simply point and click to menu selections with the mouse or use the key to create an index instantly. You can also modify and delete records in Table view.

Most PC-File users will be glad to know that you no longer have to use complex ASCII codes to modify your macros. Instead you can use plain English. By using record mode you can create up to 27 macros with a maximum of 1,000 characters each.

In previous versions of PC-File, you had to exit PC-File to use PC-Label, the labels program, the file packing utility, and several other utilities. Now you can access these programs by selecting a command from a pull-down menu from within PC-File.

In PC-File 6.0, you can specify Read-only mode to prevent users from changing a database, while allowing them to browse and search through the database.

What Can You Use PC-File For?

You can use PC-File to keep track of all the sorts of information you can imagine: mailing lists, membership lists, accounts payable and receivable, personnel records, inventory—any record-keeping task you want to perform for your office. You also can track information for your personal needs such as a collection of recipes, sports statistics, photographs, stamps, or coins.

You can custom design your reports to print selected records or all records in your database. You also can use the letter writing feature with mail-merge commands to create personalized form letters and produce mailing labels. You can graph the database by creating a line, bar, pie, or scatter graph to represent numeric information in a picture format.

PC-File's macros feature lets you record and replay frequently used information and commands as macros. You can store frequently used phone numbers in PC-File's auto dial feature that will automatically dial any phone number directly from your database.

Why a Book about PC-File?

Mastering PC-File basics is easy; however, it is important to learn the advanced features and develop a good sense of database skills to get the most out of the program. PC-File helps you store and retrieve information in the easiest and best possible way, but not everyone will be able to produce exactly what they want without getting advice from other PC-File users or studying databases.

Using PC-File helps solve the problems of both novice and experienced users. This book offers tips and hints to help you store and retrieve information produced from a wide variety of databases ranging from a customer list, a mailing list, a dBASE file, and sales reports to form letters, mailing labels, an autodialing phone log, and a line, bar, scatter, or pie graph.

This book is not intended as a substitute for Buttonware's excellent documentation. Instead, *Using PC-File* is a practical guide that goes beyond the basics of the manual and provides practical examples and hints for using the program in an office and home environment.

Who Should Use This Book

No matter what your background and experience, you will need to learn new methods and terms when you enter the world of databases. This book brings together the special vocabularies of the database user and computer operator to explain clearly the concepts from these disciplines, which are merged in database applications.

Whether you plan to buy PC-File soon, you just purchased it, or you already use PC-File at work or at home, you should consider reading this book. If you are new to database programs and feel a little intimidated by computer programs in general, this book helps you quickly master the basics.

Although PC-File looks easy to use, most beginners find it difficult to be productive and learn a computer program at the same time. You might find yourself struggling through the simplest tasks and concepts if you have had little experience with PC-File or a similar program. *Using PC-File* can quickly become your reference tool and can give you the basic information necessary to consistently store and retrieve information quickly and easily. This book may even stimulate your imagination so much that you may want to move ahead to learn the advanced features in a shorter period of time rather than trying to learn the program on your own.

If you are an experienced PC-File user and want to sharpen your database skills, this book helps you develop the proficiency needed to produce complex reports, mail-merge applications, and graphs. Even the most experienced PC-File users occasionally may not be able to design a perfect report, document, or graph the first time. *Using PC-File* contains step-by-step instructions to help you learn new techniques quickly along with numerous examples and tips to help you develop advanced skills.

Although this book is addressed to the latest PC-File program, those using the earlier versions of PC-File on the IBM also will find these examples and suggestions useful.

How To Use This Book

The best way to use this book is to start at the beginning and read through to the end. You will benefit from the logical sequence of ideas and be able to understand the concepts as they are introduced. If you're new to PC-File, you may find that the fastest way to learn how to use the program is to get hands-on practice with the Quick Start lesson in Chapter 2. If you're an experienced user, you may want to skim quickly through the basic material presented in Chapters 2, 3, and 4 and then jump right into Chapter 5, "Adding Records."

All users, however, should read Chapter 1, "Getting Started," to learn more about the fundamentals of databases and PC-File's technical specifications. This chapter gives you a good overview of the concepts you need to think about before you even start the program.

What Is in This Book

Using PC-File is divided into four main sections, plus two appendixes, including a quick reference section.

Part I, "Learning the Basics," provides an overview of working with a database and explains the fundamentals of database design.

Chapter 1, "Getting Started," demonstrates how to start the program, introduces you to parts of the PC-File screen display, basic maneuvering techniques, the PC-File menus, and the on-line Help feature, and shows you how to exit PC-File.

Chapter 2, "Quick Start: Create a Database," introduces and reinforces some key concepts. After you complete the sample database, you should have enough confidence to get started producing your own database, even as you continue working through the remaining chapters.

Chapter 3, "Designing a Database," teaches you how to design a database from beginning to end. It provides an overview of database concepts and the fundamentals of preparing a database, including database terminology and PC-File technical specifications. You examine various ways to communicate your ideas effectively by using PC-File and gain deeper insight as to what constitutes a good working database.

Part II, "Creating Database Files," teaches you everything you need to know about designing a database as well as adding, searching and retrieving records in the database.

Chapter 4, "Creating a Database," shows you how to create a database using the Fast method and the Paint method.

Chapter 5, "Adding Records," shows you how to display a list of existing database files, select existing database files, and add records to a database, and teaches you how to enter data in records in various ways.

Chapter 6, "Searching for Records," introduces you to PC-File's Find feature to search for records in a database using a simple search. Using formula and global search commands to find specific records is discussed. You also learn how to display specific records in a database.

Part III, "Working with PC-File Records," explains how to modify and update records in a database. You examine PC-File's special editing commands for changing the data in your records. This section also shows you how to index and sort records in various ways. Changing the design of a database file is also explored.

Chapter 7, "Modifying Records," shows you how to navigate through records with the keys and the mouse in Record view and Table view. This chapter steps you through working with PC-File's editing commands to edit data in records. You learn how to use the Restore command to undo editing commands. Deleting and undeleting records are also explained.

Chapter 8, "Indexing Records," demonstrates working with PC-File's indexing feature and teaches you how to reorganize records in ascending and descending order. You also learn how to perform index operations by creating, switching, deleting, and renaming indexes.

Chapter 9, "Changing the Design of a Database," discusses all aspects of restructuring the format of your database file. You also learn how to manage PC-File functions which include copying, renaming, and deleting files. This chapter also shows you how to use the Drop to DOS feature to exit PC-File temporarily and run DOS commands and other programs from the DOS prompt. Exporting and importing data are also discussed.

Part IV, "Working with Other PC-File Features," brings everything you learned in earlier chapters together. This section introduces generating reports, merging documents for producing form letters and labels, and creating graphs. You also examine how to pack databases, create macros, and explore PC-File's autodialing feature.

Chapter 10, "Generating Reports," shows you how to create and print reports. You see the power of PC-File's report formats so that you can create and print impressive and professional-looking reports.

Chapter 11, "Producing Form Letters and Mailing Labels," shows you how to produce form letters using PC-File's mail-merge feature. This chapter shows you how to use PC-File's Snapshot and PC-Label features to produce mailing labels. You also learn how to incorporate mail merge formatting commands in a merge document to enhance the appearance of your form letters.

Chapter 12, "Creating Graphs," walks you through creating bar, line, scatter, and pie graphs. You also learn how to print the graphs.

Chapter 13, "Using Other PC-File Features," provides you with information on packing databases. You discover how to repair damaged databases. You explore PC-File's autodialing feature. You learn how to create macros to automate your work in PC-File.

Appendix A, "Installing and Configuring PC-File," is especially provided for the benefit of new PC-File users who need extra help setting up PC-File.

Appendix B, "Quick Reference," presents a complete list of PC-File's hot keys. Use this section to refresh your memory and to access information quickly.

Enjoy *Using PC-File*, and you'll benefit from the many useful tips offered in this book.

Part I

Learning the Basics

Includes

Getting Started

Quick Start: Creating a Database

Designing a Database

1

Getting Started

B efore you begin using PC-File, you will want to read Appendix A on installing PC-File and configuring your system. This chapter describes the fundamentals you need to know to operate PC-File. You learn how to start and exit the program and how to identify different parts of PC-File's window. Then you move on to selecting menu commands and using the Help system. If you're new to PC-File, plan to read this chapter in sequence.

Starting PC-File

You can start PC-File in three ways—from a floppy disk, from the hard disk, and from Windows. This section discusses each of these methods.

Starting PC-File from a Floppy Disk

In a PC-File floppy disk installation, there are two basic steps:

- Preparing the program and data disks
- Starting the program from a floppy disk system

You need to create a working program disk by copying the PC-File program disk on to a 5 1/4-inch floppy disk. PC-File's program disk has no copy protection, so you may make as many copies of the program disk as you want.

Additional disks must be formatted to store the PC-Files you create.

To make a working program disk, format a disk as a system disk with the /S switch option (see your DOS manual if you need help with this step). This process formats the disk and copies part of the DOS operating system onto it. This disk becomes your PC-File start-up disk. Label the disk PC-File Working Disk.

When you are ready to copy the original program disk to your newly formatted disk, follow these steps:

1. Replace the DOS disk in drive A with the original PC-File program disk.

2. Replace the formatted disk in drive B with the newly formatted system disk labeled PC-File Working Disk.

3. Type *copy* *.* *b:* and press Enter.

After the copying is complete, you are ready to start the PC-File program.

NOTE

To prevent damage or wear to your original program disk, use your PC-File Working Disk for day-to-day work. Store the original disk in a safe place.

Format two other disks and label them PC-File Data Disk.

To start PC-File from a floppy disk, follow these steps:

1. Insert the PC-File Working Disk in drive A and turn on your computer.

2. When prompted, enter the date and time (if your computer doesn't enter them for you automatically).

3. At the A> prompt, type *pcf* and press Enter to load PC-File into memory. PC-File's menu bar appears. (The menu bar is examined in detail later in this chapter.)

Starting PC-File from a Hard Disk

You can start PC-File from a hard disk to design a new database or work with an existing database. Make sure you begin at the DOS directory where you installed PC-File.

To start PC-File from a hard disk, perform these steps:

1. At the C> prompt, type *cd\pcfile* and press Enter to change to the PC-File directory.

2. At the prompt, type *pcf* and press Enter to load PC-File into memory. PC-File's menu bar appears. (The menu bar is examined in detail later in this chapter.)

You are ready to begin using PC-File.

Starting PC-File from Windows

If you are using Microsoft Windows, you can add PC-File as a non-windows application and start the program from Windows. Refer to your Windows documentation or see *Using Windows* published by Que Corporation.

To start PC-File from Windows, double click the PC-File icon. PC-File's menu bar appears. (The menu bar is examined in detail later in this chapter.)

You can begin using PC-File.

Examining the PC-File Menu Bar

When you start the PC-File program, you are presented with the PC-File menu bar. Figure 1.1 shows the screen you see after you start the program.

PC-File commands are listed in the menu bar at the top of the PC-File window. The nine command names describe the types of action the commands perform—file, edit, views, search, print, utilities, tools, macros, and help. For a complete list of PC-File commands, refer to the Quick Reference in Appendix B.

To access a command from the menu bar, you can use the arrow keys and press Enter or type the underlined letter in the command. For example, the letter *f* is underlined in the File command. You can type the underlined letter in upper- or lowercase. Alternate ways of selecting commands in PC-File are discussed later in this chapter.

Table 1.1 lists the commands in the menu bar, their letter keys, and the tasks these commands perform.

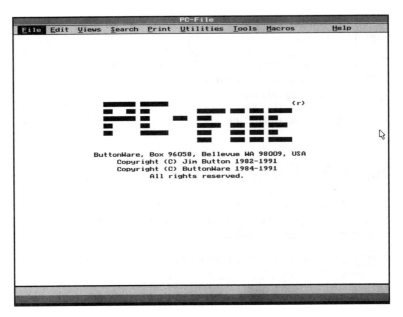

Fig. 1.1. The PC-File menu bar.

Table 1.1
The Commands in the Menu Bar

Command	Letter Key	Description
File	f	Opens, creates, closes, and saves database files; sorts records and performs indexing operations; exits PC-file
Edit	e	Adds, deletes, and modifies records in a database; performs global editing operations
Views	f	Shows records in a table or record view
Search	s	Searches and retrieves records in a database
Print	p	Prints reports and letters

Command	Letter Key	Description
Utilities	u	Exports and imports data from databases created with other programs, manages your PC-File files, configures the PC-File program. Also prints mailing labels, packs a database to compress unused space in the database file, repairs a damaged database, and prints a database description
Tools	t	Temporarily exits to the DOS prompt, automatically dials phone numbers, prints single labels, and performs calculations
Macros	m	Records, modifies, deletes, and loads macros
Help	h	Accesses the Help system

Examining the PC-File Screen

When you open a PC-File database file, you press f to select File, enter the name of the file, and press Enter.

The first record in the database appears in the PC-File screen. Figure 1.2 shows a record in the PC-File screen.

The PC-File screen is divided into six parts—the title bar, menu bar, work area, dialog box, button bar, and status line.

Title Bar

The title bar at the top of the screen displays the program name and the name of the open database. If you enter a description for the database, PC-File displays the description next to the database name. If no database is open, PC-File displays only the program name in the title bar.

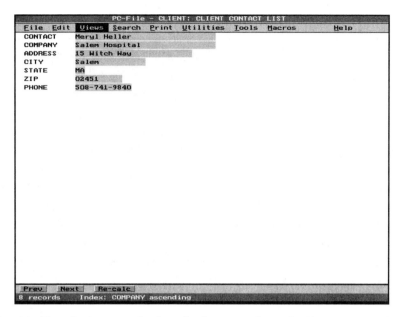

Fig. 1.2. *The PC-File screen displays the first record in a database.*

Menu Bar

The menu bar runs across the top of the screen under the title bar. It contains the main PC-File commands. When you select a command from the menu bar, PC-File displays a pull-down menu. From the pull-down menu, you can select commands to perform specific tasks.

Work Area

The work area takes up most of the PC-File screen and displays the contents of a file. Depending on where you are in the PC-File program, the work area may display a record, an edit window for defining a database, a report, or a letter.

Dialog Box

A dialog box displays in the bottom half of the screen when PC-File needs additional information to carry out a command. It can prompt you to complete or cancel the command or it can request information. If you are already familiar with Microsoft Windows dialog boxes, you will find that PC-File dialog boxes are similar and just as simple to use.

PC-File offers five different areas in the dialog box where you can enter information, depending on what kind of information is needed. These areas include command buttons, option buttons, text boxes, list boxes, and check boxes.

To move around in a dialog box with the keyboard, use the arrow keys or press the Alt key and the appropriate underlined letter. You can press the Tab key to move to the right or down and Shift-Tab to move up or to the left. To accept current options, press Alt-O or click the OK button with the mouse. To cancel the operation and return to the previous step, press Alt-C or the Esc key. Or, click the Cancel button with the mouse.

To move a dialog box with the keyboard, press Alt-F7. Then use the appropriate arrow keys to reposition the box. Once the box is positioned where you want it, press Enter.

To move a dialog box with the mouse, point at the title bar, hold the left mouse button down, and drag the dialog box where you want it.

If PC-File is set to graphics mode, the mouse pointer changes to the shape of a hand when you move the mouse pointer onto a title bar in a dialog box.

Command Buttons

Command buttons are rectangular buttons displayed in a dialog box. Figure 1.3 shows a sample dialog box with command buttons. The buttons have labels, such as OK, Cancel, Yes, No, All, and Quit to indicate what the buttons do. PC-File also displays the command buttons on the button bar, as discussed later in this section.

To select a command button with the keyboard, move the cursor to the command button you want, and press Enter or press the underlined letter. To select the OK and Cancel buttons, press Alt-O or Alt-C.

To select a command button with the mouse, click on the command button.

Fig. 1.3. A sample dialog box with command buttons.

Option Buttons

Option buttons are circular shaped buttons that are displayed as a group in a dialog box. Figure 1.4 shows a sample dialog box with option buttons.

You can select only one option at a time. For example, to print all the records in your database, you can press the Print option button labeled All records. Or you can print specific records by selecting the Some records Print option button.

To select an option button with the keyboard, move the cursor to the option button you want and press Enter, or press Alt and the underlined letter.

To select an option button with the mouse, click on the option button.

A sample PC-File screen provides a highlighted text box where you can type information into a dialog box. Figure 1.5 shows a highlighted text box in a sample dialog box.

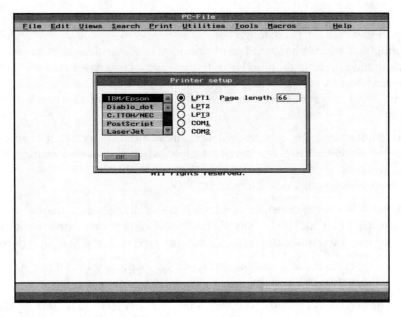

***Fig.** 1.4. A sample dialog box with option buttons.*

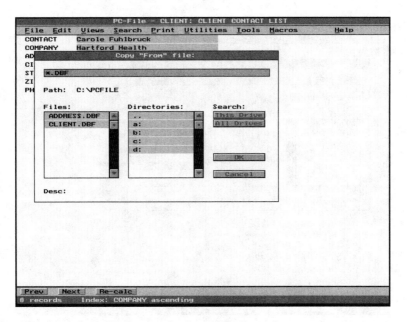

***Fig.** 1.5. A sample dialog box with a highlighted text box.*

There is a limit to the number of characters you can type in a text box. Some text boxes have a fixed length and allow you to type only within the highlighted box. Other text boxes are scrollable and let you type more information in the highlighted box. In this case, as you type in the text box, the text scrolls to the left. When you enter the maximum number of characters in a text box, PC-File beeps to indicate that you have reached the limit.

Sometimes a text box appears with text already in it. You can either accept the default text or type over it. For example, when you save an existing file, the file name appears in the text box. You can accept the current file name or type over it with a new file name.

When you move the cursor to a text box, PC-File changes the cursor from an arrow to an I-beam. The I-beam is a flashing curly vertical bar that indicates where you start typing and is sometimes referred to as the insertion point.

As you type, PC-File displays the text to the left of the I-beam, which pushes any existing text to the right.

A list box contains a menu of options. Some list boxes let you select only one option. Other list boxes, called check-off lists, allow you to select more than one option. Figure 1.6 shows a sample dialog box with a list box.

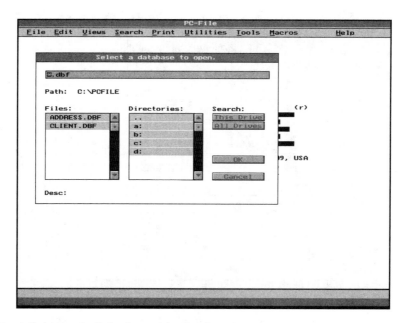

Fig. 1.6. *A sample dialog box with a list box.*

To scroll through a list box with the keyboard, use the up- and down-arrow keys. To select a menu option, move the highlight to the option you want and press Enter.

Often, a list box has vertical scroll bars when all available menu options do not fit in the list box. You can scroll through the vertical scroll bars with the up and down arrows. When you find the option you want, highlight it and press Enter.

PC-File gives you three ways to scroll through a list box with the mouse. You can click above or below the scroll box, click on the up or down scroll arrows, or drag the scroll box by clicking on the scroll box, holding the mouse button down, and dragging the box up or down the scroll bar. Once the menu option is highlighted, you can click on it to select that option.

Check-off list boxes let you select multiple options, and PC-File displays a check mark next to each option you select. Figure 1.7 shows a sample dialog box with a check-off list box. In some cases, if the order of selection is important, PC-File displays a number next to the check mark indicating the order specified. For example, when you want to print a report from a database that contains fields in a particular order, you can select the fields you want with check marks and numbers in a check-off box.

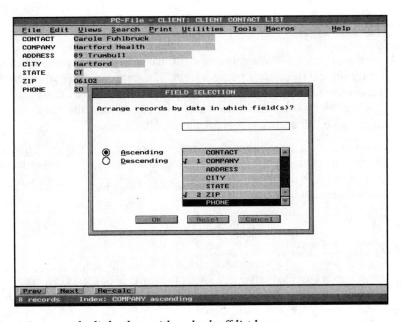

Fig. 1.7. *A sample dialog box with a check-off list box.*

To select an item in a check-off list box with the keyboard, use the up- and down-arrow keys to highlight the option and then press Enter.

To select an item in a check-off list box with the mouse, simply click on an option.

If you change your mind, you can remove all check marks and numbers by selecting the Reset button in the check-off list box.

Check Boxes

A check box is a square button in a dialog box that functions as a toggle. You select it once to turn an option on; select it again to turn the option off. PC-File displays an X in the box to indicate that the option you've selected is turned on. Figure 1.8 shows a sample dialog box with a check box.

To turn an individual option on and off with the keyboard, press the Alt key and the underlined letter of the box label.

To turn an individual option on and off with the mouse, click within the check box, not the label.

Button Bar

At the bottom of the PC-File screen, the button bar displays various buttons, depending on the operation you perform. The buttons work most easily with a mouse. For example, click the Prev button to move to the previous record, click the Next button to move to the next record, and click the Re-calc button to recalculate the formulas in the database.

If you do not have a mouse, use the hot keys. For example, press Ctrl-P to move to the previous record, press Ctrl-N to move to the next record, and press Ctrl-A to recalculate formulas. For a complete list of hot keys, refer to the Quick Reference in Appendix B.

Status Line

The status line is located on the last line at the bottom of the PC-File screen. It shows the number of records in the open database and the current index name.

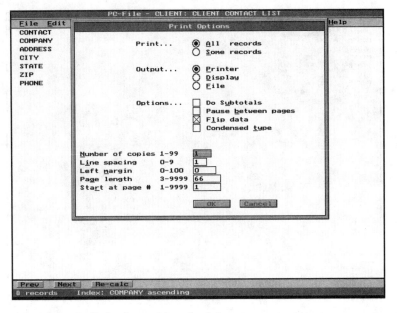

Fig. 1.8. A sample dialog box with a check box.

Using Pull-Down Menus

All PC-File menus branch from the menu bar, and PC-File commands are listed in the pull-down menus. Figure 1.9 shows the Edit pull-down menu. From the pull-down menus, you can select the command you need. For a complete list of PC-File commands, refer to the list of commands in the Quick Reference in Appendix B. This section describes how to access and use these pull-down menus.

There are four features about menu options that you need to be acquainted with—the active option, the grayed-out option, the ellipsis, and the check mark.

The active option is the black bar that points to the name of the command that is currently active. For example, in the Edit menu, the Add command is the active option.

The grayed-out option is a command name that appears grayed out in the menu. It means that the command is inactive and that you cannot use it at this time. For example, in the Edit menu, Modify mode is the grayed-out option.

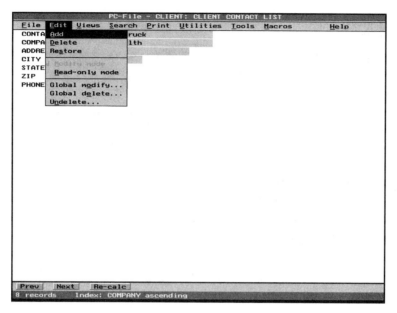

Fig. 1.9. *The Edit pull-down menu.*

The ellipsis (...) following a command name indicates that a dialog box will appear when that command is selected. For example, in the Edit menu, the Undelete command is followed by an ellipsis and displays a dialog box when selected.

The check mark option displays a check mark to the left of the command name. It indicates that one of two options is selected. For example, in the Edit menu, you can toggle between Modify mode and Read-only mode. You select the unchecked option to switch options.

Selecting Commands from Menus

PC-File provides three ways to select commands from menus. You can use the arrow keys, the letter keys, or the mouse. Novice PC-File users may find it easier to select commands by using the arrow keys at first. With some practice, you probably will prefer to use the letter keys as keyboard shortcuts.

Selecting Commands with the Arrow Keys

PC-File allows you to select commands from its menus with the keyboard. The highlighted bar pointing to a command indicates the command is current or active. In the menu bar, use the left- and right-arrow keys or the Tab key and Shift-Tab keys to move the highlighted block. Then press Enter to process your selection. In the pull-down menus, use the up- and down-arrow keys to move the highlighted bar and the Enter key to process your selection.

To see how pull-down menus work, begin by opening a database file. To select File Open from the menus, follow these steps:

1. Press Enter to select the File command from the menu bar.

2. Press the down-arrow key to highlight the Open command.

3. Press Enter.

Selecting Commands with the Letter Keys

Using the letter keys is a quick way to execute PC-File commands. The letter key corresponds to the underlined letter in the command name. For example, to select the File command, type the letter *f*. You can type the letter in lower- or uppercase.

To select the File Open command from the menus, follow these steps:

1. Type *f* to select the File command from the menu bar.

2. Type *o* to select the Open command.

Throughout this book, the letter key shortcut procedures are used.

If you are not in the menu bar or in a pull-down menu on the screen and you want to select a menu, press Alt and the underlined letter of the menu bar option to display the pull-down menu. For instance, press Alt-P to display the Print menu.

TIP

Selecting Commands with the Mouse

You can use the mouse to select commands from any PC-File menu. The mouse pointer appears as an arrowhead on the screen. Move the mouse pointer to the command you want to select and click the left mouse button.

To select the File Open command from the menu bar, follow these steps:

1. Position the mouse pointer on the command name File in the menu bar.

2. Click the left mouse button and then release it to open the File pull-down menu.

3. Position the mouse pointer on the Open command in the File menu.

4. Click the left mouse button and then release it to select the Open command.

Exiting Menus

You can exit a pull-down menu by pressing Esc. The pull-down menu disappears from the top of the screen. To exit a pull-down menu with the mouse, click at the very top of the screen. Then you can continue working on your database.

Using the Help Feature

If you do not know or cannot remember how to perform a task in PC-File, you can get fast on-line help. PC-File provides two kinds of help—Help Now and General Help.

Both Help Now and General Help are instantly available to you while you are working any place in the PC-File program.

Help Now

When you want to get quick help on a particular function, command, or task, you can use Help Now. This Help feature contains information about the current option, dialog box, or screen to help you accomplish tasks. You can access Help Now at any time and from any place in the program.

The Help Now feature is context-sensitive to the task you are performing. When you are in the middle of performing a task, you can get Help, read the relevant Help screen, and return to your work, ready to proceed.

There are two ways to access Help Now—choose Help Now from the Help menu or press the F1 Help HotKey. However, before you can get help on a topic, you must select a command or open a database. When you ask PC-File for help, it displays the Help information in a window on the screen.

To see how Help Now works, follow these steps:

1. Select File from the menu bar.

2. Select Open from the File menu.

3. Press F1 to access Help Now. The Help window appears on the right side of your screen, as shown in figure 1.10.

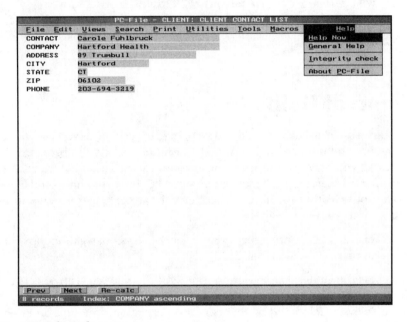

Fig. 1.10. The Help menu.

When Help information takes up more than one screen, you can scroll through the multiple screens one line at a time with the arrow keys. When you press the up-arrow key, the Help information scrolls up one line at a time so that you can view new information about the topic. When you press the down-arrow key, the Help information on the screen moves down one line at a time so that you can view the previous information again. You also can move around in the Help window with the mouse. You move the scroll box up and down in the vertical scroll bar on the right side of the Help window by clicking and dragging the scroll box.

4. When you are finished reading the relevant Help information, press Esc or select OK to exit Help and return to your original place in the program.

To get Help on any topic, simply press the F1 hot key. A Help window appears in the bottom right portion of the screen and provides information on the topic. When you have finished reading the relevant Help information, press Esc to exit Help and return to your original place in the program.

TIP

If a help screen is covering something you want to see, you can move the help window around the screen. Press Alt-F7 and then use the arrow keys to move the help window. With the mouse, move the mouse pointer to the title bar, press the left mouse button, and drag the window where you want.

General Help

If you're a new PC-File user and you want to learn PC-File as you go, you can get general help on any topic immediately after starting the program. For example, you may want to learn more about the program before creating your first database. If you're an experienced PC-File user and would like to learn about a feature you haven't used yet, you can get help on any new topic you want to learn more about.

The General Help option provides a list of keys, navigation tips, and information on PC-File menus.

To access the General Help option, press Alt-F1. You also can select Help from the menu bar and then select General Help from the Help menu. PC-File displays a Help window that contains general information on PC-File (see figure 1.11). To exit the Help window, press Esc or select OK. You are returned to your original place in the program.

Exiting PC-File

Before you exit the PC-File program, it is a good idea to save the files you are working on. In the event of a power failure, a program crash, or other disaster, saving your files with the File Save command will ensure that you won't lose any of your work. Instructions on how to use the File Save command are provided in Chapter 4 of this book.

Fig. 1.11. The General Help window.

To exit the PC-File program and return to DOS, complete the following steps:

1. Select File from the menu bar.

2. Select Exit from the File menu. PC-File displays an exit window. The number of records processed during the current session appears in the exit window.

3. Select Exit from the exit window. The DOS prompt appears.

If you change your mind, select Resume to return to PC-File.

If you are using Microsoft Windows, you are returned to the Windows Applications window in Windows.

Summary

In this chapter, you have learned how to start the PC-File program and you have been introduced to parts of the PC-File screen display so that you can identify them throughout this book and while using PC-File. You examined basic maneuvering techniques in the PC-File pull-down menus. You explored the on-line Help feature, and you learned how to exit PC-File. Now that you have been introduced to PC-File's menus and commands, it is time to begin to learn how to use them. In Chapter 2, you learn how to create a database from start to finish and develop some basic database skills.

Quick Start: Creating a Database

Getting started in PC-File is easy. Just follow the steps in this Quick Start lesson to create a typical database and get some hands-on experience with PC-File. When you complete this session, you will have a good understanding of how to create simple databases using PC-File. And you will be ready to start creating databases of your own.

First, you learn how to open a database file and give it a name so that you can store the file on a disk and recall it later. Then you are ready to learn how to design a database and add records to it.

In addition, you learn how to use PC-File's search and editing commands. You can search for specific information in your database and then use several editing commands to modify the records you've created.

You can change the order of the records in your database with the Sort feature. Using Sort, you can arrange records alphabetically and numerically in ascending and descending order.

When you are finished working on your database, you learn how to end the PC-File session by exiting the program.

 For the purposes of the quick start lesson, it is assumed that you are working on a computer with a hard disk.

Starting PC-File

To start PC-File, follow these steps:

1. Change to the directory containing the PC-File program by typing *cd\pcfile* at the C> prompt and pressing Enter.

2. At the DOS prompt, type *pcf* and press Enter.

PC-File appears on your screen, and you are ready to create a new database.

Creating a New Database

In this section, you create your first database from the PC-File window. PC-File offers two methods for creating a database: the Fast method and the Paint method.

When you select the Fast method, PC-File provides columns where you can enter your data. You can create a quick and simple database by entering the field names and defining the type of information you want to include.

If you select the Paint Method, PC-File allows you to enter information in a blank form on the screen. You create the structure and layout you want for your database.

For the purposes of this lesson, you use the Fast method to create your first database.

To create a new database file, follow these steps:

1. From the menu bar, press **f** to select File. PC-File displays the File menu.

2. From the File menu, press n to select New. The Which method? dialog box appears on your screen. Now you can select either the Fast method or the Paint Method.

3. Press **f** to select the Fast method.

4. Press Enter.

The Fast method screen design appears as shown in figure 2.1.

(For more information on creating a new database using both the Fast method and the Paint method, refer to Chapter 4.)

Now you are ready to start defining your database in the Fast method screen.

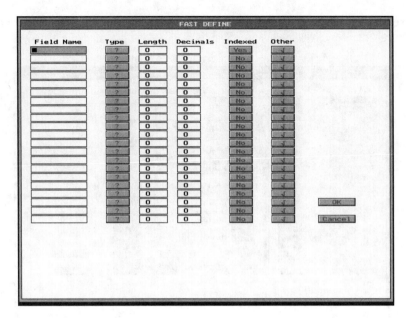

Fig. 2.1. The Fast method screen design.

Defining a Database

Before you can begin entering data in the Fast method screen, you must define the database you are creating.

Each record in a database is comprised of variable items of information called fields. For example, the fields in your database may include name, address, and phone number. To set up the fields the way you want them to appear in the database, you first must identify and format the field information in the Fast method screen.

As you can see in figure 2.1, the Fast method screen provides six columns for fields. The columns are labeled: Field Name, Type, Length, Decimals, Indexed, and Other.

In the first or Field Name column of the Fast method screen, enter a name to identify the kind of data you will be typing into the field. For instance, Last_Name indicates that only the last name should be entered in that particular field.

The Type field defines the kind of data contained in each field. This restricts the contents of the data you can enter in that field. The Fast method provides five field types: Character, Numeric, Date, Logical, and Memo as shown in figure 2.2.

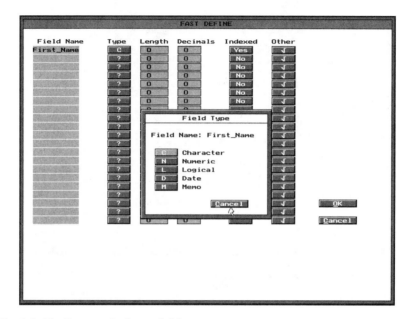

Fig. 2.2. *The Fast method type field pop-up menu.*

The Character field is generally used for text. The Numeric field stores numbers that can be used in calculations. The Date field type holds dates. The Logical field type displays true or false values in the field. The Memo field can contain text up to 5000 characters long.

A field length consists of the number of characters a field can contain. PC-File displays 65 characters in a field. If you have a field that requires more than 65 characters, you expand the memo field as explained in Chapter 5, "Adding Records."

The decimals column is where you indicate the number of decimal places you want to display for numbers in a numeric field only. The default number of decimal places is 0 (zero). The maximum number of decimal places is 8.

The Indexed column lets you organize the information in a field in a specified order. For example, you can index the names in a last name field in ascending order. The names are displayed alphabetically.

The last column, Other, allows you to enter a wide range of default data—the current date, calculations, a mask to define and limit the characters you enter in a field, a relational lookup, the current time, an automatic duplicate, and a unique number. For more information on Other field information, refer to Chapter 4, "Creating a Database."

To enter information on the Fast method screen, use the Tab key to move to the column you want and simply begin typing. To move to the previous column, use the Shift-Tab key. Some columns let you make choices from a pop-up menu.

When you're typing, don't worry about making errors. Correcting typing errors is a simple task with PC-File. If you do catch a mistake while typing, you can use the Backspace key, usually located in the upper-right corner of your keyboard, to erase the error. Pressing the backspace key erases one character to the immediate left of the cursor. Then you can retype your entry.

After you enter all the field information in the Fast method screen, you must give the database a file name and save it in a file on disk. For example, a database containing the names, addresses, and phone numbers of all your clients can be created and stored with the name CLIENT.

Suppose that you are entering field information in the Fast method screen to store typical client information for a biomedical company called Biolab. The client information consists of the contact name, company, address, and phone number.

You can enter the field names in capital letters so that they will look different from the data you input later. That way, you can tell the difference between the field name and the actual data within a field.

To define this database, complete the following steps:

1. To enter the first field name, type *contact* and press Enter. The cursor moves to the Type field.

2. Press Enter again. PC-File displays a pop-up menu that contains field types. Type *c* to select the character field type.

3. Type *30* and press Enter. This defines the field length.

4. Press Enter to skip the decimals column.

5. Press Enter again to indicate that you do not want the Contact field to be indexed. No appears in the Indexed column.

6. Press Tab to skip the Other column. The cursor moves to the second field name in the first column. You have now completed defining the field information for the first field (see figure 2.3).

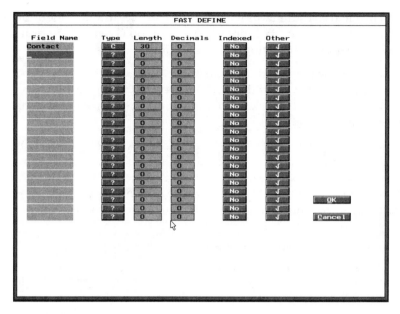

Fig. 2.3. *The first completed field in the database.*

7. To enter the rest of the field information, type the following information in the Fast method screen:

Field Name	Type	Length	Decimals	Indexed	Other
COMPANY	C	30		Y	
ADDRESS	C	25		N	
CITY	C	15		N	
STATE	C	2		N	
ZIP	C	10		N	
PHONE	C	12		N	

Figure 2.4 shows the completed Fast method screen.

8. To save the design of your database in a file, click the OK button on the right side of the Fast Method screen. PC-File prompts you to enter a name for the file.

9. Type *client* and press Enter. This saves the design of your database and all of the field information.

PC-File prompts you to enter a description for the database file.

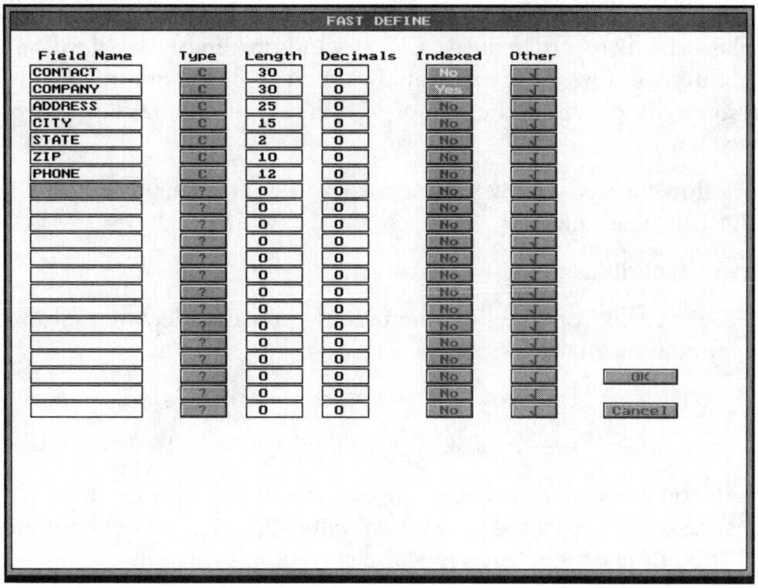

Field Name	Type	Length	Decimals	Indexed	Other
CONTACT	C	30	0	No	√
COMPANY	C	30	0	Yes	√
ADDRESS	C	25	0	No	√
CITY	C	15	0	No	√
STATE	C	2	0	No	√
ZIP	C	10	0	No	√
PHONE	C	12	0	No	√
	?	0	0	No	√
	?	0	0	No	√
	?	0	0	No	√
	?	0	0	No	√
	?	0	0	No	√
	?	0	0	No	√
	?	0	0	No	√
	?	0	0	No	√
	?	0	0	No	√
	?	0	0	No	√
	?	0	0	No	√

Fig. 2.4. The completed Fast method screen.

10. Type *client contact list* and press Enter. PC-File prompts you to enter a name for the index file.

11. Type *cli comp* and press Enter.

    PC-File displays a dialog box that confirms you have completed your entries in the Fast method screen.

12. Select OK to finish creating your database.

Refer to Chapter 4 for more information on defining a database. If you want information on how to change the design of your database, read Chapter 5.

Now that you have defined your database, you can learn how to add records to it, the topic of the next section.

Adding Records

A record is a collection of fields within a database file. Within the client database each client's account number, name, address, date, phone number, and purchase amount represents one record. If you include 25 clients' names, addresses, and phone numbers, you will have 25 records in that file.

To enter new data in a PC-File database, select the Edit All command. PC-File displays a blank record in the data entry window. Simply begin typing in the data entry window. In the first field at the top of the first record, PC-File automatically positions the cursor, a blinking horizontal line where you enter data.

The following steps show you how to add data for eight records in the CLIENT database file:

1. Select Edit from the menu bar.

2. Select Add from the Edit menu, and enter the following information for each field.

CONTACT	COMPANY	ADDRESS	CITY	STATE	ZIP	PHONE
Meryl Heller	Salem Hospital	15 Witch Way	Salem	MA	02451	508-741-9840

If you make a mistake, use the Backspace key to erase the error. Pressing the backspace key erases one character to the immediate left of the cursor. Then type the correct information.

Press the Tab key to move to the next field and use the Shift-Tab key to move to the previous field.

Figure. 2.5 shows the first record of your database.

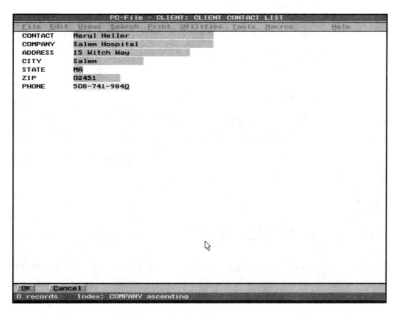

Fig. 2.5. *The first record of a sample database.*

3. When you have entered all of the data, press F10. PC-File displays the Add Record dialog box.

4. Select Yes to add this record to the database. PC-File clears the screen and provides you with a new, blank record for the next entries.

Follow these same steps to add the following records:

CONTACT	COMPANY	ADDRESS	CITY	STATE	ZIP	PHONE
Karen Giventer	Newton Clinic	8 Washington	Newton	MA	02330	617-966-3423
Cindy Verga	Jersey Hospital	100 Princeton	Princeton	NJ	07320	201-455-9083
Sam Malone	Boston City Health	222 Beacon	Boston	MA	02110	617-258-3409
Carole Fuhlbruck	Hartford Health	89 Trumbull	Hartford	CT	06102	203-694-3219
Terri Digiro	Hartford Health	89 Trumbull	Hartford	CT	06102	203-694-3218
Gary Kaz	Hartford Hospital	30 Seymour	Hartford	CT	06108	203-232-5800
Ed Cheffetz	Tampa Hospital	153 Eisenhower	Tampa	FL	33409	305-845-8937

6. When you are finished entering all of the records, press F10. PC-File displays the Add Record dialog box.

7. Select OK, then Stop Adding to add the last record to your database and exit from Add mode.

Refer to Chapter 6 for more information on adding records to a database. Now that you have added records to your database, you can search for specific information, as discussed in the next section.

Searching Records

Once data is stored, you can search and retrieve a single piece of information or a group of related data. Searching for information from the database is a procedure used to select what you want to see in the database while ignoring what you don't want to see.

PC-File offers many ways to search and retrieve information. The type of searches you can perform on a database range from simple to complex. You can use a simple search to find exact information, such as a specific phone number, for example. You can use a complex search to find values that have a meaning of larger, smaller, or equal to associated with it. For example, a date later than 03/01/91.

With the client records you have entered, you can use the Search Simple command to retrieve the records for all of the clients who are located in Hartford.

To search records, complete the following steps:

1. Type *s* to select the Search command from the PC-File menu.

2. Select Simple from the Search menu.

3. Select the City field.

4. Type *Hartford*. PC-File retrieves only the specified records containing a particular city, in this case, Hartford.

5. Select the OK button to begin the search. PC-File retrieves and then displays the first record containing the city you specified, as shown in figure 2.6.

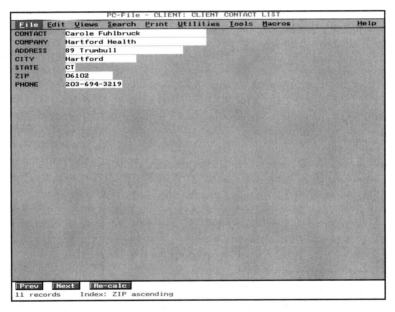

Fig. 2.6. The first record containing the city specified.

6. When you are finished looking at the first record, select the Search Again button to view the next record.

7. Use the Search Again button or press Ctrl-S to view each record one at a time. PC-File retrieves 3 records. The number of records retrieved displays on the Status line at the bottom of the screen. For example, 3 Records.

Refer to Chapter 6 for more information on searching records. Now that you have searched for the records containing the city of Hartford, you can learn how to make changes to records with the Modify command.

Modifying Records

You can explore PC-File's Table View command as you change the information in your records. PC-File gives you several ways to modify the records you retrieve with the Search command.

When PC-File is set to Modify Mode, you can delete and insert data at any time. In this section, you learn how to update records by typing over existing data with new data. You also learn how to delete a record using the Modify Delete command.

After you search for records in your database, you can make any changes to the information stored in the record. You position the cursor in the field you want to change and enter the new information.

Refer to Chapter 5, "Adding Records," for a detailed examination of these and other modify commands.

Suppose that two of the Hartford clients moved from Hartford to Cromwell. With the records you have retrieved, you can change the city very easily by typing over Hartford with Cromwell. One client, Hartford Hospital, is now doing business with a subsidiary of Biolab. You can delete the record to remove that information from the database.

To modify records, follow these steps:

1. The first record displayed on your screen should contain the city Hartford. If Hartford isn't displayed, refer to the section "Searching for Records."

2. Press the Tab key to move the cursor to the City field.

3. Type *Cromwell*.

4. Press Ctrl-S to view the next record.

5. To see the records in a table view, select Views from the menu bar. Then select Table from the Views menu.

Notice that two fields display across the table, as shown in figure 2.7. A maximum of 28 records can be displayed in the table at one time. You use the arrow keys to move around the table.

Fig. 2.7. Two fields are displayed in Table View.

You also can edit the records in the Table View.

6. To change the city for the second Hartford record, move to City field in the record and type *Cromwell*.

7. Press the down-arrow key to move the cursor to the city for the third Hartford record. Since Hartford Hospital is doing business with a subsidiary of Biolab, the Hartford hospital record should be deleted.

8. Select Edit from the menu bar.

9. Select Delete from the Edit menu. PC-File asks you to confirm deleting the record.

10. Select Yes to confirm the deletion. PC-File deletes the entire record and shows the Table View screen again without that record.

11. Select Views Record View from the menu bar to return to the PC-File window. Figure 2.8 shows the modified database in Table View.

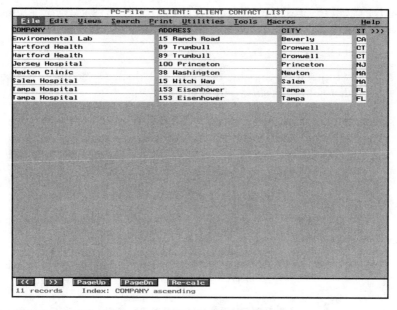

Fig. 2.8. *The modified database is displayed in Table View.*

Sorting Records

One of the major features of PC-File is its capability to sort records. You can easily rearrange records so that they appear in virtually any order that is convenient for you—alphabetical, numerical, or chronological.

The records for the CLIENT database were purposely not entered in any special order. You don't have to organize your paperwork before you enter the data in your database. What's nice about PC-File is that you can take the data from the paper forms in your office just the way it appears and enter it in a PC-File database. Then later you can sort the information to suit your needs.

PC-File uses indexes to sort data. When you created the database you already indicated that the COMPANY field is an indexed field. You can create many indexes for one database. Of course, sorting three or four fields at one time is usually the maximum you might ever use.

Suppose that you want to see the records grouped in alphabetical order by company. Or you might sort the records by zip code.

Sort the client records in numeric order by zip code. To sort records, follow these steps:

1. Select File from the PC-File menu bar.

2. Select Index from the File menu. PC-File displays the index operation dialog box, as shown in figure 2.9.

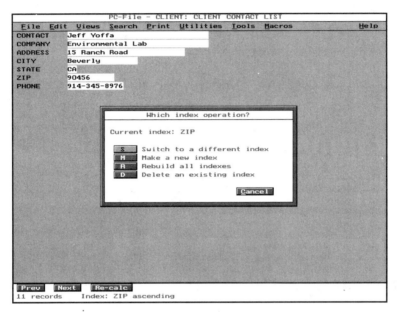

Fig. 2.9. *The index operation dialog box.*

3. Select Make a New Index from the list of operations. PC-File asks you to select the type of index.

4. Select Simple Index. PC-File displays a field selection dialog box (see figure 2.10). The sorting order default is ascending order.

5. Use the down-arrow key to highlight the ZIP field. This is the field you want to sort.

6. Select the OK button.

7. Select the ZIP field again. This is the field to which you want to attach the index.

   PC-File prompts you to enter a name for the index file.

8. Press Enter to accept the index file name CLIE_ZIP. This index file name indicates a zip code index in the Client database. Click the Cancel button to exit the index dialog box.

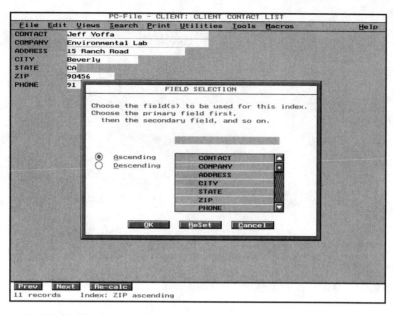

Fig. 2.10. The field selection dialog box

9. To view all of the records in sort order, select Views from the menu bar.

10. Select Table from the Views menu. PC-File displays all of the records in numeric order according to zip code, as shown in figure 2.11.

11. After you're finished looking at your records, select OK to exit Table View.

Exiting PC-File

Now that you've completed your first database, you can quit PC-File and return to DOS. To do this, you must select the File Exit command from the PC-File menu. If you have made any changes to your database since the last time you saved your database, PC-File automatically saves the file and closes it before quitting. For more information on exiting PC-File, refer to Chapter 1.

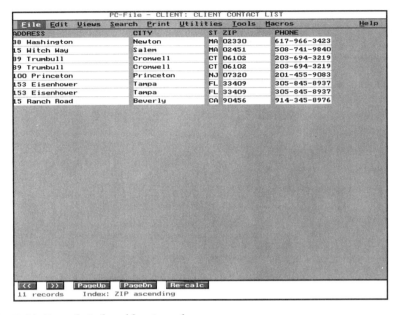

Fig. 2.11. Records indexed by zip code.

To exit PC-File and return to DOS, follow these steps:

1. Press **f** to select File from the PC-File menu bar.

2. Press **x** to select Exit PC-File from the File menu. PC-File displays the Exit window.

3. Select Exit to leave the program. PC-File closes the database.

   The DOS prompt appears.

Summary

In this chapter, you completed your first PC-File database. In addition to reviewing what you learned in Chapter 1, you previewed the Modify record commands you'll learn about in later chapters. If you're a new PC-File user and didn't finish the lesson, or you skipped over parts of it, take the time to go back through the entire lesson before you start Chapter 3. This Quick Start lesson gives you a solid foundation and prepares you for learning other PC-File features and functions in the rest of this book.

Now that you have sampled creating a database, Chapter 3 gives you information on planning and designing a good database.

3

Designing a Database

In this chapter you gain deeper insight into what constitutes a good working database. You learn database terms and concepts and PC-File's technical specifications. And you examine ways to communicate your ideas effectively by using PC-File.

Learning Database Terms and Concepts

To be comfortable with the way PC-File works, you need to be acquainted with three important terms used when talking about databases.

The first term is *file*. A file is a collection of records containing related information that is stored in one file on a disk. Each database represents a file, and as each database is created, it is given a filename. For example, a database containing the names, addresses, and phone numbers of all your business associates can be created and stored with the name PHONE.

The second term is *record*. A record is a unit of information within a file. Within the PHONE file, each business associate's name, address, and phone number represents one record. If you include 25 business associates' names, addresses, and phone numbers, you have 25 records within that file.

The third term is *field*. A field contains variable items of information comprising each record. If only names, addresses, and phone numbers are included in the PHONE file, each record will contain three fields, name, address, and phone number. If title is included as a field name, each record will contain four fields. Figure 3.1 illustrates a record that contains eight fields.

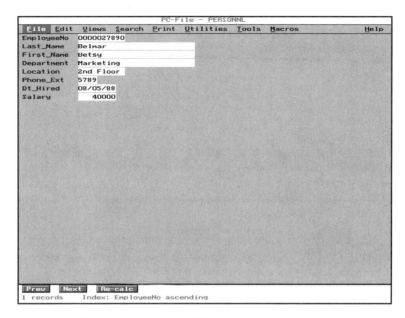

Fig. 3.1. A record that contains eight fields.

Planning the Design of a Database

A well-designed database requires some planning before you actually create the database. There are several guidelines, hints, tips, and techniques that you may find helpful when planning your database design. These techniques are presented as thinking tools for organizing your work so that you may become more productive in a shorter period of time. They also can help you gain deeper insight as to what constitutes a good database design.

Before creating a database, it is a good idea to identify the format and information you will need. Here are some general questions to answer when creating a database file.

- What fields do you want?

- What names will you give to the fields?

- What types of information will these fields contain? For example, will the fields contain character, numeric, date, logical, or memo types of information? Field types are covered in Chapter 4, "Creating a Database."

- What will be the lengths of these fields?

- How much space should you leave for each item of information?

There are several other considerations to take into account when you create a database:

- Determine the type of reports you expect to generate from the database and the information necessary for those reports. Refer to Chapter 10, "Generating Reports," for more information on creating reports.

- Identify all the uses for the database to ensure that you include the required information in each record. Examine typical paper forms and reports to get an idea of the information you may need. Refer to Chapters 10, 11, 12, and 13 for more information on generating reports, producing form letters and labels, creating graphs, and using other PC-File features.

- Aim for simplicity. Determine the number of important points you must communicate, and organize your database to include these key points.

- Design the database. First make a sketch of the database on a piece of paper, using pencil so that you can change it as many times as necessary. You also can use an existing database file design as a model. You can copy familiar paper forms you have on hand, or you can design a new form. After you decide on the format of the database, create the database design in PC-File. The record in figure 3.1 illustrates a typical personnel record.

- Determine the layout of your database design. Will the layout be an exact on-screen replica of the paper form you are using or do you want to make improvements to it? For example, you could use more descriptive labels, include more fields, or use fewer separate fields.

- Decide how to arrange the fields you want to store in your file. For example, do you want First Name before Last Name, Last Name before First Name, or a single file called Full Name? Such decisions depend on how you plan to search for and retrieve records. If you plan to search and retrieve records by Last Name only, but you also want to print mailing labels, you could use the field Full Name, and then the fields FIRSTNAME and LAST_NAME.

- Choose field names that best describe each piece of information within a field. Keep them as short as possible. Long names require more typing than short ones. For example, if you need one field for each month of the year, you could name the fields January, February, and so forth. Or you could use the shorter and equally descriptive, Jan, Feb, and so on.

- Each field must have a unique name. You must not enter any duplicate names. Otherwise you won't be able to search on a particular field to find the specific information you want.

- Combine the data kept on several paper forms into one database file or store the information kept on different forms in several database files. PC-File lets you work with multiple databases. Refer to Chapter 6, "Searching for Records," for more information on working with multiple databases.

- Decide how much data to include in the design of your database. Consider how much information you want to store at present and how much you anticipate the information to increase in the future. This potential growth determines the size of the file and how many records will be stored in the file. This also helps you decide if your information should be stored in one or more database files. For example, a database file with 500 records is more manageable than a file with 5,000 records. The larger the file, the slower the response time when editing, updating, sorting, or searching and retrieving records from the file.

- Consider the amount of storage space available in your computer. If you work with two 720K floppy disk drives, each 5 1/4-inch double-density disk will hold up to 720,000 characters of data. A high-density disk holds up to 1.44 million characters. If you work with a hard disk, the design of your database and the number of records is limited only by the specifications set up by PC-File, as discussed at the end of this chapter.

If your database is not properly planned or if you find you must track some new data that is not provided for in the original design, you can make changes to the database with the File Redefine command. It will not disturb the data already entered into your existing database. PC-File lets you add, change, and delete fields at any time, without losing any of the data that you have already entered. For more information on changing the design of your database, refer to Chapter 5, "Adding Records."

If you want to use PC-File for record keeping, you can plan a design so that PC-File actually helps direct the operator when filling in entries in the records, thus cutting down on the number of input errors. You can do this by restricting the kinds of data that can be entered, by setting ranges of acceptable values, and by setting initial entry values that can be copied and used in new records. For more information on these features, refer to Chapter 4, "Creating a Database."

Now that you are familiar with planning a good database design, you can learn about the technical specifications for setting up databases in PC-File, as described in the next section.

Examining PC-File Technical Specifications

When you are setting up your database files, you need to be acquainted with several technical specifications established by ButtonWare for the PC-File program. Table 3.1 lists the type of technical specification and the maximum limit for that specification.

Table 3.1
PC-File Technical Specifications

Technical Specification	Maximum Limit
Records per database	1 billion
Record length	4,000 characters
Field length (nonmemo)	254 characters
Memo field length	5,000 characters
Fields per database	128
Entry screens per database	5
Calculated fields per database	128
Indexes per database	9

Summary

In this chapter, you studied database terms and concepts and you were given a solid foundation for planning a well-designed database. The guidelines presented in this chapter for planning and designing a database include important concepts and techniques to reference any time you work with a database program.

If you are new to PC-File, read the next chapter to learn how to create a database. If you are an experienced PC-File user, you may want to turn to a specific chapter to learn more about a particular PC-File feature.

Part II

Creating Database Files

Includes

Creating a Database

Adding Records

Searching for Records

4

Creating a Database

In this chapter, you learn how to create a new database file. You learn how to name fields, determine field length, define data types, and set up index fields. You also learn how to name database files. And finally, you learn how to enter a description for a database file.

Creating a New Database File

To create a new database in PC-File, you create a new database file with the File New command, define the database, give the file a name, and save it in a file on disk. Then you can use the File Open command to open the new database you have created in order to add or edit the records it contains. When you are ready to end the session, you exit your PC-File database by invoking the File Exit command.

PC-File gives you two ways to create a database—the Fast method and the Paint method. To decide which method is best for your needs, refer to the section Examining Ways to Define a PC-File Database later in this chapter. No matter which method you choose, here are the general steps you follow to create a database:

1. From the menu bar, press **F** to select File. PC-File displays the File menu (see figure 4.1).

2. From the File menu, press **N** to select New. The Which method? dialog box appears on the screen.

3. Select either the Fast method or the Paint Method to define your database.

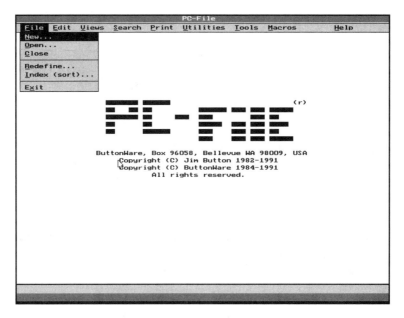

Fig. 4.1. *The File menu.*

4. Whether you choose the Fast method or the Paint Method, the next step is to assign names and define your fields. Information on assigning names is covered in detail in the section on Entering Field Names later in this chapter. Defining fields is covered in the sections on Defining Field Types and Examining Field Length later in this chapter.

5. When you are finished designing your database, select OK. PC-File prompts you to enter a name for your database.

6. Type the file name for your database and press Enter. For information on naming a database, refer to the section on Naming PC-File Databases in this chapter.

7. PC-File prompts you to enter a file description for your database. The file description is optional.

   For information on describing a database file, refer to the section in this chapter on Entering a File Description.

8. Press Enter to bypass the file description or type a description and press Enter.

9. PC-File displays the message, Creating database. At this point, the database is saved to disk. Then PC-File asks you to name each index file and specify the sorting order.

10. Enter a name for each index file and select the appropriate sorting order.

    For information on indexing files, see Chapter 9, "Changing the Design of a Database."

11. PC-File tells you to add records to the database with the Edit Add command. Select OK to end the process of creating a new database file.

The next section shows you how to define a database using either the Fast method or the Paint method.

Examining Ways To Define a PC-File Database

PC-File offers two methods for defining a database: the Fast method and the Paint method. The Fast method lets you create a quick and simple database by entering the field names and defining the type of information you want to include in your database. The Paint method allows you to enter information in a blank form on the screen. You can create an image of the form you want. The Paint method is more flexible than the Fast Method, but it takes more time to set up the design of your database.

> If your database contains 21 fields or less, and each field takes up one line, you probably want to use the Fast method to define your database.
>
> If your database contains more than 21 fields, and several fields are contained on one line, and if you want to draw lines and boxes on the form, use the Paint method to define your database.

Using the Fast Method

When you want to set up a simple database quickly and easily, use the Fast method. With the Fast method, you enter the field names in the order you want them to appear in the database. Then you define the type of information you want to include for each field. Defining the field information in a database must be done before you input the actual data.

The Fast Method screen contains six columns: field name, type, length, decimals, indexed, and other. Detailed information on field names, field types, field lengths, decimals, indexed fields, and other fields is explained later in this chapter.

To define a database using the Fast method, follow these steps:

1. From the Which method? dialog box, press **F** to select the Fast method. PC-File displays the Fast method screen (see figure 4.2). This screen contains a blank data entry form that looks like a list.

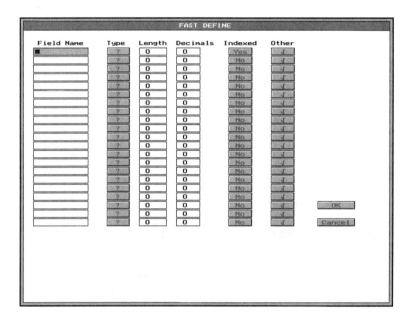

Fig. 4.2. The Fast method screen.

2. Type the first field name in the field name column and press the Tab key. You can enter a maximum of 10 characters for the field name. For example, type FIRST_NAME and press Tab. The cursor moves to the field type column.

TIP

Enter field names in capital letters so that they will look different from the data you input later. That way, you can tell the difference between the field name and the data within a field.

TIP

If you make a typing error, use the Backspace key to erase the error. Pressing the backspace key erases one character to the immediate left of the cursor. Then you can re-type the data.

3. Press Enter. PC-File displays a pop-up menu that lists the field types, as shown in figure 4.3.

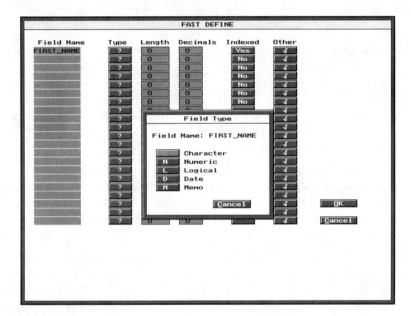

Fig. 4.3. *The Fast method's field type pop-up menu.*

4. Press the appropriate letter to select the field type you want. For example, press **C** to select Character.

    PC-File enters in the Type column the code that represents the field type you selected. (The field types are discussed in detail in the section on Defining Field Types in this chapter.)

    The cursor moves to the field length column. The default field length of 25 characters appears in the column.

5. You can leave the number as is or you can type the field length you want and press the Tab key.

    Refer to Table 4.2 later in this chapter for a list of the default lengths for all field types. If you select a Date, Logical, or Memo field type in the type column, PC-File does not let you change the field length. If you want the length that appears in the column, press the Tab key. If you want to change the length for Character and Number fields, type over the default number and then press the Tab key.

To estimate the length of a field, count the number of characters in the longest entry you will enter in that field. Add a few more characters to your estimate of the longest entry to accommodate any longer entries you might enter in the future.

6. If the field type is Numeric, enter the number of decimal places.

7. Press the Tab key to move to the Indexed column. The letter Y, which stands for Yes, appears in the Indexed column.

8. If you want to index the field, leave the Yes and press the Tab key. If you do not want to index the field, press Enter. Be sure to index at least one field in the database.

   Your needs determine which fields you index. For example, if you want to print a phone directory, you index your LAST_NAME field to sort the list alphabetically by last name. If you want to print mailing labels according to zip code, you would index your ZIP_CODE field.

9. In the Other column, you can select other characteristics for the field. Press Enter to select Other, and PC-File displays a pop-up menu that contains the Other field types. Select the Other operation that you want and define the field option. If you do not want to assign another field type, press the Tab key to return to the first column on the screen.

   (For more information on the other field types, refer to the section in this chapter on Defining Other Field Characteristics.)

10. Repeat steps 2 through 7 to define the rest of the field information.

11. When you are finished defining the field information, select OK. PC-File prompts you to enter a name for your database and press Enter.

12. Type the file name CUSTADDR, for example.

    A file name can have a maximum of 8 characters and consist of letters, numbers, or both.

13. PC-File prompts you to enter a description of your database. This is optional.

14. If you do not want to enter a description, click the OK button or press Alt-O. Otherwise, type a description and click the OK button. You can enter up to 30 characters—a customer mailing list, for example.

    PC-File displays the message Creating a Database. You are prompted to name an index file. PC-File displays an Index file name that consists of the first four characters of the field that you indexed. For example, CUSTLAST represents the LAST_NAME field and is indexed in the CUSTADDR database.

15. Click the OK button to accept the index file name. PC-File tells you that the database is empty. To add records, use the Edit Add command.

16. Click the OK button to end the process of creating a database with the Fast method.

Using the Paint Method

If you want to create an elaborate database, you can use the Paint method to design the structure and the layout of your database in a data entry screen. PC-File's Paint method is more flexible than the Fast method because you can enter more than one field on a line and up to five screens of fields.

PC-File gives you two options for working with the Paint method to design a database. You can create a new data entry screen by filling in a design screen with the field information you want to include in your database. Or you can use an existing database that is similar to the design you want. This last option gives you a model database design to start with instead of having to fill in the data entry screen from scratch.

If you use an existing database design to create a new database design, PC-File makes a copy of the existing design. Therefore, when you make the changes for the new database you are working on the copy. The original database design remains unchanged.

Using an existing database as a model is covered in Chapter 9, "Changing the Design of a Database."

A PC-File database can have a maximum of five data entry screens. Each screen contains 21 lines. Three screen pages fit on a standard 8 1/2-by-11-inch printed page of 66 lines. Fitting all of the data on a single screen is most convenient, but if you have to enter the data on more than one screen, use the additional screens.

> If your data takes up five or more data entry screens, you might want to organize the data by creating two or more databases to accommodate all of the information.

Use the arrow keys and the PgUp and PgDn keys to move around the data entry screens in the edit window.

To define a database using the Paint method, follow these general steps. For more detailed information, refer to the appropriate sections that follow.

1. From the Which method? dialog box, press **P** to select the Paint method. PC-File displays the Paint method edit window (see figure 4.4). This screen contains a blank data entry form.

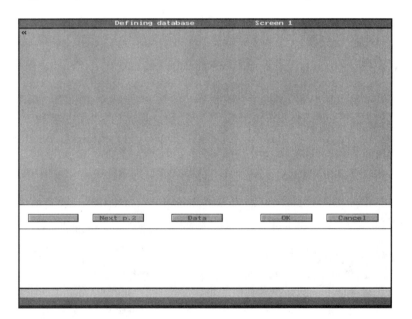

Fig. 4.4. The Paint method edit window.

At the top of the edit window are the title, Defining database, and the status message, Screen 1. The status message tells you on which screen the cursor is currently positioned.

The middle portion of the screen is a blank area where you type the design of the form. Notice that the cursor is in the upper-left corner of the shaded area. The cursor shows you where to start typing.

2. Type the field label where you want it to appear.

There are no restrictions on the length or on the characters you enter for a field label. That way, you can enter a field label as long as necessary and with any characters you want. Some examples of field labels you can use in a last name field include LAST_NAME, CUSTOMER'S LAST NAME, and ENTER THE LAST NAME HERE.

Field labels differ from field names in three ways:

A field name can have up to 10 characters; a field label can be any length you want.

A field name can contain only letters, numbers, or both; a field label can contain any character.

A field name can be used in both the Fast and Paint methods; A field label can be used only with the Paint method.

If you catch a mistake while typing, you can use the Backspace key to erase the error. Pressing the backspace key erases one character to the immediate left of the cursor. Then you can retype the field label.

You can use the Insert key as a toggle; press Ins to enter additional characters. Press Ins again to type over existing characters.

Enter the field labels in capital letters so that they will look different from the data you input later. That way, you can tell the difference between the field name and the actual data within a field.

Leave the first line on your screen blank so that there is a space between the menu and the first group of fields. You also can indent a couple of spaces from the left side by leaving space at the top and the left and right sides of the data entry screen. Then you can easily draw lines and boxes to enclose the groups of fields later.

3. When you have finished designing your database screen, position your cursor at the first field. Then select the data button or type your field markers. Repeat this step for each succeeding field.

Using the Data Button

Select the Data button at the bottom of the window. PC-File prompts you to enter the field type as shown in figure 4.5. Select the field type by pressing the appropriate letter. For example, press C to select Character.

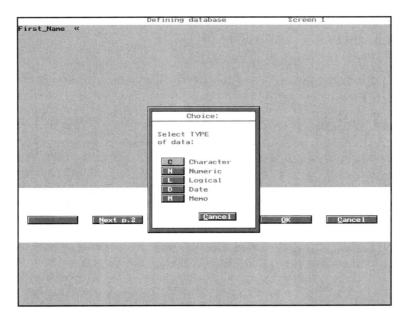

Fig. 4.5. *Selecting the Paint method Field type menu with the Data button.*

PC-File prompts you to enter a field length for all field types as shown in figure 4.6. PC-File remembers the previous default field length you entered and displays it in the dialog box. Leave the default field length or type over the default field length with the new length you want. For character fields, enter the number of characters. For numeric fields, enter the total number of characters, including the numbers on each side of the decimal point.

Refer to Table 4.2 for a list of default lengths for all field types. The default lengths are the same for both the Fast method and the Paint method.

Select OK. PC-File enters the appropriate field markers in the field.

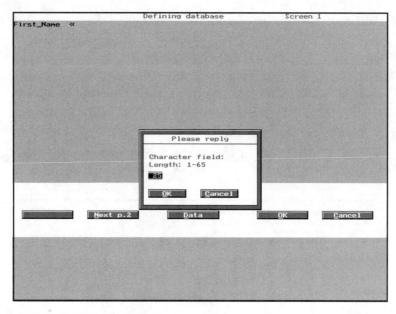

Fig. 4.6. The field length dialog box.

Typing

Type the appropriate field marker once for each character length. For example, if you are creating a character-type field that is 25 characters long, enter 25 @s (at symbols) in a row.

Table 4.1 shows the field types and field markers that PC-File uses. The field markers do not display when you use the database.

Table 4.1
Field Markers

Field Type	Field Marker
Character	@ (at sign)
Numeric	# (pound sign)
Date	\ (backslash)
Logical	| (pipe)
Memo	~ (tilde)

4. Add other fields as necessary.

   Note that you can add two fields on the same line. Be sure to leave enough space around the field labels so that you can draw lines to enclose the information in a box later. Do not crowd the screen. Use blank rows, lines, and boxes to separate the data into groups on the screen and leave ample white space.

5. When you are finished, select OK.

   PC-File displays field buttons on top of each field you have entered as shown in figure 4.7.

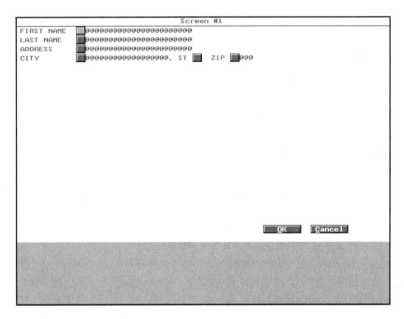

***Fig. 4.7.** The field buttons.*

A field button lets you further define each field. You can change the field information you defined on the data entry screen such as the field type and length. You also can enter define field characteristics such as the field name, indexed field, mask, constant, and calculation.

A field name can have a maximum of 10 characters with no spaces; a field label has no restrictions . The field name can be used in a report, letter, or mailing label. The field label is used in the data entry form to make it easier to enter data for each record.

If you do not want to change or further define any fields, you do not have to choose all of the field buttons. However, you must select at least one field and define it as an indexed field. The field characteristics are covered in detail in the section on Defining Field Information later in this chapter.

6. Select the field button of the field you want to change. The first field is chosen automatically as an Index field, but you can change it.

    PC-File displays a Field Characteristics dialog box as shown in figure 4.8. The first entry in this box is the default field name in the Name text box. It may be different from the field label you entered in the data entry screen.

    For example, if you entered FIRSTNAME and LASTNAME field labels, PC-File automatically enters NAME1 and NAME respectively for field names in the Field Characteristics dialog box.

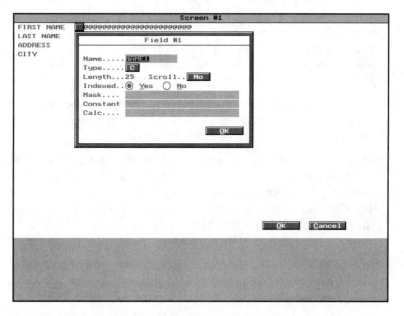

Fig. 4.8. The Field Characteristics dialog box

7. Press Tab to leave the default name and continue to the next field. Or if you want to change the name, type a field name in the NAME text box and press Tab.

Be sure to change the field markers on the data entry screen to match the new field type.

8. Press Enter to leave the default name and continue to the next field. Or if you want to change the name, type a field name in the Name text box and press Tab. You move to the field type box.

   For information on field names, refer to the section on Entering Field Names later in this chapter.

9. Press Tab to keep the field type the same. Or press Enter and then choose the field type from the dialog box that appears on the screen.

   Be sure to change the field markers on the data entry screen to match the new field type. To do this, press Esc to exit the dialog box and type over the old field markers with the new field markers.

   You cannot change the field length in the dialog box. You must adjust the field length by adding or deleting field markers. You can change the display length in the Scroll field only for a character field in the dialog box. The display length is the length of the field that appears in the data entry screen. If the data in a field is longer than the display length, you can scroll right and left to see all of the data.

   The field length specifies the number of characters you can type in a field. The default Scroll mode is set to No. This means the display length is the same length as the field length.

   When you press Enter to select Scroll, PC-File displays the Scroll dialog box, as shown in figure 4.9. Type a number to specify shortening or lengthening the display length. For example, type 35 to shorten the display length for a field that contains 45 characters. The scroll field displays Yes. This means you can use the arrow keys to scroll left and right in the field.

10. To index a field, select the Yes option button in the Indexed field. Enter a name for each index file, and specify the sorting order. If you do not want to index a field, select the No option button.

    For information on Indexed fields, refer to the section on Using Indexed Fields later in this chapter.

    The other options, Mask, Constant, and Calc, are covered later in this chapter.

After you make a change in the Field Characteristics dialog box and select OK, PC-File displays a check mark in the field button for that particular field.

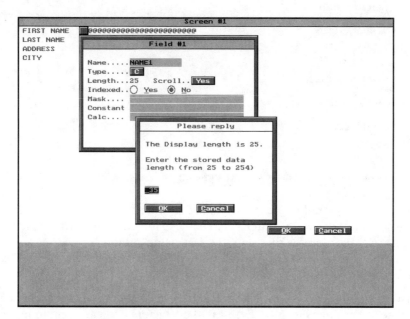

Fig. 4.9. The Scroll dialog box.

11. When you are finished defining your database, select OK. You are now asked to name your database and give it a description.

12. Type the file name for your database and press Enter. PC-File tells you to add records to your database with the Edit Add Command.

13. When you have finished adding records to your database, select OK to return to the PC-File menu bar.

Defining Field Information

Whether you choose the Fast method or the Paint method to define your database, there are several guidelines you need to be acquainted with when you define the field information. The next few sections provide you with the rules for the following field information:

- Field name

- Field type

- Field length

- Data length

- Display length

- Decimal places

- Field order

- Indexed field

Entering Field Names

A field name identifies the kind of data that will be typed into a field. In the Fast method screen, you enter a field name in the first column. For instance, LAST_NAME indicates that only the last name should be entered in that particular field. The field names and field labels are the same in the Fast method.

There are restrictions on the length and the characters you enter for a field name. A field name can have up to 10 characters and can contain letters, numbers, and the underline (_). The underline (_) indicates a space. Field names must start with a letter and cannot contain spaces.

In the Paint method edit window, you enter a field label in the data entry screen and give the field a separate name in the Field Characteristics dialog box. There are no restrictions on the length or the characters you can enter for a field label. That way, you can enter a field label as long as necessary and with any characters you want. An example of a field label is ENTER LAST NAME HERE.

You may need to identify a field in an existing report or letter. In such cases, it is important that the field name you have assigned to it clearly identifies that field. For example, if you entered the field label ENTER THE LAST NAME HERE in the data entry screen, enter the field name LAST_NAME in the dialog box so that it is more understandable when you use it later in a report or form letter.

When you use the Paint method, the default field name appears in the Name text box in the Field Characteristics dialog box. The default field name is different from the field label you entered in the data entry screen. For example, PC-File defines the field name as HERE for the field label ENTER THE LAST NAME HERE.

There are several rules to keep in mind when entering field names using either the Fast or Paint method:

- Each field must have a unique name. You must not enter any duplicate names. Otherwise, you won't be able to search on a particular field to find the specific information you want.

- A field name can have up to 10 characters, including letters, numbers, or both, and the underline character. The first character in a field must be a letter.

- A field name can be entered in upper- or lowercase. It is a good idea to enter the field names in uppercase to distinguish between field names and the data you enter in a field.

- Spaces are not allowed. For example, LAST NAME is an invalid field name. To separate characters in a field name, enter the underline character (_). For example, LAST_NAME and LASTNAME are valid field names.

Several rules you might keep in mind when entering field labels in the Paint method edit window are as follows:

- A field label can include spaces.

- A field label can contain several words.

- A field name can be omitted. It is optional. However, you must enter a field label.

Defining Field Types

PC-File handles different kinds of data in different ways. You need to tell it which kind of data is contained in each field by defining a field type. This restricts the contents of the data you can enter in that field. One of the following field types must be defined for every field in your database. The five field types available for a field are character, numeric, date, logical, and memo.

If you use the Fast method, each field type is represented by a code. The field type also can determine the length of a field or a range of lengths. The field types, field lengths, field code, and descriptions for the Fast and Paint methods are summarized in table 4.2.

Table 4.2.
Field Types

Field Type	Field Length	Code (Fast Method)	Description
Character	1 to 254	C	Text
Numeric	1 to 19	N	Quantities, dollar amounts, statistical data
Date	8 or 10	D	Dates only, birthdates, due dates, expiration dates
Logical	1	L	Answers to Yes/No, True/False questions
Memo	0 to 5000	M	Large amounts of text

Character Field Type

The character field type is generally for conceptual information that contains letters, numbers, and special characters. Typical character fields contain names, addresses, phone numbers, social security numbers, part numbers, and descriptions. Why isn't the phone number, social security number, or part number assigned a numeric field type? Yes, they are all numbers, but a good rule of thumb is to assign character field types unless the numbers are to be used in arithmetic calculations.

The Numeric Field Type

The numeric field type is for numbers that may be used in calculations. It can contain numbers, decimal points, minus signs, and plus signs. A numeric field is accurate to eight decimal positions. You might, for instance, include numeric fields for quantity, price, salary, or population.

The Date Field Type

The date field type is for valid dates that contain 8 or 10 characters. PC-File lets you enter dates in two formats: YYYYMMDD or MM/DD/YY. For example, August 2, 1991, can be entered as 19910802 or 08/02/91. PC-File displays the date in the MM/DD/YY format and stores the date in the database file in the YYYYMMDD format. Thus, if you enter 08/02/91, PC-File displays it exactly the way you entered it and stores the 19910802 format in the database file. Some uses of a date field are receipt date, ship date, birth date, and expiration date.

The Logical Field Type

The logical field type displays true or false or yes or no values in a field. A logical field is one character long, and it can contain only one of the following characters: T for True, F for False, Y for Yes, or N for No. You can use either upper- or lowercase letters. Some uses of logical fields are recording whether students attended a class or not, an insurance claim was paid or not, or a check has cleared the bank or not.

The Memo Field Type

The memo field type, which can contain up to 5000 characters, usually is used to store large amounts of text. It can contain the same characters as the character field. You can enter notes, comments, or special information about a particular record in a memo field. You cannot index a memo field.

Examining Field Length

Field length refers to the number of characters a field can contain. PC-File's maximum field length is 254 characters per nonmemo field. A memo field's length is a maximum of 5000 characters. Thus, if you define a field length of 25 characters for an Address field, you can enter any address that contains a maximum of 25 characters.

In some cases, the field length is determined by the field type. Date fields, for example, must be eight characters long. The logical fields must be one character long. You cannot alter the field length for a date, logical, or memo field.

In summary, the field length is the number of characters you choose for a field. The data length is the maximum number of characters possible. And the display length is the number of characters that will appear on a screen.

Determining Data Length and Display Length

The data length is the total number of characters the field can contain. The maximum data length for a character field, for example, is 254 characters. This means you can enter up to 254 characters in a field.

The display length is the number of characters of a field that PC-File displays in the data entry screen at one time. The maximum display length for any type of field is 65 characters. For example, if you set the display length in a character field to 65 and the data length to 85, you can still enter more than 65 characters in that field. You can enter more characters than the screen displays for this field.

If you define your database with the Paint method, you can set the field length separately from the display length for character fields only. The field length is sometimes referred to as the data length in the Paint method.

If the data length is longer than the display length, you can see only part of the data in the field at any one time. To see other portions of the field, you can scroll within that field by using the left- and right-arrow keys to move the visual window across the data.

Setting Decimal Places

PC-File lets you specify the number of decimal places you want to display to the right of the decimal for numbers in a numeric field only. The default number of decimal places is 0 (zero). A numeric field is accurate to eight decimal positions. The maximum number of decimal places you can specify is the field length minus two. Suppose you define a numeric field as 10 characters long. You can place up to eight of those characters to the right of the decimal.

Examining Access Order

The access order is the order that fields are normally accessed in the database. In Table View, the access order is the order in which the fields are positioned across the screen.

When you add or modify records, PC-File moves the cursor in the order that you entered the fields, from left to right and top to bottom.

If you want the cursor to move through the fields in a different order, you can tell PC-File to do just that—but only if the database was created with the Paint method. For example, you can place the fields that rarely contain data at the end of the access order. That way, if there is no data to enter in those fields, you can quickly skip to the next record.

You cannot change the access order when you use the Fast method to create a database. For more information on changing the access order, refer to Chapter 5, "Adding Records."

Using Indexed Fields

An indexed field lets you organize the information in a field in a specific order. You can index a field alphabetically and numerically, in ascending or descending order. Indexing a field sorts your records so that PC-File can locate information faster during a search in indexed fields than in unindexed fields.

For example, in a name and address database you might want to index the LAST_NAME and the ZIP_CODE fields in ascending order. Because you want your database to be arranged by last name or zip code, and you would search for records in the LAST_NAME or the ZIP_CODE fields, you indicate Yes to the index option for either field or both. On the other hand, you would not arrange your database by address and would not search for records in the ADDRESS field, so you indicate No to indexing that field

PC-File sorts the indexed fields and automatically updates the index fields when you add, modify, and delete records. You can switch from one index to another using the File Index command, and the database reorders itself, based on the current index field.

For information on switching indexes, refer to Chapter 7, "Modifying Records."

When you create a database, you must define at least one index, and you can specify a maximum of 9 index fields per database. Memo fields, however, cannot be indexed. Generally, one or two index fields are specified in a database. If you need additional indexes, you can use the File Index command to create more indexes later.

In the Fast method screen, you specify the index field by selecting Yes in the Indexed column. To specify an index field using the Paint method, select the field button for the field you want indexed. Then select the Yes option button in the Indexed field. This tells PC-File that you want a particular field indexed. You name the index file later.

For more information on working with indexes, refer to Chapter 8, "Indexing Records."

Defining Other Field Characteristics

With the Fast method, you can define other field characteristics in the last column called Other. With the Paint method, you determine other field characteristics in the Field Characteristics dialog box.

The other field characteristics options include default data, calculations, edit mask, automatic data, and update limiter.

Default Data

You can specify an exact value for the field with the Default Data option. PC-File inserts the same data in a field in most records or in any new records added to the database. For example, if most of the cities in a database are Sacramento, you can specify Sacramento as the default data in the CITY field (see figure 4.10). That way, you do not have to type Sacramento every time a new record is added. Instead you can skip over that field most of the time.

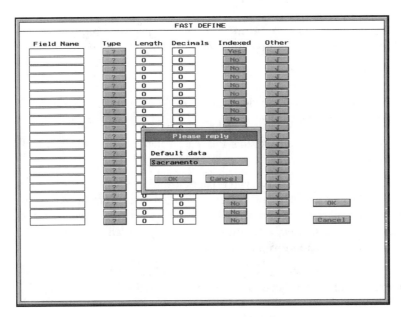

Fig. 4.10. Entering the default data in the CITY field with the Fast method.

In the Fast method screen, follow these steps to specify default data:

1. Select the field for which you want to specify the default data. For instance, select the CITY field.

2. Select the Other option and PC-File displays a pop-up menu that contains the Other field types as shown in figure 4.11.

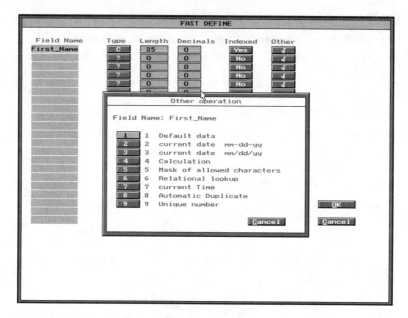

Fig. 4.11. *The Other options menu.*

3. Select the Default data option.

4. Type the default data. For instance, type *Sacramento*.

5. Select OK.

PC-File prompts you to select a limiter operation. A limiter operation specifies when default data is added to a record. If you select NEW, PC-File enters the default data in the field during data entry only, and not during data modification. For example, if you replaced Sacramento with Denver when you entered the record, you wouldn't want PC-File to replace Denver with Sacramento automatically if you displayed the record later for some other modification.

6. Select N for New and then select OK to enter default data only when you enter a new record.

7. If you want the default data entered when you modify an existing record, select Modify.

8. If you want to enter data in an empty field, select Blank.

9. If you want to enter default data in both new and existing records, select Always.

In the Paint method edit window, follow these steps:

1. Select the field button for which you want to specify default data. PC-File displays the Field Characteristics dialog box (see figure 4.12).

2. In the Constant field, type the default data—*Sacramento*, for example—and select OK.

PC-File prompts you to select a limiter operation. In both the Paint method and the Fast method, a limiter operation specifies when default data is added to a record. If you select NEW, PC-File enters the default data in the field during data entry only, and during date modification. For example, if you replaced Sacramento with Denver when you entered the record, you wouldn't want PC-File to replace Denver with Sacramento automatically if you displayed the record later for some other modification.

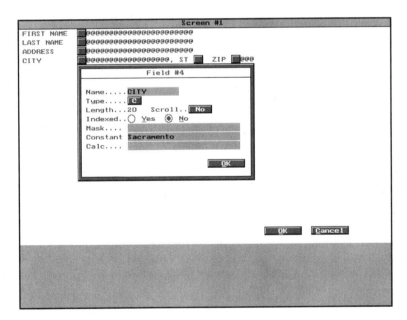

Fig 4.12. *Sample default data.*

Calculations

The Calculations option lets you enter a calculation in a field. Instead of entering the data in a field yourself, you enter the calculation in the field definition. PC-File performs the calculation for each record and inserts the results in the field.

You can enter mathematical calculations to add, subtract, multiply, divide, or exponentiate. You also can enter date calculations that perform calculations on dates to determine the number of days between dates or a future date.

A mathematical calculation contains fields, numbers, or both as well as arithmetic operators. Use a + (plus sign) for addition, a − (minus sign) for subtraction, an * (asterisk) for multiplication, and a / (slash) for division. For example, you might request INCOME − EXPENSES. Another example is YR_SALARY / 12.

PC-File allows you to enter relational lookups in fields to retrieve data from other databases. A relational lookup is a special calculation that is used to link two databases. For example, you can look up an insurance policy number in one database and retrieve it into another database to print out with each insurance claim form. The relational lookup would look like this:

<(@POL_NO, CAR_INS, POL_NO, CLAIMS)>

For more information on relational lookups, see Chapter 11, "Producing Form Letters and Mailing Labels."

When you enter a calculation, PC-File encloses it in parentheses automatically. You can leave as much space as you want between the fields, numbers, and operators (see figure 4.13).

In the Fast method screen, follow these steps:

1. Select the Other option. PC-File displays the Other operation dialog box.

2. Select Calculation and type the calculation.

3. Select OK.

4. Select the limiter operation you want.

For more information about limiter operations, refer to the section on Default Data earlier in this chapter.

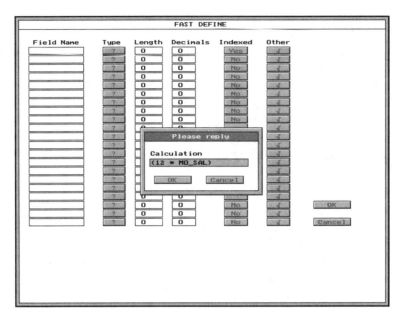

Fig. 4.13. *A sample calculation.*

In the Paint method edit window, follow these steps:

1. Select the field button for which you want to enter a calculation. PC-File displays the Field Characteristics dialog box.

2. In the Calc field, enter the calculation. For example, to calculate profit enter *INCOME – EXPENSES*. You must have INCOME and EXPENSE fields in your database. Do not enter fields that are not in your database.

3. Select OK.

4. Include the limiter option you want, as described later in the section on Update Limiter.

Edit Mask

The Edit Mask option allows you to define the range of characters allowed in a field beyond those limits imposed by the field type. PC-File provides default edit masks in fields that you define for numeric and logical field types. For example, you can enter only the characters *t, f, y,* or *n* in a logical field.

You can create a mask for a particular field to allow only uppercase characters. For example, a mask in a state field lets you enter only uppercase letters such as *CA* or *FL*. Or you can prepare a field for information such as phone numbers to limit data entry to the digits 0-9 and hyphens.

Table 4.3 lists the edit marks and describes each mark.

Table 4.3
Edit Masks

Edit Mask	Example
:AZ:	Uppercase letters only
:AZaz:	Uppercase and lowercase letters only
:AM:	Uppercase letters A through M only
:BA:	No characters allowed
:AZaz09:	Uppercase and lowercase letters, digits and a space.
:09//:	Digits and a slash
:$$09..:	A dollar sign, digits, and a decimal point
:09---:	Digits and hyphens

To create an edit mask, you enter characters in pairs in the edit mask field. For example, to specify uppercase letters only, you enter AZ. To specify the digits 0-9 and hyphens, enter *09---*. When you set up an edit mask, PC-File encloses it in colons (:) automatically (see figure 4.14).

In the Fast method screen, complete the following steps to select an Edit mask:

1. Select the Other option. PC-File displays the Other operation dialog box.

2. Select Mask of allowed characters and type the edit mask. For example, type *AZ* to specify uppercase letters only. Type *$$09.* if you want to specify a dollar sign, digits, and a decimal point. This edit mask is used to enter currency.

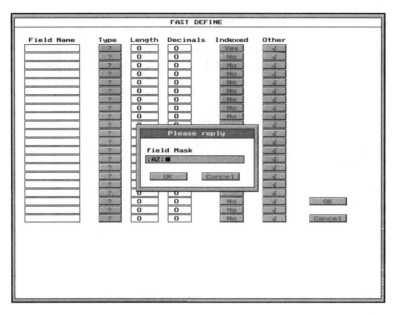

Fig. 4.14. The Edit Mask field.

3. Select OK.

4. Select the limiter option you want and select OK.

In the Paint method edit window:

1. Select the field button for which you want to enter an edit mask. PC-File displays the Field Characteristics dialog box

2. In the Mask field, enter the edit mask and select OK (see figure 4.15).

You also can include the limiter option you want, as described in the section Update Limiter in this chapter.

Automatic Data

The Automatic Data option generates data in a field automatically either from a function or from the computer. An automatic field is another type of mask. The data may include the current date and time, a unique number, and a duplication of the previous record.

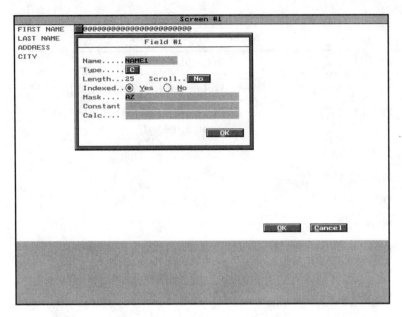

Fig. 4.15. A sample edit mask.

For example, you can set up an automatic field for a CLAIM_DATE field in an insurance claim database. PC-File would then enter the current date each time you added a new record for a claim.

An example of a unique number mask is a unique number for each record. You can specify that the first record you enter is the number 1, the second record is number 2, and so on. When you sort the database, PC-File does not change these numbers. When you delete a record, PC-File does not reuse the numbers.

A duplication mask can be compared to default data with one exception. Default data always adds the same data in a field, but a duplication mask inserts the data that appeared in the previously viewed record. For instance, you can set up a duplication mask for a State field. This would allow you to enter all of the CA addresses first, then the NH addresses, and finally, the FL addresses.

With the Fast method, PC-File gives you five automatic field options. With the Paint method, you can choose from 11 automatic field options. The six extra options are variations on entering a date. Table 4.4 shows the 11 automatic field options with examples. You can use only the first five options with the Fast method. You can use all of the options with the Paint method.

Table 4.4
Automatic Field Options

Mask	Example
:UNIQUE*:	568 (a unique record number)
:DUPE*:	CA (duplicates from previously viewed record)
:MM/DD/YY*:	12/22/91
:MM-DD-YY*:	12-22-91
:DD/MM/YY*:	22/12/91
:MM*:	12
:DD*:	22
:YY*:	91
:YYMMDD*:	911222
:YYYYMMDD*:	19911222
:HH:MM*:	15:31

To enter a mask for an automatic field, type one of the masks mentioned in Table 4.4 and include an asterisk (*) after each mask. For example, type *12/22/91** to enter this date in a particular date field in every record. PC-File encloses the mask in colons (:) automatically.

To enter a mask in the Fast method screen, select the Other option and PC-File displays the Other operation dialog box. Select either the current date, current time, automatic duplicate, or unique number option. Type the mask and select OK. Select the limiter option you want and select OK.

In the Paint method edit window, select the field button for which you want to enter a mask for an automatic field option. PC-File displays the Field Characteristics dialog box. In the Mask field, enter the mask and select OK. You can also include the limiter option you want, as described in the following section Update Limiter.

Update Limiter

The Update Limiter option specifies when default data, calculations, and automatic data appear in a field. Because PC-File enters the data in a field automatically, you must tell PC-File when it should and should not update the field. Normally, PC-File updates the field by entering information in the field automatically when you add and modify a record. Since PC-File is set to Modify mode, the field is updated each time you display the record.

Normally, PC-file updates a field automatically by entering information to the field when you add or modify a record. However, when you create default data, calculations, or automatic data, you must tell PC-File when it should and should not update the field. The Update Limiter option specifies when to enter the information.

If you do not specify a limiter option, PC-File defaults to the Modify mode and the field is updated each time you display the record.

For example, if you create an automatic field mask with a date, PC-File inserts the current date when you enter a new record and when you display the record for modification.

PC-File lets you override the default if you select an update limiter operation from the operations dialog box for default data, calculation, or automatic field mask.

There are four update limiter symbols: N, M, B, and A. The N stands for New and tells PC-File to update the field only when you enter a new record. This is useful with default data as well as the unique number and duplication automatic field masks.

The M stands for Modify. It tells PC-File to update the field only when you modify data and display the record. The Modify update limiter is handy when you set up date and time automatic fields and calculations.

The B represents Blank and tells PC-File to update the field only when the field is blank. This is useful for automatic fields, default data, and calculations. The Blank update limiter prevents PC-File from performing a calculation when you enter data in the field.

The A represents Always and tells PC-File to update the field for new and existing records. This is the default for updating automatic fields. With both the Fast and Paint methods, PC-File displays a dialogue box that contains the limiter options. You select the option you want. For example, select N to specify entering automatic data in new records only.

Drawing Lines and Boxes

When you use the Paint method, you can make your database design on the screen look like the paper form you use in your office; that is, you can draw lines and boxes as part of a structure. That way, you can visually divide one area of the database structure from another or focus attention on specific parts of the database.

PC-File lets you draw lines and boxes in the data entry screen in the Paint edit window with characters from the ASCII table. You can find the ASCII Tables in Appendix D in the PC-File documentation. Each line or box character is represented by a decimal value.

To draw the lines and boxes, hold down the Alt key, type the decimal value for the ASCII character, then release the Alt key. For example, to create the upper left corner of a box, you hold down the Alt key, type the numbers 218 using the numeric keypad, then release the Alt key. You must repeat this process for each line and box character you want to draw on the screen.

Use the arrow keys to move to the location where you want to draw a line. Each decimal value you enter appears next to the ASCII character on the screen. For more information on drawing lines and boxes, refer to your PC-File documentation.

Naming PC-File Database Files

When you finish your database with the Fast or Paint method, PC-File prompts you to enter a file name for your new database. Type the file name and press Enter. PC-File automatically assigns the file extension .DBF to the file name. DBF stands for database file and is used to distinguish database files from other files in PC-File. An example of a complete file name is CLIENT.DBF.

File names must be unique and follow the DOS naming conventions. Follow these guidelines when you name your file:

- Use one to eight characters for the file name.

- Use letters, numbers, or a combination of both.

- Don't use spaces.

- Don't use punctuation such as periods, commas, or colons.

- Don't use question marks or asterisks. These characters are reserved for use as wild cards when searching for files in DOS. (A wild card is a symbol that represents any character or any sequence of characters.)

You should use a file name that describes the contents of the database in abbreviated form. The file name CUST, for example, might hold the database containing the names, addresses, and phone numbers of your customers.

TIP

If you type an invalid file name in PC-File, you see the message *Not a valid file name.*

Entering a File Description

PC-File lets you attach a file description to a new database file name for easier file identification. This feature is optional. If you enter a file description, the descriptive comment appears next to the database file name when you choose a database.

A file description is a good reminder of what kind of information the database contains or what the database is used for.

A file description can have up to 50 characters. It may contain letters, numbers, or a combination of both.

When you name a new database file, PC-File prompts you to enter a file description. Type the file description and press Enter. If you do not want to enter a file description, select OK to bypass the prompt.

Naming Index Files

When you name and describe your database, you are prompted to enter file names for your indexed fields. PC-File displays a default index file name for each indexed field. The name consists of the first four letters of the database and the first four letters of the indexed field name. For example, CLIELAST indicates that the last name field is indexed in the CLIENT database.

It is recommended that you accept the default name because it is a unique index file name created by PC-File, and you cannot have duplicate index file names in PC-File.

You can change the default index file name, but make sure the name you choose is a unique name. Otherwise PC-File tells you the index file name is a duplicate. Then you must enter a new name.

Summary

In this chapter you learned how to create a new database file from start to finish. You examined two ways to define a PC-File database using the Fast method and the Paint method. You learned about the rules and guidelines for defining field information. You found out how to name PC-File database files and attach a file description to the file name.

If you want to make changes to the design of your database or learn how to manage your files, read the next chapter. If you are satisfied with the design of your database, skip to Chapter 6 to learn how to add records to your database.

5

Adding Records

This chapter explains how to add records to your database. You learn how to open an existing database and enter data for each record. You examine field limitations and leaving fields blank. You find out how to use the calculation fields and the memo field. You learn how to save a record and exit Add mode. You discover several shortcuts to make it easier to add records to your database, such as duplicating fields and records, memorizing data, and using the flip data character feature.

Opening an Existing File

To add records to an existing file, you must open that database. In PC-File, you use the File Open command to open the database.

Follow these steps:

1. Select File from the menu bar.

2. Select Open from the File menu. PC-File displays the File Open dialog box that contains a list of files and directories (see figure 5.1).

3. If you know the name of the database file you want to open, type the file name in the text box at the top of the dialog box.

4. If you do not know the name of the database file you need to open, scroll through the list to find the database file you want. If the database file is stored in a different directory, select the directory, and then scroll through the list to find the database file. Select the database file you want to open by using the arrow keys to move the highlight to it or by clicking on it with the mouse.

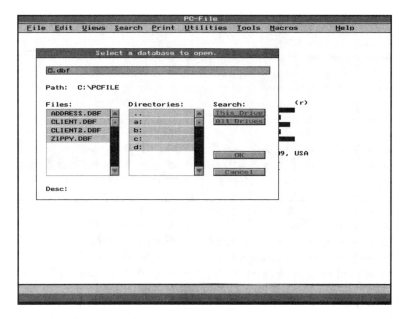

Fig. 5.1. *The File Open dialog box.*

5. Press Enter or click OK to open the database. PC-File opens the database and displays a blank record on the screen.

Now you can add records to your database, as described in the next section.

Adding Records to a Database

You can add data to the database at any time after the file has been created. To add records to a database, open the database first with the File Open command.

You can add records in any order you like. There is no need to enter them in alphabetical or numerical order. PC-File takes care of finding the information you want when you need it.

In PC-File, you add records to your database with the Edit Add command. If you are in Record View or Table View, you can choose the Edit Add command. However, you can add records only in Record View. If you are in Table View, PC-File automatically switches to Record View.

The Edit Add command displays a blank data entry screen that provides the field names, field labels, and space for you to enter the data for each field.

It is a little like having an electronic 3×5 card for each record. PC-File positions the cursor at the top of the data entry screen, ready for you to enter the data for the first field, as shown in figure 5.2.

```
                   PC-File - CLIENT: CLIENT CONTACT LIST
     File  Edit  Views  Search  Print  Utilities  Tools  Macros       Help
   CONTACT      __
   COMPANY
   ADDRESS
   CITY
   STATE
   ZIP
   PHONE




    OK    Cancel
   8 records    Index: ZIP ascending
```

Fig. 5.2. A blank data entry screen.

Entering Data

You can enter up to one billion records in a PC-File database. PC-File also lets you add records to a database by importing records from other PC-File databases or from a database created with a different program, as explained earlier in Chapter 4.

While you are entering data, the commands in the menu bar are displayed in gray. This means that you cannot select the commands in the menu. If you want to access the menu again, you must exit data entry mode.

To enter data, follow these steps:

1. Select Edit from the menu bar.

2. Select Add from the Edit menu. PC-File displays the data entry screen.

3. Type the data for the first record as shown in figure 5.3. Use the Enter or Tab key to move the cursor to the next field. Use the Shift-Tab key to move the cursor to the previous field.

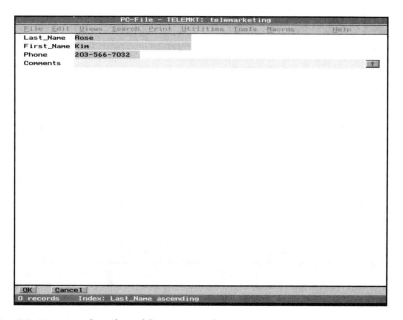

Fig. 5.3. Entering data for adding a record.

What happens if you make a mistake? Use the Backspace key to erase the error. Then type the correct information. Use the arrow keys, the Enter key, or the Tab key to move forward again.

4. When you finish entering data for the first record, press F10 or click OK to store the record in your database. PC-File displays the Add Record dialog box (see figure 5.4).

5. If you want to add the current record and exit from Add mode, select OK.

6. If you want to add the current record and display the Add Record dialog box after you enter the next record, select Yes to this record.

7. If you want to add the current record and all subsequent records without displaying the Add Record dialog box, select Always yes.

Fig. 5.4. The Add Record dialog box.

8. If you want to cancel adding the current record and return to the current record, select Cancel.

9. If you chose Yes to this record or Always yes, repeat steps 3 and 4 to enter more records until you are finished entering all of the records you want to add to the database.

When you are finished adding records to your database, select OK. PC-File exits Add mode. Now you can search and retrieve records as explained in Chapter 6, "Searching for Records."

> If your database contains multiple data entry screens, PC-File displays the next screen automatically when you enter data in the last field on the current data entry screen and press the Enter or Tab key.

You will find that certain field types and all edit masks pose some restrictions on the characters you enter in a field. You cannot enter letters in a numeric field, for example, and you can enter the letters y, n, t, and f only in logical fields. The edit masks put further restrictions on the characters that you can enter, as explained in Chapter 4, "Creating a Database."

If you try to enter a character that is not allowed in that particular field, PC-File beeps.

Leaving Blank Fields

If you leave a field blank, PC-File handles each field in a different way, depending on the field type. If the field is numeric, PC-File displays a zero (0) in the blank field. If the numeric field is set to a specific number of decimal places, PC-File displays a zero (0) before the decimal and a zero (0) for each character to the right of the decimal. For example, a numeric field with three characters to the right of the decimal displays 0.000 when you leave it blank.

In all other field types, PC-File displays no characters in the field if you leave it blank.

For information on entering data in calculation fields and memo fields, read the next two sections.

Using Calculation Fields

A calculation field contains data that is a result of a calculation. If you accidentally enter data in a calculation field, PC-File ignores it.

If you used the Blank Only limiter (*B) when you defined the calculation field, as described in Chapter 4, PC-File does not perform a calculation when you enter data in that field.

You can restrict the entry of data in a calculation field by defining an edit mask that prevents the entry of all characters. The edit mask you can use is BA. BA allows the entry of all characters greater than B and less than A, of which there are none. You can create the edit mask for the calculation field with the File Redefine command. For more information on entering edit masks refer to Chapter 9, "Changing the Design of a Database."

Using the Memo Field

A memo field is used to store large amounts of text, such as memos and short documents. The data you enter in a memo field is not stored in the DBF and HDB database files. It is stored in a separate file called a database text file. This file has the same name as the other database files and is automatically assigned an HDB file extension. The maximum size of a memo field is 5000 characters.

In a memo field, you can expand the display to a window so that you can see most or all of your entry. A memo field contains an up-arrow button at the end of the field that allows you to expand the field to a window, as shown in figure 5.5. If the display length of a memo field is less than three characters, PC-File does not display the up-arrow button.

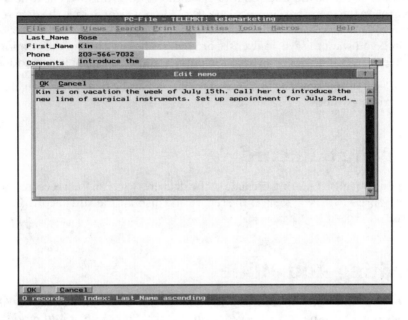

Fig. 5.5. *A memo field.*

To expand a memo field, click on the up-arrow button at the end of the field with the mouse. If you want to use the keyboard, move the cursor to the memo field with the Tab key and press Ctrl-E. PC-File expands the field to a window.

You can expand the window to full size or shrink the window with the resize buttons. The maximize button is in the upper-right corner of the window. Click on it with the mouse to expand the window to full size. To shrink the window to its original size, click on the maximize button again.

If you want to resize the window using the keyboard, press Alt-F10 to expand the window and press Alt-F10 again to shrink the window.

You also can move the memo window with the mouse by clicking on the title bar called Edit Memo and dragging the window where you want it.

Once you expand the window, you can type anything you want in the memo field. If you make a mistake, you can use the Backspace or Delete key to erase the error. Then type the correct information. Use the arrow keys to move around the memo window.

To save the data you entered and close the memo window, click the OK button in the menu bar or press F10. If you do not want to save the data you entered, click the Cancel button in the menu bar or press Esc. PC-File asks you if you want to save your entry or changes before closing the window. Select No. PC-File does not save the entry and closes the memo window.

PC-File displays only the first line of the memo in the field when you close the memo window.

Saving a Record

When you finish entering the data in the data entry screen for a record, click OK or press F10. PC-File saves the record and displays the Add Record dialog box.

Exiting Add Mode

When you finish adding records, you must exit Add mode. Otherwise, PC-File does not let you perform any other operations. You can exit Add mode in two ways—from the Add Data dialog box or from the last record you entered.

To exit Add mode from the Add Data dialog box, follow these steps:

1. When you have entered the data for the last record, click OK to save the record. PC-File displays the Add Record dialog box.

2. Select the option OK. PC-File exits Add mode and you are returned to the menu bar. The last record you entered remains displayed on the screen.

To exit Add mode from the last record you entered, follow these steps:

1. Once you enter the data for the last record, click Cancel. PC-File prompts you to save the current record.

2. Select Yes. PC-File saves the record, exits Add mode, and returns to the menu bar. The last record you added remains displayed on the screen.

Duplicating Fields and Records

In PC-File, you can use several shortcuts and hot keys to reduce the amount of typing required. The larger and more complicated your database, the more helpful these procedures can be.

One way to save keystrokes and time is to duplicate fields and records. The Duplicate feature allows you to fill the fields for each new record with duplicate information automatically. For example, if you have many records that have the same information for a field called CITY, you can use the Duplicate feature to display the city name in each new record you add to the database.

PC-File copies the data from the previously viewed or added record into the current record. You can duplicate one field or all of the data from the current field to the end of the record. This feature can save you time and typing.

> If you duplicate a field, PC-File overrides any default data you entered in a field when you defined the database.

Duplicating a Single Field

You can duplicate a single field when that field repeats itself without duplicating the fields that follow. This is useful if you are entering address information, for instance. It is likely that you could have two or more addresses in a row from the same state, but with different zip codes.

Suppose, for example, that you already have a record for Sam Sargent and you want to duplicate one field. To duplicate a single field, follow these steps:

1. Move the cursor to the field you want to duplicate.

2. Press Ctrl-F. PC-File copies the data from the previously viewed or added record into the current record, as shown in figure 5.6.

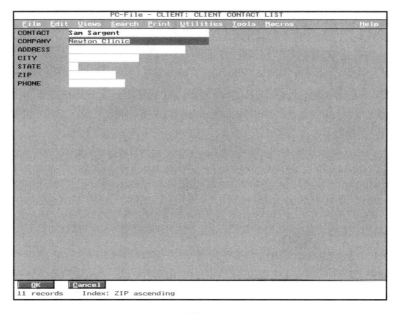

Fig. 5.6. Duplicate data in a single field.

Duplicating to the End of the Record

Suppose you have address information such as the city, state, and zip code in the current record that is the same as the address information in the previously viewed or added record. Instead of typing that information again, you can ask PC-File to duplicate all of the data from the current field to the end of the record.

To duplicate all of the data to the end of the record, follow these steps:

1. Move the cursor to the field where you want to start duplicating data.

2. Press Ctrl-R. PC-File copies the data for the current field and all subsequent fields from the previous record, as shown in figure 5.7.

This feature also is useful when two records are almost identical and you want to change only one or two fields after making the duplication. After you duplicate the fields, you can change the data in the current record before you add the record to your database.

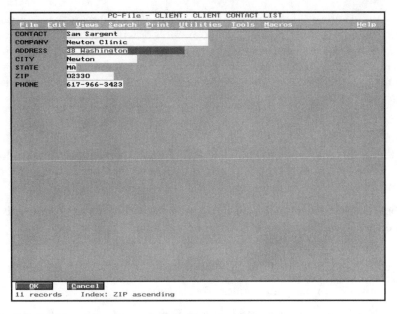

Fig. 5.7. *Duplicate data in several fields.*

You also can duplicate fields when the last few fields in a record are the same. In this case, you enter the data in the fields at the beginning of the record, then press Ctrl-R when the cursor is in the field you want to duplicate.

If you plan to duplicate fields in a database that contains a field with a unique numbering mask (:UNIQUE*:*A), lay out your database so that the unique number field is the first field in the record. Otherwise, PC-File duplicates the unique number field when you press Ctrl-R, thus giving you two records with the same number. If the unique number field is the first field in the record, you can move the cursor to the second field, and then press Ctrl-R to duplicate the rest of the fields in the record.

Memorizing Data

Another shortcut to reduce typing and time is memorizing data. Suppose that you enter the same data in a particular field frequently. For instance, you may enter the same remark in a comments field for many of the records in your database. If almost every record in your database has the same remark in the comments field, you can enter default data in the comments field using the Default Data feature, as explained in Chapter 4, "Creating a Database." Or, you can save time and typing by memorizing the data you enter in a field. PC-File lets you copy data from one field and paste it in another field.

PC-File stores the data you copy in a temporary storage area called the buffer, and you can recall the data from the buffer any time you want. The buffer holds only one block of data at one time. If you copy another block of data to the buffer, PC-File replaces the previous block of data with the new data.

The data remains in the buffer during the current working session only. If you exit PC-File, the data in the buffer is cleared.

PC-File gives you two hot keys to copy data to and from the buffer—Ctrl-Ins to copy the data to the buffer and Shift-Ins to copy data from the buffer.

To copy data to the buffer, follow these steps:

1. Select the data in a field that you want to copy to the buffer. To do this with the mouse, click and drag through the data to highlight it. With the keyboard, press the Shift key and use any arrow key to extend the selection. PC-File highlights the data in the field, as shown in figure 5.8.

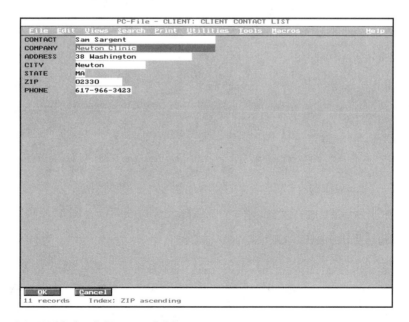

Fig. 5.8. Highlighted data in a field.

2. Press Ctrl-Ins to copy the data to the buffer.

3. Move the cursor to where you want to copy the data.

4. Press Shift-Ins. PC-File copies the data from the buffer to the new location, as shown in figure 5.9.

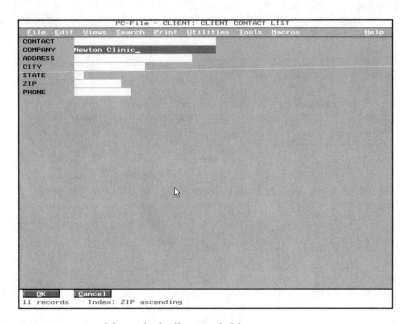

Fig. 5.9. *Data copied from the buffer to a field.*

For more information on using the buffer, refer to Chapter 7, "Modifying Records."

Using the Flip Data Character Feature

PC-File provides a flip data character feature to speed up data entry. In most databases, you place the first and last names in separate fields. However, you may already have included both the first and last name within a single field in a database. If you want to sort that database by last name, PC-File lets you flip the names around. If you want to print mailing labels, you can flip the last name and first name. The flip data character feature also is useful when you generate form letters using the mail merge format, as explained in Chapter 11, "Producing Form Letters and Mailing Labels."

To flip the data within a field, enter a tilde (~) between the two parts of the field for every record you enter. This will swap the order of the two parts within the field when you display it on the screen, print a report, or print mailing labels.

For example, type *Digiro ~terri* in the name field when you add records to your database. Be sure to type a space between the last name and the tilde. PC-File displays the name as Terri Digiro in a report, a mailing letter, or a form letter.

Summary

In this chapter you learned how to add records to your database. You also learned how to open an existing database and enter data for each record. Now you can use PC-File's data entry techniques to make it easier and quicker to add records, reducing the number of data entry errors.

Once you add records to your database, you can search and retrieve the records to update the information and keep the database current, as explained in the next chapter, "Searching Records."

Searching for Records

The capacity to search and retrieve records is one of the most powerful PC-File features. Once data has been stored, a single piece of information or a group of related data can be retrieved. This chapter shows you how to search and retrieve records in a PC-File database. You examine the Search menu, and you learn how to perform three types of searches: Simple, Formula, and Global. You also learn how to find duplicate records, and discover shortcuts for navigating through the records in your database.

A PC-File database can hold up to a billion records. The databases you will be working with will probably have many records, some with a very large number of fields. In many cases, you want to work with selected parts of a database at a time. In a client database, for example, you may search and retrieve the records for clients in the state of Connecticut and work with only those records.

Using the Search commands, specific information can be located within a database, displayed on the screen, and modified or deleted.

Retrieving specific data is relatively easy. PC-File has a fast search and retrieval feature that lets you find the data you need quickly and easily by simply selecting commands from the Search menu, as described in the next section.

Navigating through Records

You can navigate easily and quickly through the records in a database using the Search commands that appear at the bottom of the Search menu (see figure 6.1). You have four choices: you can display the next record, the previous record, the first record, or the last record in the database.

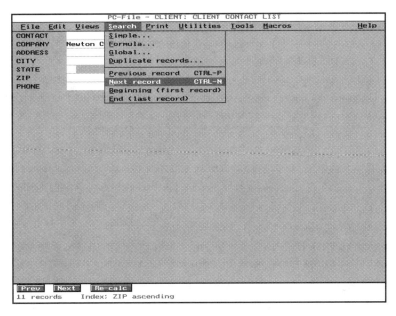

Fig. 6.1. *The Search menu with navigation commands.*

To display the previous record, select Search from the menu bar. Then select Previous record from the Search menu. PC-File displays the next record in your database. You also can use the hot key Ctrl-P to move to the previous record in your database. Repeat the steps to move backward through your database.

To display the next record, select Search from the menu bar. Then select Next record from the Search menu. PC-File displays the previous record in your database. You also can use the hot key Ctrl-N to move to the next record in your database. Repeat the steps to move forward through your database.

To display the first record in your database, select Search from the menu bar. Then select Beginning from the Search menu. PC-File displays the first record in your database.

To display the last record in your database, select Search from the menu bar. Then select End from the Search menu. PC-File displays the last record in your database.

Searching for Data

When you select the Search command from the menu bar, PC-File displays the Search menu (see figure 6.2). From the Search menu, you can perform three types of searches: Simple, Formula, and Global. The Simple and Formula search commands let you search for specific data, scan through a specific field for a word or part of a word, search for data that sound like the search criteria, and use wildcard characters to find specific information. For more information on performing a Simple search, refer to Performing a Simple search later in this chapter.

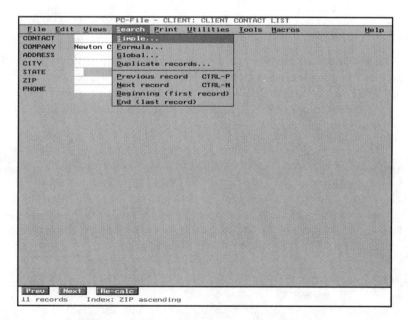

Fig. 6.2. The Search menu.

The Formula search command is more powerful than the Simple search. PC-File compares the data as it performs the search and retrieve operation. For example, a typical Formula search can ask PC-File to find all the clients in the client database who purchase more than $1,000 worth of products per month. For more information on the Formula search command, read the section later in this chapter on Performing a Formula Search.

The Global search command lets you search for specific text through all the fields except memo fields. For more information on the Global search command, read the section later in this chapter on Performing a Global Search.

PC-File also lets you check for duplicate records using the Duplicate records command in the Search menu, as described later in this chapter. The Previous record, Next record, Beginning, and End commands are shortcuts you can use for navigating through the records in your database. These shortcuts are explained at the end of this chapter.

Entering Search Criteria

When you select the type of search from the Search menu, PC-File displays a blank record. You type the search criteria in this record.

PC-File provides four ways to enter search criteria in the Simple and Formula searches. The four methods include generic, scan across, sounds like, and wildcard. You can use one of the methods or combine several methods within one search operation. The generic search is the default method for entering search criteria.

TIP

You can make searches case sensitive or case insensitive using the Utilities Configuration ? command. If you select case sensitive and you enter only uppercase letters for search criteria, PC-File retrieves records only for data that matches in uppercase letters. It does not find data that contains both uppercase and lowercase letters within a word. For example, if you enter *BOSTON* as your search criteria, a case-sensitive PC-File search retrieves records that contain BOSTON, but not Boston or BOSton. If you select case insensitive and enter only uppercase letters for search criteria, PC-File finds records that contain the data in both uppercase and lowercase letters. For example, if you enter *BOSTON,* PC-File finds not only BOSTON, but Boston or BOSton as well.

Generic

You can use the generic search to search for information that exactly matches the search criteria you enter. For example, to search your database for a client who has a specific phone number, you enter that phone number in the PHONE field.

PC-File also lets you enter the first part of a word to search for data in a particular field (see figure 6.3). If you type *ch* to retrieve records that begin with ch in a furniture field, for example, PC-File retrieves records that contain chair and chaise.

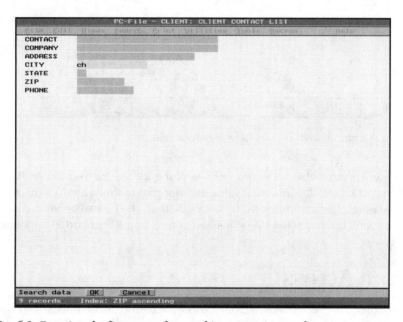

Fig. 6.3. Entering the first part of a word in a generic search.

If you want to search for a root word or part of a word, enter a space following the word, as shown in figure 6.4. For example, to find Jack, but not Jackson or Jackston, enter a space after the *k* in *Jack*.

In a Simple generic search, you do not have to enter any special characters. Simply type the search criteria in the field.

In a Formula generic search, however, you must enclose the search criteria in quotation marks (" "). The quotation marks are part of the search command syntax, as explained later in this chapter.

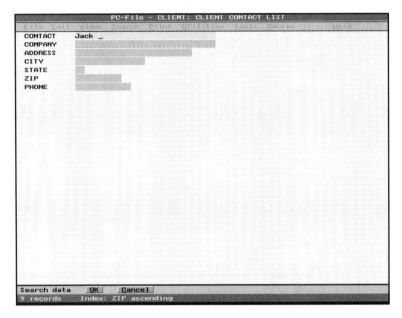

Fig. 6.4. Entering part of a word in a generic search.

A generic search also is used when searching for values in numeric fields. You must search for the actual value and not part of the value. For instance, if you enter *3* in a numeric field generic search, the records with the value 3 are found but not 30 or 300; you must enter *30* or *300* to find those values.

Scan-Across

You can use the scan-across search if you want to find occurrences of specific pieces of information in your file. PC-File scans across all the characters you specify in a particular field to retrieve the records you want.

A scan-across search can be used in a Simple and Formula search, but it cannot be used in a numeric field.

In a Simple scan-across search, you enter a tilde (~) before the search criteria as part of the search command syntax. For example, ~*K* retrieves all last names that begin with the letter K. For another example, ~*cb* in the CITY field retrieves the records for Charlotte, Charleston, Munich, and Greenwich (see fig. 6.5).

If you want to search for information that ends in a particular character, you must enter a space after the character. In a country field, for example, if you entered ~*Y* followed by a space, PC-File would retrieve records for Italy, Hungary, and Germany.

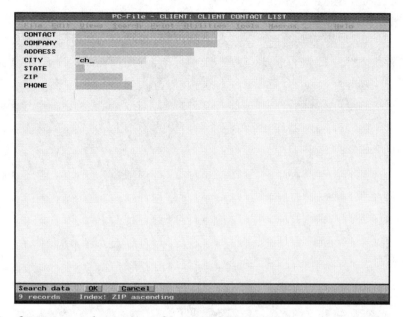

Fig. 6.5. Entering characters within a word in a Simple scan-across search.

In a Formula scan-across search, you must enter a tilde (~) before and after the search criteria. For instance, to search for cities enter ~*wich*~ in your Formula criteria. PC-File retrieves records for Greenwich, Sandwich, and Harwich.

Sounds-Like

The sounds-like search is used when you do not remember exactly how a piece of information was entered in a field. PC-File retrieves records that sound the same as the search criteria. If you want to search for names that sound like Solomon, for example, you can enter *?Solomon.* PC-File then retrieves records for Solomon, Saloman, and Solaman (see figure 6.6).

A sounds-like search can be used in a Simple and Formula search and only on character fields.

In a Simple sounds-like search, you must enter a question mark (?) before the search criteria as part of the search command syntax. The first character of the search information in a sounds-like search must be the same as the first character of the information you want to retrieve. For example, ?Kramer does not retrieve records for Cramer.

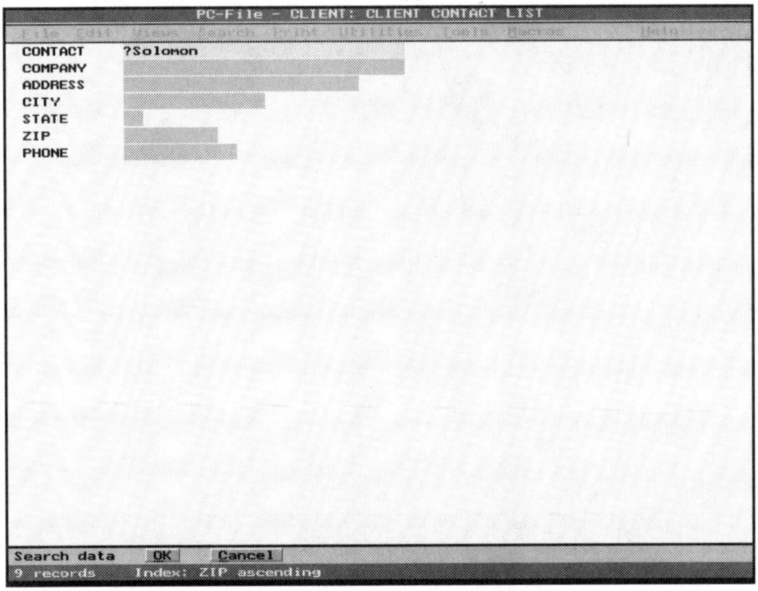

Fig. 6.6. A sounds-like search.

In a Formula search, you must enter a question mark (?) before and after the search criteria. For instance, to search for names, enter *?Novack?* or *?Rowan?* and PC-File retrieves records for Novack, Novick, and Nowak or Rowan, Rohan, Roughan, and Rowen.

Wildcard

When you do not remember exactly how a piece of information is entered in a field but you do know where some of the characters appear in fixed positions, you can use PC-File's wildcard search. Wildcards are especially useful when searching for dates.

If you want to search for birth dates in a particular month, for example, you can enter *10/_/91* to search for records that contain October birth dates (see fig. 6.7).

A wildcard search can be used in a Simple and Formula search, but it cannot be used in combination with sounds-like or Global searches or on numeric fields.

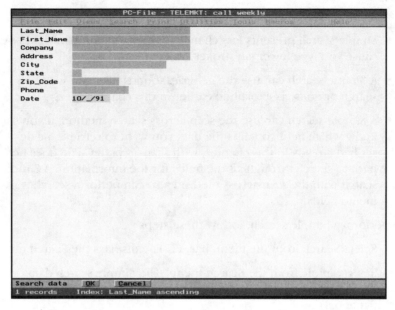

Fig. 6.7. *A wildcard search.*

In a Simple or Formula wildcard search, you must enter an underscore (_) in the search criteria as part of the search command syntax. You place the underscore where a character appears in a fixed position. In the search, PC-File accepts any character found in that fixed position. For example, to search for all tenants with a lease expiration date in the month of July, you can enter *07/_/91* in the LEASE EXPIRATION date field.

> If you want to search on a date field, you must enter the date in the YYMMDD or MM/DD/YY format. If you enter a date in the MM/DD/YY format, be sure to include both slashes in the search criteria.

Performing a Simple Search

In most cases, you perform a Simple search when you want to find specific records. In some cases, the complexity of the search might require a Formula search. To determine which type of search is appropriate, you need to know about the advantages the Simple search has over a Formula search:

- A Simple search is more intuitive.

- Simple search presents less chance for making typing mistakes because you type fewer keystrokes.

- A Simple search can use the generic, sounds-like, and wildcard search options, as explained earlier in this chapter.

- A Simple search can use the scan-across search method, if you know which field contains the data you want to retrieve. As described already in this chapter, with scan-across PC-File does not have to search through all the fields for the information. A Simple search with the scan-across method also can perform searches in memo fields.

To perform a Simple search, follow these steps:

1. Select Search from the menu bar. PC-File displays the Search menu.

2. Select Simple from the Search menu. The Simple search data entry screen appears. This is where you enter search criteria (see figure 6.8).

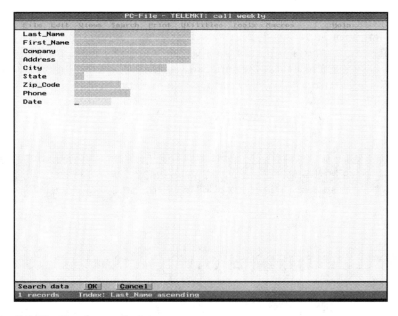

Fig. 6.8. The Simple search data entry screen.

3. Move to the field where you want to enter search criteria by pressing the Enter key.

4. Enter the search criteria. For example, type *mt* in the state field.

   You can perform generic, scan-across, sounds-like, and wildcard searches by typing the appropriate search criteria.

5. Click OK or press Alt-O to begin the search. If you change your mind and do not want to perform the search, click the Cancel button or press Alt-C.

   PC-File searches through the records in your database and displays the first record that matches the search criteria (see figure 6.9).

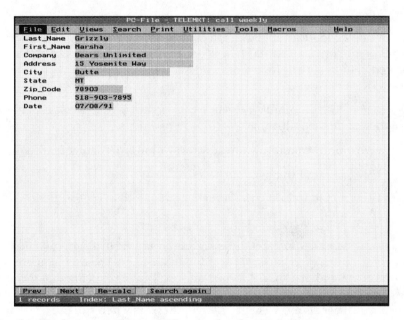

Fig. 6.9. The first record that matches the search criteria.

6. To retrieve the next record that matches the search criteria, either click on the Search button using the mouse or press Ctrl-S. Repeat this step to retrieve the rest of the records that match the search criteria.

7. When you are finished looking at all the records retrieved, you can select any command you want from the menu bar to perform a different task.

PC-File lets you search in more than one field at a time using a Simple search. For example, you can ask PC-File to search for all the clients located in New York who have purchased $10,000 worth of merchandise. In this case, you type *New York* in the CITY field and *10000* in the SALES field.

Performing a Formula Search

PC-File's Formula search is more powerful than the Simple search. The Formula search lets you search for larger, smaller, equal, or not-equal information. For example, you can search for a salary larger than $50,000 or for a date later than 07/01/91.

A Formula search also allows you to search in more than one field at a time. For example, you can tell PC-File to search for all your clients located in either New York or Florida. If you prefer, you can search for all clients located in New York or for clients who have purchased more than $10,000 worth of merchandise.

The four types of Formula searches you cannot perform with a Simple search include the following:

- Using more than one search criteria within a particular field

- Using a logical operator such as OR

- Using a comparison criteria such as greater than or less than

- Using a calculation

In a Simple search, you enter the exact search criteria in a particular field or fields for the records you want to find. In a Formula search, you enter a search command in a special format in a text box, as explained in the next section. You can enter a maximum of 250 characters in a Formula search command. There is more chance for typing errors when you use a Formula search because you must enter the correct special characters in the correct locations in a search command.

To perform a Formula search, follow these steps:

1. Select Search from the menu bar. PC-File displays the Search menu.

2. Select Formula from the Search menu. PC-File displays the Formula search dialog box where you enter the search command (see figure 6.10).

3. Type the search command in the text box. For example, type *SALES > 50000*. For information on entering search commands, refer to the next few sections.

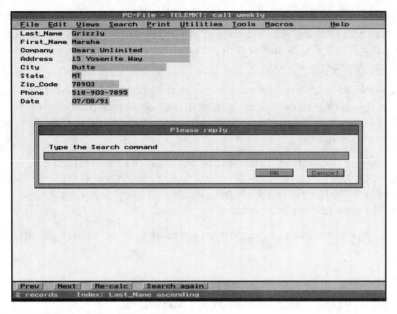

Fig. 6.10. The Formula search dialog box.

4. Click OK or press Alt-O to begin the search. If you change your mind and do not want to perform the search, click the Cancel button or press Alt-C.

   PC-File searches through the records in your database and displays the first record that matches the search criteria.

5. To retrieve the next record that matches the search criteria, either press Ctrl-S or click on the Search button using the mouse. Repeat this step to retrieve the rest of the records that match the search criteria.

6. When you are finished looking at all the records you've retrieved, you can perform any operation you want by selecting the appropriate command from the menu bar.

Entering a Formula Search Command

A Formula search command consists of three components: the search location, the operator, and the search criteria. As a rule, the search location is on the left side of the comparison operator, and the search criteria is on the right side. The general format for a formula search command using a comparison operator looks like this: search location = search criteria.

If you want to search for all records in the state of California, you enter *STATE = "CA"*. STATE is the search location, the = (equal sign) is the comparison operator, and "CA" is the search criteria enclosed in quotation marks to indicate a generic search.

The Formula search command allows up to 34 comparisons. You can enter as many spaces as necessary anywhere in the command to make the formula easier to read. PC-File recognizes both uppercase and lowercase letters in a search command.

An example of a more complex formula search command is (LAST_NAME = "Howe" | LAST_NAME = "Solomon") & CITY = "NEW YORK". This command tells PC-File first to find anyone named Howe or Solomon, and then to make sure the city is New York.

The components of a Formula search command are covered in detail in the next few sections.

Specifying the Search Location

A search location is a field in the database. It also can be a calculation. You always enter the search location on the left side of the comparison operator without any punctuation: *LASTNAME = "Howe"*.

A search location must precede each search criteria. To enter a field name for each search criteria, for example, you would type *LASTNAME = "Howe" | LASTNAME = "Solomon"*. You must not enter LASTNAME = "Howe" | "Solomon".

You can use the pipe (|) as a comparison operator to separate fields and specify an "or" comparison, as explained later in this chapter.

If you don't want to type the entire field name, you can abbreviate it. For example, you can use LA = "Howe" instead of LASTNAME = "Howe". PC-File recognizes LA as unique to the LASTNAME field if this is the only field in the database that starts with LA. Be sure that no other field name in the database contains the same characters you select for an abbreviated version of the field name. If you have a LASTNAME field and a LAWYER field and you enter *LA = "Howe"*, PC-File cannot retrieve the records you want.

PC-File lets you use a calculation as a search location as well. It can be any valid numeric or date calculation and cannot be a relational lookup, as described earlier in Chapter 4. Also, you can use more than one search location within a command. For example, SALES − EXPENSES >= 50000 tells PC-File to search for all records where the profit is greater than or equal to $50,000. One location is SALES and the other is EXPENSES. PC-File searches on both fields to retrieve the appropriate records by using the subtraction operator and comparing the answer to the calculation of the figure 50,000.

For information on using comparison operators, read the next section.

Using Comparison Operators

A comparison operator is used to compare two pieces of data. When you compare two pieces of data, PC-File retrieves the records that match the search criteria. PC-File uses the comparison operator to evelute the relationship between the search location and the search criteria.

There are six comparison operators you can use in a Formula search. Table 6.1 lists the six comparison operators.

Table 6.1
Comparison Operators

Comparison	Operator
Equal to	=
Not equal to	!=
Greater than	>
Less than	<
Greater than or equal to	>=
Less than or equal to	<=

The equal-to operator (=) is used to retrieve data that are exactly equal to each other. For example, LASTNAME = "Solomon" finds only Solomon; PC-File does not find Solamon unless you perform a sounds-like search.

The not-equal-to operator (!=) retrieves all records in which the search location does not contain the search criteria you specified. Be sure to enter the equal sign after the exclamation point. For example, CITY != Boston finds all records in which the city is not Boston.

The greater-than operator (>) means that the data to the left of the symbol is greater than the data on the right. For example, SALES > 500 finds all records in which sales are greater than $500.

The less-than operator (<) means that the data to the left of the symbol is less than the data on the right. For example, SALES < 500 finds all records in which sales are less than $500.

The greater-than or equal-to operator (>=) means that the data to the left of the greater than symbol and equal sign is greater than or equal to the data on the right. Be sure to enter the equal sign after the greater than symbol. For example, SALES >= 500 finds all records in which sales are greater than or equal to $500.

The less-than or equal-to operator (<=) means that the data to the left of the less-than symbol and equal sign is less than or equal to the data on the right. Be sure to enter the equal sign after the less-than symbol. For example SALES <= 500 finds all records in which sales are less than or equal to $500.

Notice that when the search criteria use numeric values, the criteria do not require quotation marks.

Entering Search Criteria

The search criteria are entered on the right side of the comparison operator. The criteria can be a constant, a calculation, or a field. The constant must be enclosed in special characters, which vary depending on the method you choose for entering the search criteria. However, if the constant is a numeric value, the special characters are optional. Table 6.2 lists the methods for entering search criteria, the special characters, and examples of search criteria.

Table 6.2
Special Characters for Search Criteria

Search Method	Special Characters	Example
Generic	Quotation marks (" ")	"Howe"
Scan across	Tilde (~)	~ch~
Sounds like	Question mark (?)	?Solomon?

The wildcard character (_) search method can be used in combination with generic and scan-across searches, but not with the sounds-like search.

Using Logical Operators

A logical operator is used to retrieve a group of related data or to set up either-or criteria. You can link multiple comparisons with a logical operator. PC-File gives you two logical operators: AND and OR. The ampersand (&) is the symbol that represents the AND logical operator. You enter a comparison on the left and right sides of the ampersand (&) to compare data from different fields. Using the AND logical operator means that both comparisons must match the search criteria. For example,

LASTNAME = "Smith" & CITY = "Richmond"

tells PC-File to find first anyone named Smith, then to make sure the city is Richmond.

The pipe (|) is the symbol that represents the OR logical operator. To enter the pipe (|) symbol, you must press Shift and the backslash (\) key.

When using an OR logical operator, you enter a comparison on the left and right sides of the pipe (|) to compare data from the same field. Using the OR logical operator means that either comparison can match the search criteria. For example, when given the entry

ITY = "Fairfax" | CITY = "Richmond"

PC-File retrieves records that contain the city Fairfax or the city Richmond.

PC-File lets you set up search criteria that contain multiple logical operators. In this case, you must use parentheses in the command syntax to get the results you want, as described in the next section.

Using Parentheses

In most cases, when you use multiple logical operators in search criteria, you must enter parentheses to group the comparisons logically and get the proper results. If you do not enter the parentheses, PC-File retrieves a different group of records.

For example, when you enter

State = "MA" & (Contact = "Novack | Contact = "Solomon")

PC-File retrieves all the records in which the state is MA and the Contact is either Novack or Solomon. Without the parentheses, PC-File retrieves all of the records in which the state is MA and the Contact is Novack, plus those records for which the Contact is Solomon, regardless of what the city is.

The way that PC-File reads search commands is from left to right. It ignores the previous logical operator when it reads the new logical operator. Using this example, there are two main parts to the search command that are separated by parentheses: the AND (&) operator comparison and the OR (|) operator comparison.

PC-File considers both logical operators as one unit. Thus, the two groups of comparisons are considered together. If you do not enter the parentheses, PC-File ignores the AND logical operator when it reads the OR logical operator and treats OR separately.

In most cases, you do not have to use parentheses if you use only OR or only AND in a search command. If you use only OR in a search command, for example,

> STATE = "MA" | STATE = "RI" | STATE = "VT"

PC-File retrieves all of the records in which the state is either MA, RI, or VT. Thus, you do not need the parentheses.

The following is another example, using only AND in a search command and no parentheses:

> CITY = "Boston" & BIRTHDATE = 12/_/_ & ZIP = "02110"

This command tells PC-File to first find anyone in the city of Boston, then make sure the birth date is in December and the ZIP code is 02110.

The following example shows when you need to enter parentheses because you are using only AND in a search command:

> CITY = "Boston" & (NAME != ?Howe? & NAME != ?Solomon?)

This command tells PC-File first to find anyone in the city of Boston, then make sure the name is not Howe and not Solomon. Without the parentheses, PC-File first retrieves all of the records in which the city is Boston; then it retrieves all the records for which the name is not Howe plus those for which the name is not Solomon, regardless of what the city is.

Now that you are acquainted with the details about entering search criteria for a Formula search, you can enter any of the various Formula search commands to suit your needs, as explained in the next section.

Looking at Some Examples

You have examined examples of Formula search commands in the last few sections; this section provides examples to show you how to enter the commands. The samples range from simple to complex search commands and are illustrated with figures.

The sample SALES > 50000 in figure 6.11 is not very complex, but does require a Formula search because it needs the comparison operator. In a Simple search, the comparison operator is understood to be the equal sign.

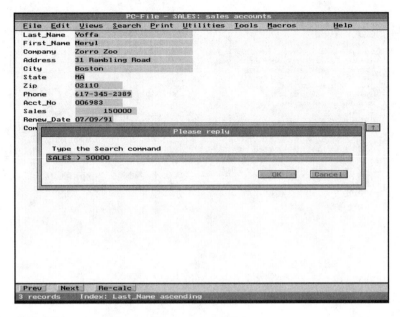

Fig. 6.11. The greater-than comparison operator.

The sample SALES < 50000 & DATE >= "07/15/91" in figure 6.12 contains two comparison operators and the AND logical operator. This means the search must meet the criteria for both comparisons. Notice that the numeric value uses no quotation marks; the DATE criteria, however, must use the quotation marks to indicate a generic search.

The sample ZIP > "01000" & ZIP < "02000" in figure 6.13 finds all the records between the two ZIP codes. It contains two comparison operators and the AND logical operator. This means the search must meet the criteria for both comparisons.

The sample ACCT_NO = "0057209" | ACCT_NO = "0082317" in figure 6.14 finds all of the records with either one or the other account number. It contains two comparison operators and the OR logical operator. This means the search must meet the criteria for either comparison.

The sample ZIP = "01816" & (ACCT_NO = "0057209" | ACCT_NO = "0082317") in figure 6.15 finds all of the records in which the ZIP code is 01816 and the account number is either one or the other. It contains the equal-to comparison operators, and both the AND and OR logical operators. This means the search must meet the criteria for the first comparison, and either criteria for the second comparison.

Fig. 6.12. The greater-than comparison operator and the AND logical operator.

Fig. 6.13. The greater-than and less-than comparison operators and the AND logical operator.

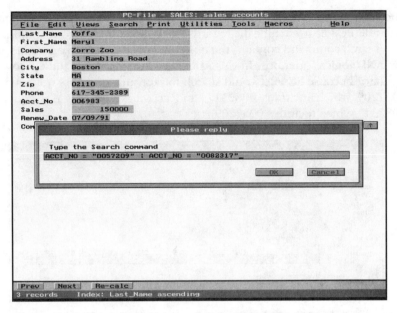

Fig. 6.14. *The equal-to comparison operators and the OR logical operator.*

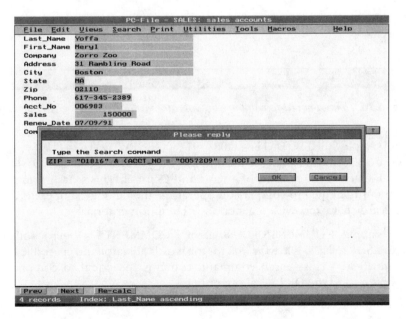

Fig. 6.15. *The equal-to comparison operators and the AND and OR logical operators.*

The sample ACCT_NO != "0057209" & ACCT_NO != "0082317" in figure 6.16 tells PC-File to exclude the records that contain both account numbers. This search command contains the not-equal-to comparison operators and the AND logical operator. In this sample, you do not use the OR logical operator because PC-File would search for account numbers not equal to 0057209 which includes 0082317, and account numbers not equal to 0082317 which includes 0057209.

Fig. 6.16. *The not-equal-to comparison operators and the AND logical operator.*

The sample RENEW_DATE = "08/_/91" | RENEW_DATE = "10/_/91" in figure 6.17 tells PC-File to use the underline (_) wildcard character to search for all dates in the months of August and October. This search command contains the equal to comparison operators, the OR logical operator, and wildcard characters within generic search option criteria

The sample, COMMENTS = ~alligator | COMMENTS = ~crocodile, in figure 6.18 tells PC-File to search for the words alligator and crocodile in all memo fields. This search command contains the equal to comparison operators and the OR logical operator.

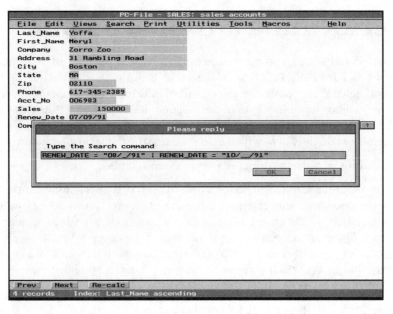

Fig. 6.17. The equal-to comparison operators, wildcard characters, and the OR logical operator.

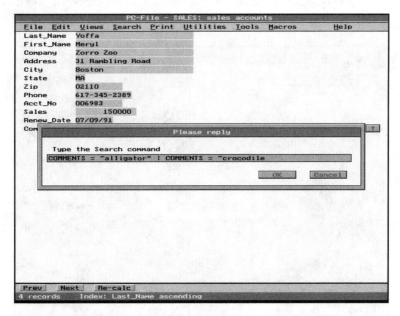

Fig. 6.18. A scan-across search in memo fields.

Performing a Global Search

With a Global search, you can search for specific text through all of the fields except memo fields. This type of search is useful when your database has several fields that contain the same kind of information. For example, your database may have more than one name field such as FIRST_NAME, LAST_NAME, FULL_NAME, and CONTACT. In this case, you can use a Global search if you do not know which field contains the data you want to retrieve.

You cannot perform a Global search in memo fields.

When you enter search criteria for a Global search, type the information the way it appears in the records. If case sensitivity is turned off in the configuration profile, as mentioned earlier in this chapter, PC-File searchs for both upper and lowercase combinations of the criteria. You do not have to enter any special characters. You cannot use wildcards and you cannot enter multiple criteria. If you want to search for dates, you must enter them in the YYYYMMDD format.

To perform a Global search, follow these steps:

1. Select Search from the menu bar. PC-File displays the Search menu.

2. Select Global from the Search menu. PC-File prompts you to enter the search criteria in the Global search dialog box (see figure 6.19).

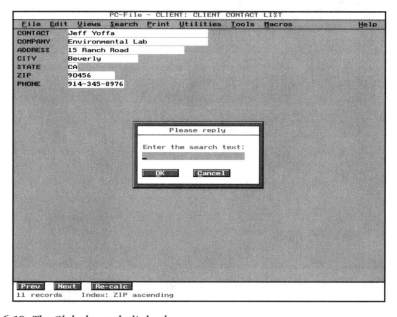

Fig. 6.19. The Global search dialog box.

3. Type the search text in the text box. For example, type *Johnson*.

4. Click OK or press Alt-O to begin the search. PC-File searches all fields (except memo fields) in your database. If you change your mind and do not want to perform the search, click the Cancel button or press Alt-C.

   PC-File searches through the records in your database and displays the first record that matches the search criteria.

5. To retrieve the next record that matches the search criteria, either click on the Search button using the mouse or press Ctrl-S. Repeat this step to retrieve the rest of the records that match the search criteria.

6. When you are finished looking at all of the records retrieved, you can perform any operation you want by selecting the appropriate command from the menu bar.

Finding Duplicate Records

Often, you find duplicate records in databases—especially in mailing lists. Duplicate records are those records which have exactly the same data in all fields. PC-File makes it easy to find and display duplicate records because you can select the fields you want to check. If any duplicates are found, you can delete them.

For example, if two records each have a name field that contains the name Joshua Tree and an address of Elm Street, PC-File identifies them as duplicates. However, if one record is J. Tree and the other is Joshua Tree, PC-File does not consider them duplicates.

PC-File gives you two ways to process duplicate records:

You can display the duplicate records side by side, then choose to delete the record on the right, on the left, both, or neither. Or you can print a report of all the duplicate records to either of three places: on-screen, a printer, or a file.

If you want to use the first method for processing duplicate records, you must display them on the screen first and then delete the duplicate records, as explained in the next section.

Displaying Duplicate Records

The first method for processing duplicate records involves two major steps: displaying the duplicate records and deleting them.

PC-File checks the records for duplication by comparing the data in one or more fields. You can choose up to 10 fields. From this comparison, PC-File assumes all remaining fields in the records also are duplicated.

PC-File identifies the duplication only when two records are identical in all of the fields being compared. Therefore, the more fields you select, the stiffer the comparison.

PC-File displays two records side by side for easy comparison. The data in the second record is compared to the data in the first and third records. The data is not compared to the data in the fourth, fifth, or any other records. The order of the records is based on the current index. The primary field of comparison you select should be the same as the current index. For example, if the database is currently indexed by ZIP code, select the ZIP_CODE field as the primary comparison field.

To display duplicate records side by side, follow these steps:

1. Select Search from the menu bar.

2. Select Duplicate records from the Search menu. PC-File displays the Duplicate records decision dialog box. The dialog box contains a warning message that specifies the current index and tells you that duplicate records may not be found if the current index is not in the same sequence as the compare data (see figure 6.20).

3. If you want to use the current index, click Yes or press Y to continue. If you want to switch to a different index, click No or press N to exit the Duplicate records dialog box. Refer to Chapter 8, "Indexing Records," for information on switching indexes. If you want to cancel the duplicate records operation, click Cancel or press C.

4. If you selected Yes in step 3, PC-File displays a list of all the fields in the database as shown in figure 6.21.

   Select the current index. A warning message tells you that duplicate records may not be found if the current index is not in the same sequence as the compare data.

5. Select one or more fields from the list by using the arrow keys and pressing Enter. Or, with the mouse, click each field you want. For example, select the LAST_NAME and FIRST_NAME fields.

Fig. 6.20. *The Duplicate records decision dialog box.*

Fig. 6.21. *The Field selection dialog box.*

6. When you are finished selecting the fields, click OK.

   PC-File displays a dialog box. You are prompted to select the method you want to use to process the duplicate records (see figure 6.22).

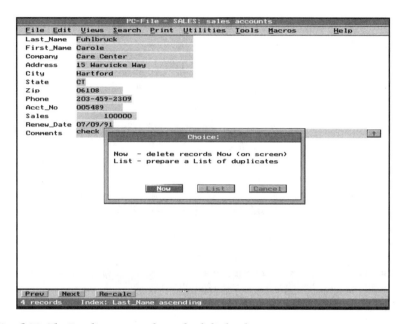

Fig. 6.22. The Duplicate records method dialog box.

7. If you selected Yes in step 3, PC-File displays a list of all the fields in the database.

8. To display the records side by side on the screen, select Now from the dialog box. PC-File displays the first pair of duplicate records on the screen with a dialog box (see figure 6.23).

9. Select Left to delete the duplicate record on the left side of the screen. Select Right to delete the duplicate record on the right side of the screen. Select Both to delete both duplicate records. Select Neither to delete neither of the duplicate records.

10. After you select which records you want to delete, PC-File displays the next two records side by side on the screen. Repeat Step 6 until you finish going through all of the duplicate records.

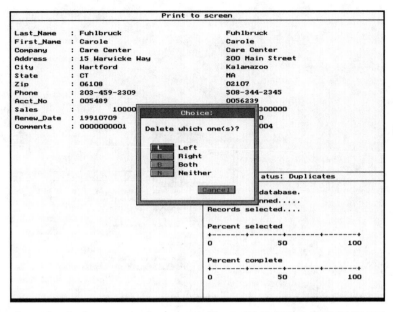

Fig. 6.23. The duplicate records compared by LAST_NAME and FIRST_NAME fields.

11. When you finish processing the duplicate records, a status box displays to tell you how many duplicate records were displayed and deleted (see figure 6.24). Click OK in the Information box to exit the Duplicate records screen.

Another way to process duplicate records is to print a report of all the duplicate records. This method is better than the display method. With a hard copy of the report, you can take the time to check for address changes and other reasons the duplicates were created. You also can examine the records carefully—by looking at the records only on the screen, you might go through them too quickly and not catch a duplicate.

You can print a report to the screen, a printer, or a disk. You also have the option to print all of the data or only the compared data.

To print a duplicates report, follow these steps:

1. Select Search from the menu bar.

2. Select the current index. A warning message tells you that duplicate records may not be found if the current index is not in the same sequence as the compare data.

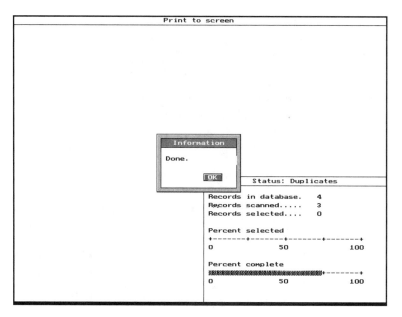

Fig. 6.24. The Duplicate records status box.

3. If you want to use the current index, click yes or press Y to continue. If you want to switch to a different index, click No or press N to exit the Duplicate records dialog box. Then refer to Chapter 8, "Indexing Records," for information on switching indexes. If you want to cancel the duplicate records operation, click Cancel or press C.

4. Select one or more fields from the list by using the arrow keys and pressing Enter. Or, with the mouse, click each field you want. For example, select the LAST_NAME and FIRST_NAME fields.

5. When you are finished selecting the fields, click OK. PC-File displays a dialog box. You are prompted to select the method you want to use to process the duplicate records (see figure 6.25).

6. Select List from the dialog box. PC-File displays another dialog box prompting you to specify where you want to print the report (see figure 6.26).

7. If you want print the report to the screen, select Screen. If you want to send the report to a printer, select Printer. If you want to send the report to a file on disk, select File. Once you select where you want to print the report, PC-File prompts you to select the amount of data you want to print (see figure 6.27).

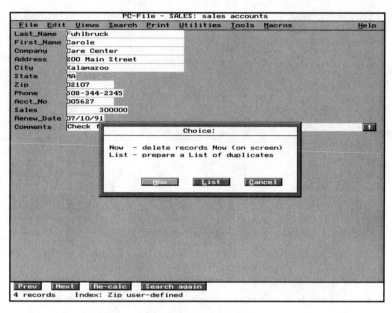

Fig. 6.25. *The Duplicate records method dialog box.*

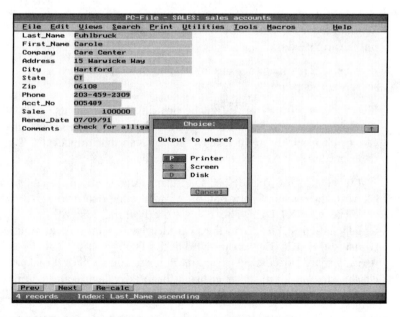

Fig. 6.26. *The Print Duplicate Records report dialog box.*

Fig. 6.27. The Data Print dialog box.

8. If you want to print all of the data, select All. If you want to print the data from the fields you have chosen for comparison, select only Compare data.

If you select print to the screen, PC-File displays the report on the screen at this point.

If you select print to a printer, the printing begins at this point. If the fields do not fit within the width of the printer, you can truncate or chop off the right side of the fields so that they do fit. When prompted, select Yes to truncate the fields.

If you select print to a file, PC-File prints a list of the duplicates to a file with the name of your database and the file extension DUP, for example, CLIENT.DUP. This file is stored on the current directory, usually called PCFILE. You then can display this text file at any time by using the DOS TYPE command at the DOS prompt. You also can use any word processing program. Refer to the DOS or word processing documentation for information on displaying and printing text files.

Once you print the report, you can check for duplicate records you want to remove, and display them on the screen, as explained earlier in this chapter. Finally, you can delete the duplicate records.

Summary

In this chapter you learned how to search and retrieve records in a database. You examined the Search menu and learned how to perform three types of searches: simple, formula, and global. Now you can see how flexible PC-File is when it comes to finding information in a database no matter how small or large the database may be. You also found out how to process duplicate records. You learned some shortcuts for navigating through the records in your database.

Now that you are familiar with how to search and retrieve records in a database, you are ready to make changes to the information in your database, as explained in the next chapter, Modifying Records.

Part III

Working with PC-File Records

Includes

Modifying Records

Indexing Records

Changing the Design of a Database

Modifying Records

PC-File's powerful set of editing tools lets you fine-tune data. After you retrieve records from your database, you can modify the information stored in each record individually or modify multiple records simultaneously. You can check your work on the screen to see that the records are satisfactory and make any last minute changes, if necessary.

PC-File has several advantages over the more traditional paper files. Editing and updating the design of your database and your data within the database are accomplished easily with PC-File's Edit commands, which let you change the data simply by pressing a few keys. PC-File's prompts direct and aid you when you fill in entries, thus reducing the number of data input errors.

In this chapter you examine the edit commands in the Edit menu. You find out the differences between Modify mode and Read-only mode. You explore the View menu, and you learn how to look at your records either one at a time using Record View or in a list format using Table View. You learn how to navigate around a database in both Record View and Table View by using the keyboard and the mouse. You find out how to recalculate data when a database contains calculations.

You explore various editing commands and techniques to change the information in the records. You also learn how to modify records in both Record View and Table View.

You find out how to save the changes you make, and you also find out how to delete the records you no longer want. You learn how to make multiple changes in records and how to delete multiple records simultaneously. Finally, you discover how to recover deleted records.

The first step toward editing and viewing your records is to take a look at the Edit menu and examine Modify mode and Read-only mode, as described in the next section.

Examining the Edit Menu

PC-File's Edit menu contains one command for adding records and five commands for editing your records: Delete, Restore, Global Modify, Global Delete, and Undelete (see figure 7.1). Table 7.1 lists the Edit commands and describes each command.

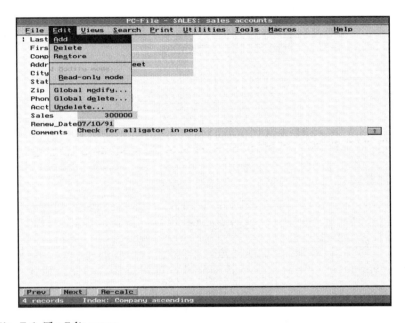

Fig. 7.1. *The Edit menu.*

Table 7.1
Edit Commands

Edit Command	Function
Add	Adds records to a database, as explained in detail in Chapter 5.
Delete	Deletes a highlighted record.
Restore	Undoes a change to a record.
Global Modify	Makes changes to multiple records.
Global Delete	Deletes multiple records.
Undelete	Undoes multiple changes to records.

Two editing modes, Modify and Read-only, are used for viewing and changing records. The editing modes are described in the next section.

Using Modify and Read-Only Mode

PC-File gives you two editing modes for making changes to records and viewing the data in records. They are Modify mode and Read-only mode. A check mark appears next to the currently active mode command on the Edit menu. Also, the active mode appears in gray on the Edit menu as shown in figure 7.1.

Modify mode lets you make changes to your records. PC-File is set to Modify mode by default, allowing you to make changes to your records at any time.

In Modify mode, you can make individual and global changes to your data as well as delete records. You can view the data and make changes to any or all of your records in either Record View or Table View, as described later in this chapter.

In Read-only mode, you can view the data and access the menu bar and the buttons in the button bar, but you cannot make changes to your data. For this reason, all the commands in the Edit menu appear in gray except Modify mode. In PC-File, you can select Read-only mode to prevent yourself or other people from making changes to your database. You can still use the commands in the other menus to create reports, print form letters, create graphs, and so on.

To switch modes, follow these steps:

1. Select Edit from the menu bar.

2. Select the mode that you want. You can select only the mode that does not have a check mark and does not appear in gray. PC-File will switch from the current mode to the other mode.

Exploring the View Menu

PC-File gives you two ways to view your records on the screen. You can view one record at a time using Record View, or you can look at your records in a list format using Table View. You can switch between the two views at any time.

You can select either option from the View menu with the keyboard or the mouse. When you do, PC-File displays a check mark next to the view that is currently selected and grays the command name. You cannot select the current option, but can select the non-gray option (see figure 7.2).

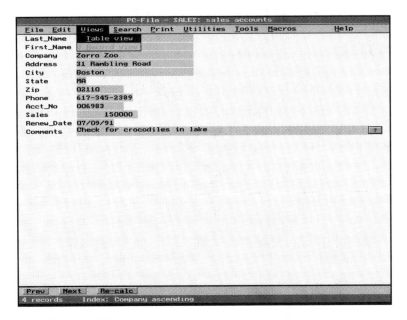

Fig. 7.2. The Record View menu.

You also can use the hot keys to switch between the two views by pressing Ctrl-T.

In either view, PC-File allows you to look at your records, navigate through those records, and make changes to them using the Edit commands, as explained in the next few sections.

If you want to set the default view to a Record View or Table View when you open a database, you can use the Utilities Configuration command. For information on changing the default view, refer to Appendix A, "Installing PC-File and Configuring Your System."

Using Record View

When you open a database or search and retrieve records, PC-File displays the first record on the screen (see figure 7.3). The screen looks just like the data entry screen that you work with when you add records or search and retrieve records. You can view up to five pages in the data entry screen. The default view in PC-File is the Record View that allows you to view one record at a time.

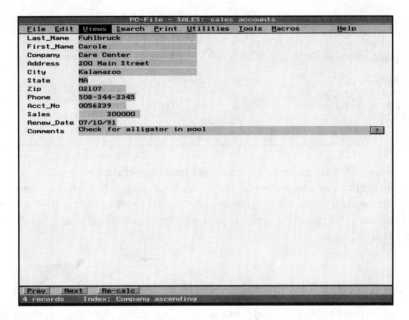

Fig. 7.3. The Record view.

You can use the keyboard or the mouse to navigate through the records in Record View, as explained in the next section.

Navigating through Records

PC-File lets you navigate in Record View using the keyboard or the mouse.

Table 7.2 lists the navigation keys and mouse actions you can use in Record View. The navigation keys are keyboard shortcuts and are referred to as the hot keys. The mouse actions are the buttons that you can click at the bottom of the Record View screen.

Table 7.2
Navigation Keys and Mouse Actions in Record View

Action	Hot Keys	Button
Next record	Ctrl-N	Next
Previous record	Ctrl-P	Previous
Continue search	Ctrl-S	Search again
Next page	PgDn	PgDn
Previous page	PgUp	PgUp
Recalculate	Ctrl-A	Calc

To move to the first record in a database based on the current index, select the Search command from the menu bar and select Beginning from the Search menu. To move to the last record in a database based on the current index, select the Search command from the menu bar and select End from the Search menu.

Navigating through Fields

If PC-File is set to Modify mode, as explained earlier in this chapter, you also can move between fields in a record. (In Read-only mode, you can't move among the fields; you can only view the records.) Use the Tab key to move forward and the Shift-Tab key to move backward. With the mouse, you can click on a field. PC-File highlights the current field in a different color or shade. The cursor appears as a flashing underscore.

If you want to view the data in a memo window but you do not want to make any changes to it, you can do this in either Modify or Read-only mode. For more information on viewing a memo field, refer to the section in Chapter 5 on Using the Memo Field.

Using Table View

You might find it more convenient and efficient to browse through many records at one time. PC-File lets you view 28 records at one time in a list format on the screen with the Table View feature. Each record appears on a separate line on the screen. The number of records displayed depends on the type of monitor you have. For information on how many lines can display on your monitor, check the documentation on your monitor.

In PC-File, the default view is set to Record View. If you want to switch to Table View, follow these steps:

1. Select View from the menu bar.

2. Select Table View from the View menu. PC-File displays the records in a table on the screen. Observe that several fields are displayed across the table in columns. The number of fields displayed depends on the length of the fields and the width of your screen (see figure. 7.4).

The current record highlighted in Record View is displayed in the first row in Table View.

The table is comprised of columns and rows. Each column contains the information for a field. The field length determines the width of a column. In Table View, only entire columns display on the screen, not partial columns. As a result, sometimes you see blank space on the right side of your Table View screen. The columns display in various colors on a color monitor and in shades of gray on a monochrome monitor.

Fig. 7.4. *The Table View.*

PC-File arranges the records on the screen in rows according to the current index. If you switch indexes, PC-File switches the order of the records in the table according to the new index. For information on the current index, refer to Chapter 8, "Indexing Records."

TIP

> You also can use the hot key Ctrl-T to switch to Table View.

You can use the keyboard or the mouse to navigate through records in Table View, as described in the next section.

Navigating through Records

You can navigate in Table View using the keyboard or the mouse. Table 7.3 lists the navigation keys and mouse actions you can use in Table View. The navigation keys are keyboard shortcuts and are referred to as the hot keys. The mouse actions are the buttons you can click at the bottom of the Record View screen.

Table 7.3
Navigation Keys and Mouse Actions in Table View

Action	Hot Keys	Button
Scroll right	Ctrl-Tab	>
Scroll left	Ctrl-Shift-Tab	<
Down one screen	PgDn	PgDn
Up one screen	PgUp	PgUp
Continue search	Ctrl-S	Search again
Recalculate	Ctrl-A	Calc

To move one record at a time in the table, use the up and down arrow keys. To move to the first record in the table based on the current index, select the Search command from the menu bar and select Beginning from the Search menu. To move to the last record in the table based on the current index, select the Search command from the menu bar and select End from the Search menu.

Navigating through Fields

PC-File lets you view a memo field in Table View in Modify mode. However, you cannot display a memo window in Table View in Read-only mode. For more information on viewing a memo field, refer to the section in Chapter 5 on Using the Memo Field.

> If PC-File is set to Modify mode, as explained earlier in this chapter, you can use the Tab key to scroll right one column at a time. You can use the Shift-Tab key to scroll left one column at a time.

TIP

Modifying Records

In earlier versions of PC-File, you could view your data only in Table View. In PC-File 6.0, you now can view your data as well as modify records in Table View.

In Record View or Table View, you can update the contents of records using PC-File's edit commands to keep your database current. You can modify records as you page through them in your database or after you perform a search and retrieval of the records.

Suppose that you did not have all the information you needed at the time you added records to your database, and you left some of the fields blank. After you retrieve the records from your database, you can enter the information in those empty fields. Information also changes in response to changes in your business environment—for example, the renewal date for an insurance policy changes, a sales projection figure increases, or a last name changes.

PC-File lets you modify records only in Modify mode, as described at the beginning of this chapter.

There are two ways you can make changes to the data. You can edit one record at a time in Record View or you can edit the records in a list format in Table View. The following instructions for adding and changing information pertain to both methods.

To move to a field, follow these steps:

1. Using the keyboard, press the appropriate arrow keys. Or if you want to use the mouse to move the cursor to a particular field, move the mouse pointer to the field and click.

   The cursor changes to an I-bar, as described in Chapter 1 (see figure 7.5).

2. Add or change the information for the current entry.

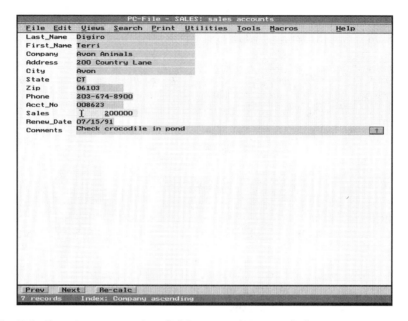

Fig. 7.5. Changing an entry in a field in Record View with the I-Bar.

When you move to the next record or select another command from the PC-File menu bar, the current record is saved. Even if you exit PC-File, the current record is saved.

PC-File gives you two ways to change the information in a field. You can type over the current entry, or you can erase the data in the field by pressing Ctrl-B and then typing in the new entry.

To erase the current entry in a field, use the Backspace or Delete keys. The Backspace key erases characters to the left of the cursor and the Delete key erases characters to the right of the cursor.

To delete text with the mouse, first highlight the entry by clicking on the first character in the entry and dragging the mouse through the characters. PC-File highlights the characters. Then press the Delete key. PC-File erases the entry.

You also can use a shortcut to reduce typing and time when you add or change information in your database. PC-File lets you memorize data, as described in Chapter 5. If you enter the same data in a field for many of the records in your database, PC-File lets you copy data from one field and paste it in another field. The data you copy is held temporarily in a storage area called the buffer.

There are two copy buffer commands. You can use Ctrl-Ins to copy or read the data to the buffer and Shift-Ins to copy or write the data from the buffer. To delete the data from the current location and copy the data to the buffer, press Shift-Del.

If you want to undo the last copy buffer command, press Alt-Backspace. PC-File reverses the command. For example, if you press Ctrl-Ins to read data to the buffer, and then press Alt-Backspace to undo the command, PC-File reads the data from the buffer and writes it back to the record.

If you save other changes to your records after you perform one of the copy buffer commands, the Undo feature does not work.

For step-by-step instructions on using the buffer, refer to Chapter 5, "Adding Records."

Using the Restore Command

Sometimes when working in a database you make typing mistakes, choose the wrong commands, erase data accidentally, or decide to restore things as they were originally. PC-File's Edit Restore command lets you reverse commands and erase changes you have made to entries.

If you save the changes for the current record by moving to the next record, selecting a command from a menu, or selecting File Exit, PC-File cannot restore the changes for the current record.

To restore the changes in a record, follow these steps:

1. Select Edit from the menu bar.

2. Select Restore from the Edit menu. PC-File undoes the changes for the current record.

Saving Your Changes

Once you leave a record after making changes, PC-File saves the changes automatically. Leaving the record is defined as moving to another record, selecting a command from a menu to begin a new operation, or selecting File Exit to exit the program.

PC-File saves the changes in a record in Record View the same way it does in Table View. After you make the changes to a record in Record View, you move to another record by clicking the OK button. PC-File saves the changes in the record and displays another record.

In Table View, you move the cursor from one record to another by using the up- and down-arrow keys. PC-File saves the changes you made to the previous record.

Recalculating Data

If you change data in a record that contains calculations, you must use the Calculation feature to recalculate the fields that contain the calculations. This feature is useful for relational lookups when you link databases and the data in the lookup database has changed. The Calculation feature is also handy for recalculating date calculations when one or more dates have changed. For information on relational lookups and date calculations, refer to Chapter 10, "Generating Reports."

In Record View or Table View, you can use the hot key Ctrl-A or click the Recalc button with the mouse to rerun the calculations (see figure 7.6). PC-File updates the current record and displays the new answer.

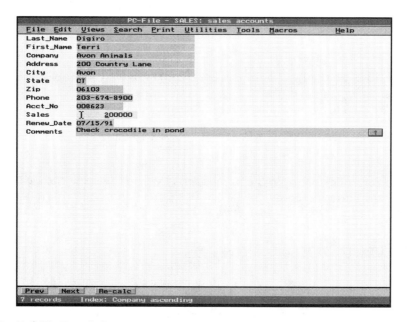

Fig. 7.6. *The Re-calc button.*

Making Changes to Multiple Records

What if you want to change a selected group of records or all of the records in your database at one time, rather than one record at a time? No problem. PC-File lets you do this with the Edit Global Modify command.

Changing one record at a time can be time-consuming whereas changing a group of records or all of the records takes less time and is easier to do. For example, you can change all records containing the city Boston to Hartford.

You can update information by making a change in one field that is dependent on the contents of another field. For example, if you want to change all assistant managers with salaries over $35,000 to Managers, you can use the Edit Global Modify command to do just that.

Suppose that an area code changes for a particular exchange in a phone number. For example, the area code 617 changes to 508 for any phone number with the exchange 552. In this case, you select all of the phone numbers that contain the 617 area code and 552 exchange and change them to a 508 area code.

You can modify a group of records only if there is a common denominator that you can use as search criteria to select these records. For example, the change in the area code provides search criteria that allows you to select specific records. However, in most cases changes in addresses do not provide search criteria that let you select specific records—you have to change the addresses individually. Most addresses in a database do not have a common denominator that you can use to find specific records and change a group of addresses. Generally, addresses in a database are not identical.

When you make changes to multiple records using the Edit Global Modify command, PC-File does not display the records on the screen. You can select changing all of the records, or you can perform a search to change a selected group of records, as explained in Chapter 6, "Searching for Records."

To prevent changes to specific characters within a field that you are changing, use the underline (_) wild-card character. You enter the wild-card character where you do not want a particular character to change. For example, if you are changing an area code in a phone number and you do not want the seven digits in the rest of the phone number to change, enter an underline (_) for each digit you do not want PC-File to change. You would enter 617-_ _ _-_ _ _ _ in the phone field.

If you want to blank out characters you are changing, use spaces. For example, if you are changing a group of 9-digit zip codes to 5-digit zip codes, enter the first five digits of the zip code followed by five spaces. The spaces blank out the dash and the last four digits of the 9-digit zip codes.

You can use the example of the area code change to make changes to multiple records. Follow these steps:

1. Select Edit from the menu bar.

2. Select Global Modify from the Edit menu. PC-File prompts you to select all or some of the records (see figure 7.7).

3. If you want to change all of the records in your database, select All. If you want to change a group of records in your database, select Some. PC-File prompts you to enter search criteria, as explained in Chapter 6 (see figure 7.8).

   If you specify Some, move the cursor to the field where you want to enter the search criteria. For example, to change all the 203 area codes to 302, move the cursor to the PHONE field.

   Type the search criteria. For example, type *203* in the PHONE field.

   Click the OK button, and PC-File retrieves all of the records that contain the 203 area code.

   After you select All records or perform the search, PC-File displays the data entry screen with an empty record.

4. Type the changes in the data entry screen. For example, type *302-___-____* to enter a new area code. A dash and three wild-card underline (_) characters indicate no change to the exchange; another dash and four wild-card underline (_) characters indicate no change to last four digits in the phone number.

5. Click the OK button.

   PC-File displays the first record selected and a dialog box that asks whether you want to make changes to the record.

6. If you want to change the current record and display the next record, select Yes. Repeat this step to make changes to the records individually.

   If you do not want to make changes to the current record and you want to display the next record, select No. Repeat this step to make changes to the records selectively.

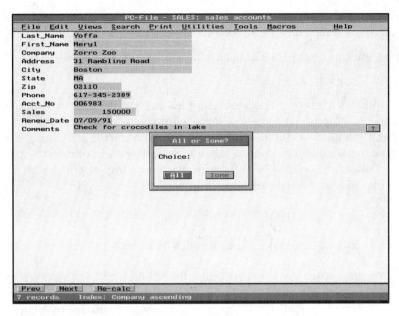

Fig. 7.7. *Global Modify command All or Some records dialog box.*

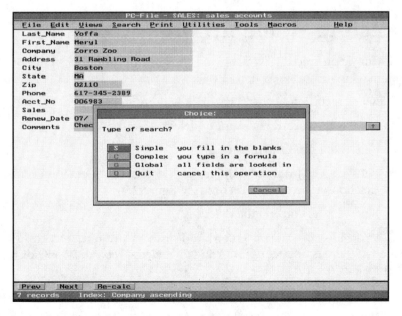

Fig. 7.8. *Global Modify command search criteria.*

If you want to make the specified changes to the current record and the rest of all of the selected records, select All.

If you want to cancel the Global Modify operation, select Quit.

PC-File makes the changes accordingly.

You must use a macro to perform complex global changes; you cannot use the Global Modify command. Some complex Global changes include variable length data and inserting data within other data. For example, you may want to remove the comma following each city name or insert a hyphen in a 9-digit zip code. For information on creating macros to perform complex global changes, refer to Chapter 13.

Deleting Records

PC-File lets you delete records individually in Record or Table View. You also can delete multiple records with the Edit Global delete command. One of the nicest features in PC-File is recovering the records you delete. All of these features are covered in the next few sections.

Deleting Single Records

You can delete records you no longer want by using the Edit Delete command in Record View or Table View.

To delete a record in Record View, follow these steps:

1. Display the record you want to delete.

2. Select Edit from the menu bar.

3. Select Delete from the Edit menu. PC-File asks you to confirm the deletion of the current record (see figure 7.9).

4. Select Yes to confirm the deletion.

PC-File deletes the current record and displays the next record on the screen. If there is no record following the deleted record, PC-File displays the previous record.

To delete a record in Table View, follow these steps:

1. Position the cursor anywhere in the record you want to delete.

2. Select Edit from the menu bar.

3. Select Delete from the Edit menu. PC-File asks you to confirm the deletion of the current record.

4. Select Yes to confirm the deletion.

PC-File deletes the record and displays the table again. The deleted record no longer displays in the table.

You can change your mind after you delete a record and undelete the deleted record. The steps for recovering a deleted record are explained in the section on Recovering Deleted Records at the end of this chapter.

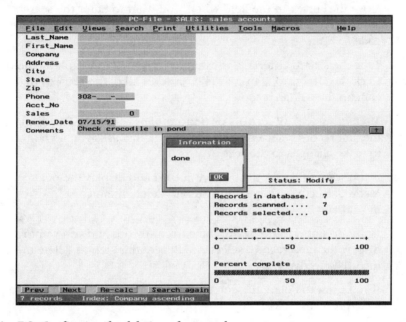

Fig. *7.9. Confirming the deletion of a record.*

Deleting Multiple Records

Suppose that you want to delete all the records or a group of selected records in your database, instead of deleting one record at a time. PC-File lets you do this with the Edit Global Delete command.

As with the Edit Global Modify command, you can delete a group of records only if there is a common denominator that you can use as search criteria to select these records. This is explained in the section on Making Changes to Multiple Records earlier in this chapter.

To delete multiple records, follow these steps:

1. Select Edit from the menu bar.

2. Select Global Delete from the Edit menu. PC-File prompts you to select all or some of the records.

3. If you want to delete all of the records in your database, select All.

   If you want to delete a group of records in your database, select Some. PC-File prompts you to enter search criteria.

   Move the cursor to the field where you want to enter the search criteria. For example, to delete all of records that contain the area code 617, move the cursor to the PHONE field.

   Type the search criteria. For example, type *617* in the phone field. Click the OK button, and PC-File retrieves all of the records that contain the 617 area code.

   After you select All records or perform the search, PC-File displays the first record selected and a dialog box that asks you if you want to make changes to the record.

4. If you want to delete the current record and display the next record, select Yes. Repeat this step to delete the records individually.

   If you do not want to delete the current record and you want to display the next record, select No. Repeat this step to delete the records selectively.

   If you want to delete the current record and all the rest of the selected records, select All.

   If you want to cancel the Global Delete operation, select Quit.

   PC-File deletes the records accordingly.

Recovering Deleted Records

PC-File is forgiving and lets you restore records with the Edit Undelete command. You can recover the records you deleted individually with the Edit Delete command or recover the multiple records you deleted with the Edit Global Delete command.

PC-File can recover your deleted records because it does not actually erase the records when you delete them. It just removes them from the screen so that you no longer see them.

However, if you add new records to your database, PC-File replaces the deleted records with the new records. You cannot recover those records that have been written over.

If want to get rid of the records altogether, you can pack the database and PC-File erases the deleted records from your database. Information on packing a database is covered in Chapter 13, "Using Other PC-File Features."

To recover deleted records, follow these steps:

1. Select Edit from the menu bar.

2. Select Undelete from the Edit menu.

   PC-File displays the deleted records one at a time on the screen and prompts you to select the records you want to restore.

3. If you want to undelete the current record, select Yes. If you do not want to undelete the current record you can select No and skip to the next deleted record. If you want to undelete all deleted records at one time, select All. If you want to cancel the undelete operation, select Quit.

4. If you select Yes in step 3, continue selecting Yes or No until you finish undeleting the deleted records. PC-File displays the Information dialog box when you finish the undelete operation. Click OK or press Alt-O to remove the dialog box.

5. In Record or Table view, navigate through the records to verify that the deleted records are recovered.

Summary

This chapter gave you hands-on experience with making changes to the information in your database. You found out how to use PC-File's powerful editing tools for easy and quick modification of your records. You examined the Edit Menu and learned about the differences between Modify and Read-only mode. You also learned how to view your data in two ways using Record View and Table View.

You learned how to change and delete individual records as well as multiple records. You found out how to undo the changes you make in fields and recover deleted records.

Now you have learned how to perform most of the operations you often use in a database. This includes adding records, searching and retrieving records, and modifying records. One more feature that you use often in a database is the sorting feature. Sorting records is covered in detail in the next chapter.

8

Indexing Records

One of the most helpful features of PC-File is its capability to sort records. You can easily rearrange the records so that they appear in virtually any order that is convenient for you—alphabetical, numerical, or chronological.

You might want to reorganize your database for a variety of reasons. In the example of the CLIENT database, you might want to see the records grouped by contact name to print a phone list, or you might want to print mailing labels by zip code.

You do not have to organize your information before entering the data in your database. PC-File can copy data just the way it appears from the paper forms or from another database and enter it in a PC-File database. Later you can sort the information to suit your needs.

PC-File sorts data by using indexes, as explained in the next section. In this chapter, you examine indexing operations that include switching, creating, rebuilding, and deleting indexes. You learn how to create varying indexes from start to finish.

Indexing Data

Indexing sorts records and helps PC-File locate records quickly and easily during a search. Searching for records on an indexed field is faster because the computer organizes records based on the index. Thus, the computer can retrieve files faster when they have been indexed. In PC-File, you must use indexes to sort records.

An index is a special file that makes the database appear to be sorted. The index file is created automatically by PC-File when you create a database and specify that a field be indexed, as explained in Chapter 4.

An index file is a separate file from the database files. After you assign a file name to an index file, PC-File automatically assigns the file extension .NDX. For instance, LASTNAME.NDX is an index file that sorts records by last name.

When you add, modify, and delete database records, PC-File automatically updates the index files.

At least one index file must be defined when you create a database. In practice, indexing one or two fields at one time is customary. After you create a database, you can create additional indexes by using the File Index command. PC-File lets you set up a maximum of 9 indexes in a database. A memo field, however, cannot be indexed.

In the Fast method, you specify an index simply by entering a *Y* in the Indexed column for a particular field. In the Paint method, you specify an index by selecting Yes to accept the Indexed option for a particular field in the Field Characteristics dialog box.

The sort order can be alphabetical, numerical, or chronological. You can set up indexes in ascending or descending order.

Suppose that you want to print mailing labels by ZIP code. If you specify an ascending index on a ZIP_CODE field, for example, PC-File arranges the records numerically in ZIP code order beginning at 00000 and ending at 99999. Another example is an ascending index on a LAST_NAME field; PC-File arranges the records alphabetically by last name, from Aaronofsky to Zymon.

You also can create indexes that sort on more than one field. For instance, you can create an index that sorts first on the COMPANY field, then on the CITY field. As a result, when you get to Bears Inc., Anchorage appears first, then Fairbanks, then Nome.

PC-File provides four indexing operations for working with index files, as explained in the next section.

Examining Indexing Operations

PC-File has four indexing operations that you can perform using the File Index command. They include

- Switching indexes

- Creating indexes

- Rebuilding indexes

- Deleting indexes

Switching indexes: Lets you switch from one index to another. For instance, PC-File arranges the order of the data, based on the current index field. For more information on switching indexes, read the next section.

Creating indexes: Lets you define additional indexes in a database. Usually, you use only one or two indexes in a database to sort, for example, by LAST_NAME and ZIP_CODE. However, you can use the File Index command to create more indexes, as explained later in this chapter. Using more than two indexes at one time might not give you the results you want.

Rebuilding indexes: Fixes a damaged index file or rebuilds an index when there are two indexes with the same name, as explained later in this chapter. An index file can be damaged when you try to create two index files with the same name in the same directory. Damage also can occur if one of the index files contains corrupted data or if an index is stored on a damaged disk.

Deleting indexes: Deletes index files that you no longer want, as explained later in this chapter.

To perform an index operation, follow these steps:

1. Select File from the menu bar.

2. Select Index from the File menu. PC-File displays the Index Operation dialog box (see figure 8.1).

3. Select the index operation you want to perform.

Switching Indexes

You can switch from one index to another, and PC-File rearranges the order of the data, based on the current index field. When you want to perform various operations such as printing mailing labels, a phone list, or form letters, you might want to switch to a different index.

For example, if you want to print mailing labels, you might want to switch to the ZIP_CODE index to sort the records in ZIP code order. If you want to print a phone list, you might want to switch from the ZIP_CODE index to the LAST_NAME index to sort the records alphabetically by last name.

If you are viewing your data in Record view, you can switch to a different index. PC-File sorts the records accordingly and displays the first record, based on the current index.

If you are paging through records in your database in Table View, you can switch indexes. PC-File switches the order of the records on the screen as you are viewing it.

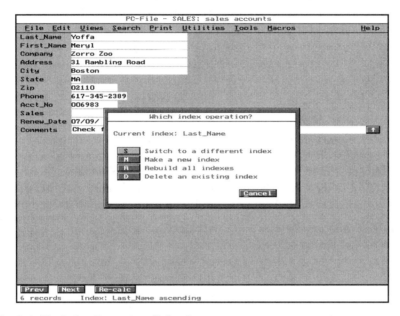

Fig. 8.1. *The Index Operation dialog box.*

The name of the current index appears on the status line at the bottom of the main screen.

PC-File gives you three ways to switch indexes: using the hot key Ctrl-I, selecting the Index Switch command from the File menu, or letting PC-File switch the index automatically. Using the hot key is the fastest way to switch an index. If you prefer to use menu commands, you can select the Index Switch command from the File menu. Or if the field you are searching on is indexed, PC-File automatically switches to that index when it performs the search.

Using a Hot Key

Using the hot key Ctrl-I to switch indexes is the fastest way to switch an index. To see how PC-File lets you switch indexes quickly by using Ctrl-I, follow these steps:

1. In Record View or Table View, the records are indexed by last name, as shown in figure 8.2. When you press Ctrl-I, PC-File displays a list of the indexes that are defined for the current database, as shown in figure 8.3.

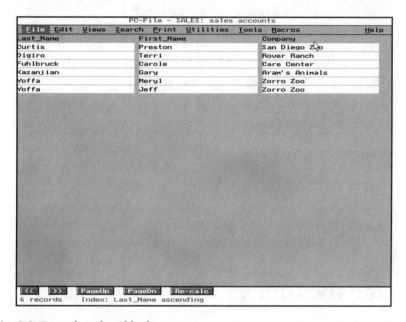

Fig. 8.2. *Records indexed by last name.*

2. PC-File indicates a category next to each index name.

There are three index categories: A for Ascending order, D for Descending order, and F for Formula index. The index categories tell you the type of index and the sort order. These categories are covered in detail in the section Creating Indexes later in this chapter.

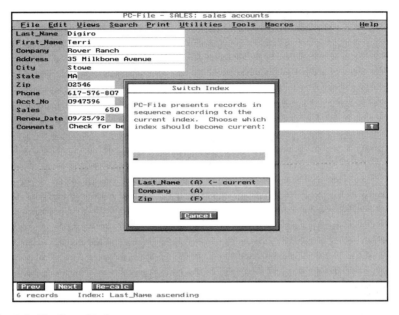

Fig. 8.3. *The list of indexes.*

3. Select the index you want from the list. PC-File sorts the data accordingly and displays the records, based on the current index. For example, select the ZIP_CODE index to sort the data by ZIP code, as shown in figure 8.4.

Using the Index Switch Command

Another way to switch indexes is to choose commands from a menu. You can use the File Index Switch command to switch an index at any time.

To switch indexes by using the Index Switch command, follow these steps:

1. Select File from the menu bar.

2. Select Index from the File menu. PC-File displays the Index Operation dialog box.

3. Select Switch to a different index from the dialog box. PC-File displays the Switch Index dialog box, as shown in figure 8.5. Notice that an arrow and the word, "current," appear next to the current index. PC-File indicates a category next to each index name.

There are three index categories: A for Ascending order, D for Descending order, and F for Formula index. The index categories tell you the type of index and the sort order. These categories are covered in detail in the section "Creating Indexes" later in this chapter.

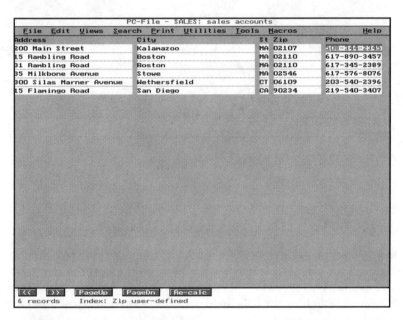

Fig. 8.4. *Records indexed by ZIP code.*

4. Type the name of the index you want to use. Or select an index from the list by using the arrow keys to highlight the index name and pressing Enter. If you want to use the mouse to select an index, just click on the index name you want.

PC-File sorts the data according to the index you specified.

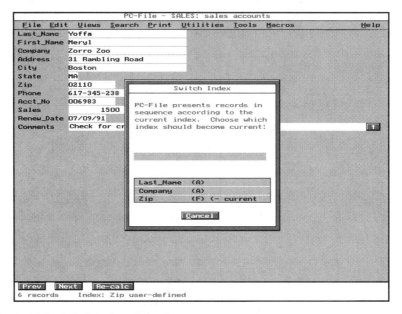

Fig. 8.5. *The Switch Index dialog box.*

Switching Indexes Automatically

When you perform a search for records and the field you are searching on is indexed, PC-File automatically switches the index to the field you are searching on. As a result, PC-File sorts the records according to the indexed field you are searching on. If the field is not indexed, PC-File uses the current index to sort the records.

You can prevent PC-File from automatically switching indexes by pressing Ctrl-X to lock in the current index. The index remains locked until you either press Ctrl-X again or close the database. Both methods unlock the index.

For example, if you search on a LAST_NAME field that is indexed, PC-File displays the records in a particular order—by last name. If you want to see the records organized by company when you search on the LAST_NAME field, you can switch to the COMPANY index by pressing Ctrl-I and then pressing Ctrl-X to lock in the COMPANY index. Thus, when you search on the LAST_NAME field, PC-File displays the records by company name.

If you want to speed up a search, select an A or D index category. The F index category, a Formula index, is generally slower than an Ascending or Descending index.

TIP

Creating Indexes

In PC-File, you must index at least one field when you create a database. You can create a maximum of 9 indexes per database file. As you use the database more and more, you might find that you need additional indexes. The need may arise when you create reports that require certain sorting options, as explained in Chapter 10, "Generating Reports." When PC-File prompts you to create an additional index for a report, you can define the new index at that time.

To create a new index, follow these general steps:

1. Select File from the menu bar.

2. Select Index from the File menu. PC-File displays the Index Operation dialog box.

3. Select Make a new index from the dialog box. PC-File displays the Make a New Index dialog box.

4. Select Simple index or Formula index to specify the index type. For information on the index types, refer to the next section.

5. If you select Simple index, PC-File displays a Field Selection dialog box (see figure 8.6). Specify the sort order, Ascending or Descending, for the first field you want to sort. Then specify which field you want to sort. Repeat this step for each field you want to sort. For information on Simple indexes, refer to the section Creating a Simple Index later in this chapter.

    If you select Formula index, enter an index expression (see figure 8.7). PC-File prompts you to select the field to which you want to attach the index. For information on Formula indexes, refer to the section Creating a Formula Index later in this chapter.

6. Select the field to which you want to attach an index. Use the arrow keys to move to the field name and press Enter. With the mouse, you can click on the field name. Only one index can be attached to a field; usually you attach it to the primary field, which is the first field you are sorting on.

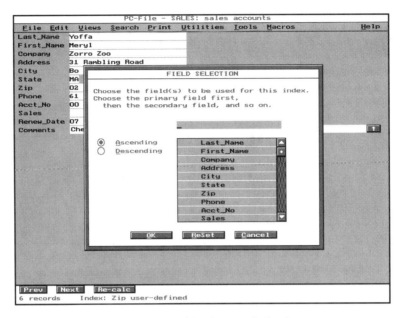

Fig. 8.6. *A Simple index from the Field Selection dialog box.*

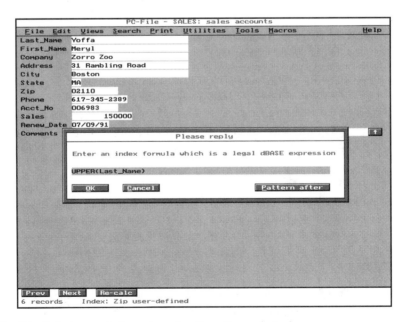

Fig. 8.7. *Entering an index expression for a Formula index.*

For example, if you are sorting on last name and company, attach the index to the LAST_NAME field. For information on attaching indexes, refer to the section Attaching an Index to a Field later in this chapter.

7. If you want PC-File to search on a group of selected records and sort only those selected records rather than sorting all of the records in a database, use the Subgroup index feature. Instead of selecting a field to which you attach an index, you select Subgroup index from the field selection list (see figure 8.8).

   Notice that Subgroup index is the first option in the field selection list. Select a Simple or Formula search, then enter the search criteria, as explained in Chapter 6. PC-File performs the search and defines the index. For information on assigning subgroup indexes, refer to the section Assigning a Subgroup Index later in this chapter.

8. After you attach an index to a field or define a subgroup, PC-File prompts you to enter a name for the index. Each index has both a name and a file name. The index name is the name of the field to which you attach an index. The index file name is the name you assign to an index when PC-File prompts you to enter a name for the index.

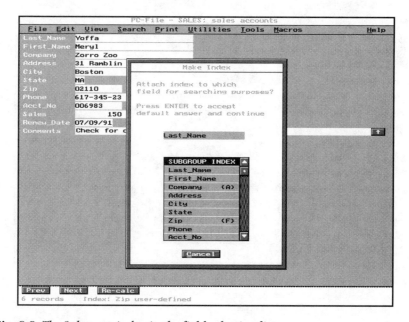

Fig. 8.8. *The Subgroup index in the field selection list.*

Press Enter to accept the default index file name or change the
default index file name. PC-File automatically assigns the file extension .NDX to the index file name. For example, SALES_ZIP.NDX
indicates a ZIP code index in the SALES database (see figure 8.9).
For information on naming index files, refer to the section Naming
Index Files later in this chapter.

Selecting the Index Type

PC-File gives you two index types: Simple and Formula. When you create a
new index, you can select the type of index you want to create.

A Simple index is used to sort data directly on the contents of one or more
fields. You can sort up to 10 fields at a time, each one sorting within the
previous field. This means if you want to sort on two fields, last name and
department, PC-File sorts first by last name, then by department. You can
sort each field in ascending or descending order. PC-File also lets you sort
on partial fields. The Simple index option is covered in detail in the next
section.

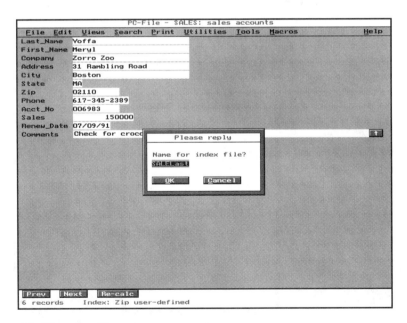

Fig. 8.9. The index file name.

In most cases, a Simple index will fulfill your indexing needs. But you can build more flexible and sophisticated indexes by defining Formula indexes. To define a Formula index, you enter an expression. The Formula index expression, which can contain dBASE and PC-File functions and calculations, is explained later in this chapter.

Creating a Simple Index

With a Simple index, you can sort data directly on the contents of one or more fields. For instance, you can create a Simple index to sort records on a single last name field. You can also create a Simple index to sort records on both a last name field and a department field.

PC-File lets you specify a maximum of 10 fields in a Simple index. You specify which field or fields of data take precedence in sorting the data. Using a phone list database as an example, you can specify the LAST_NAME and the FIRST_NAME fields for sorting. PC-File sorts the last names first, then it sorts the first names within the last names. The Sulstons appear before the Taylors; within the list of Sulstons, Eleanor appears before Frank and Frank before Sarah.

Each field can be sorted in ascending or descending order. Ascending order, the default sort order, sorts data from lowest to highest. For example, it sorts A to Z, 0 to 9, and earlier to later. Descending order sorts data from highest to lowest. It sorts Z to A, 9 to 0, and later to earlier.

If you want to sort on more than one field, you can specify the sort order for each field you define as an index field. For example, using a database that tracks sales, you can specify the SALES_VOLUME field in descending order and the DEPARTMENT in ascending order.

PC-File also lets you sort on partial fields. This can be done in both single and multiple field indexes. You can index first on a company field, then on just the first three digits of a phone number in a phone field.

You cannot sort on several types of fields, however. For example, you cannot sort on memo fields. And, although you can sort dates in date fields, you cannot sort dates with a Simple index that you entered in a character-type field. If you try to sort dates in character fields, for example, PC-File sorts 09/15/89 after 04/15/91; because the date is recognized as a string of characters, 09 comes after 04.

To create a Simple index, follow these steps:

1. Select File from the menu bar.

2. Select Index from the File menu. PC-File displays the Index Operation dialog box.

3. Select Make a new index from the dialog box. PC-File displays the Make a New Index dialog box.

4. Select Simple index to specify the index type. PC-File displays a Field Selection dialog box (see figure 8.10).

5. Specify the sort order, ascending or descending, for the first field you want to sort. The default sort order is Ascending. You can accept the Ascending sort order, or you can select the Descending sort order by clicking the Descending option button.

6. Specify the first field you want to sort—the primary sort field. Use the arrow keys to move to the field and press Enter. Or, with the mouse, click on the field. PC-File displays a check mark and the number 1 to the left of the primary sort field, and either an A for Ascending order or a D for Descending order to the right of the primary sort field (see figure 8.11).

   If you want to change the sort order, click on the Ascending or Descending option buttons to the left of the field list by using the left mouse button. Then select the field you want.

7. If you want to define only a single field index, click on the OK button to continue creating a Simple index.

   If you want to create a multiple field index, repeat Step 6 to select the additional fields you want to sort. If you select a second field to sort, PC-File displays a check mark and the number 2 to the left of the secondary sort field, and either an A for Ascending order or a D for Descending order to the right of the secondary sort field. PC-File inserts a check mark, the appropriate number, and sort order letter next to each field you select to sort (see figure 8.12). When you are finished selecting multiple fields, click on the OK button to continue creating a Simple index.

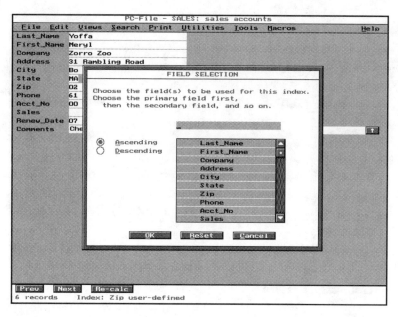

Fig. 8.10. The Field Selection dialog box.

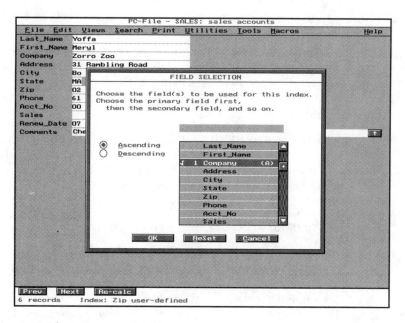

Fig. 8.11. The primary sort field.

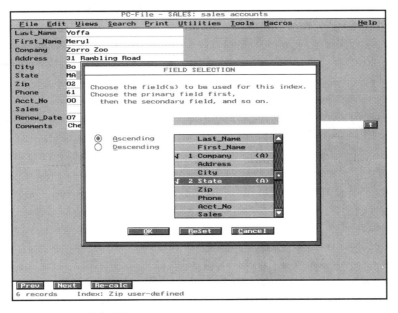

Fig. 8.12. *A multiple field sort.*

8. If you want to sort on a partial field instead of an entire field, type the field name and enter the starting position and length of the partial field in the text box at the top of the Field Selection dialog box. For instance, type *zip,1,5* to specify the first five characters of a nine character ZIP code field (see figure. 8.13). When you are finished specifying a partial field, click on the OK button to continue creating a Simple index.

   PC-File prompts you to attach an index to a field. Only one index can be attached to a field; usually, you attach it to the primary field, the first field you are sorting on. For example, if you are sorting on last name and company, attach the index to the LAST_NAME field.

9. To select a field to which you want to attach an index, use the arrow keys to move to the field name and press Enter. With the mouse, you can click on the field name.

   After you attach an index to a field, PC-File prompts you to enter a name for the index. Each index has both a name and a file name. The index name is the name of the field to which you attach an index. The index file name is the name you assign to an index when PC-File prompts you to enter a name for the index.

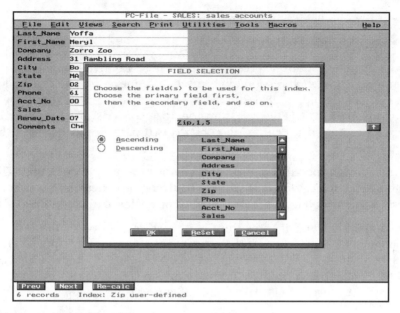

Fig. 8.13. *A partial field sort.*

10. Type the index file name and press Enter. PC-File automatically assigns the file extension .NDX to the index file name. For example, CLI_ZIP.NDX indicates a ZIP code index in the CLIENT database.

If you want to create a Formula index to perform a more complex sort, refer to the next section.

Creating a Formula Index

By using Formula indexes in PC-File, you can create more flexible and sophisticated indexes. Thus, you can build numerous types of indexes to suit your sorting needs. To create a Formula index, you enter an index expression that defines the data you want to sort. The following is a list of some of the most frequently used Formula index expressions. Information on these index expressions is covered in detail later in this chapter.

- PC-File and dBASE formula functions

- PC-File and dBASE calculations

- Multilevel sorting

- Multiple noncharacter fields

- Character fields containing numeric data

- Record number sorting

You can define index expressions that range from uncomplicated to complex. An index expression can be used to define a single field index for a field. For example, UPPER(dept) specifies a single field index for a department field. UPPER is a function that converts all characters to uppercase. An index expression contains two parts: a function and the arguments.

A function is a special command that performs a specific operation. The arguments can include a field name, a field length, a calculation, a starting position, or a condition. Arguments must be enclosed in parentheses.

The UPPER function ignores the Case Sensitivity option in the Utilities Configuration profile. By default the Case Sensitive option is turned off. The UPPER function also assumes that the Case Sensitivity option is turned off in the Configuration profile. (The Case Sensitivity option is explained in Appendix A, "Installing PC-File and Configuring Your System.")

When you use a Simple index and the Case Sensitivity option is turned off, PC-File uses the UPPER function automatically to convert all characters to uppercase. Therefore, you can create an index to convert all characters to uppercase more quickly by specifying the Simple index rather than the Formula index. If the Case Sensitivity is turned on, the UPPER function converts all characters to uppercase anyway.

A more complex index expression can be used to define an index for more than one field, as in the following example:

UPPER(Dept) + STR(Acct_no,8,0) + TOSTR(Renew_Date)

This index expression specifies an index for three fields. The Dept field is a character field. The UPPER function converts all department names to UPPERCASE when it sorts the department field. The Acct_no is a numeric field. STR converts a numeric field to a character string. The number 8 specifies the length of the field; in this case, the length is 8 characters. The number 0 specifies the number of places to the right of the decimal; in this example, there are no decimal places. The Renew_Date is a date field. TOSTR converts the date into a character string before sorting.

To specify an index with more than one function, use a plus sign (+) to connect the different parts of the expression. For easier readability, enter a space before and after the plus sign. In addition to simple and complex index expressions, you can create a new index from an existing index. To do this, you use the Pattern After button in the Formula Index dialog box; select the index you want to use, and then modify the expression to suit your needs as explained later in this chapter.

To create a Formula index, follow these general steps:

1. Select File from the menu bar.

2. Select Index from the File menu. PC-File displays the Index Operation dialog box.

3. Select Make a new index from the dialog box. PC-File displays the Make a New Index dialog box.

4. Select Formula index to specify the index type. PC-File displays a text box (see figure 8.14).

5. Enter an index expression in the text box. For example, type *UPPER(Last_Name)* and press Enter (see figure 8.15).

   When you are finished entering an index expression, PC-File prompts you to select the field to which you want to attach the index.

6. Select the field to which you want to attach an index. Use the arrow keys to move to the field name and press Enter. With the mouse, you can click on the field name. Only one index can be attached to a field; usually you attach it to the primary field, the first field you are sorting on. For example, if you are sorting on last name and company, attach the index to the LAST_NAME field.

   After you attach an index to a field, PC-File prompts you to enter a name for the index. Each index has both a name and a file name. The index name is the name of the field to which you attach an index. The index file name is the name you assign to an index when PC-File prompts you to enter a name for the index.

7. Type the index file name and press Enter. PC-File automatically assigns the file extension .NDX to the index file name. For example, you can type *CLI_ZIP* to indicate a ZIP code index in the CLIENT database.

Information on various ways to use Formula indexes to sort your data is covered in detail in the next few sections.

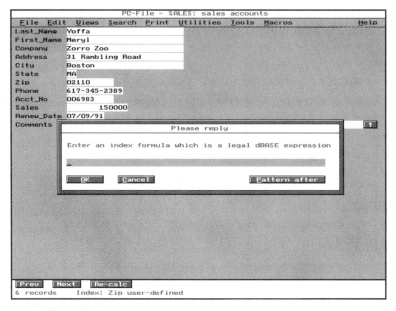

Fig. 8.14. *The Formula index text box.*

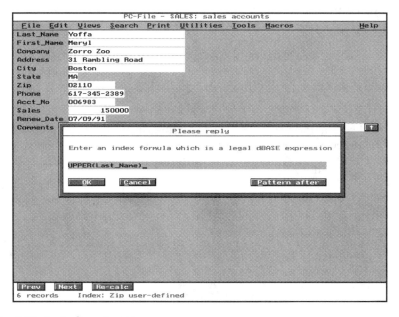

Fig. 8.15. *An index expression.*

Using PC-File and dBASE Formula Functions

A formula function is a special command that performs a specific operation. You can use a formula function in an index expression to define the index for one or more fields.

PC-File lets you enter any PC-File or dBASE function in an index expression. There are 13 PC-File functions. For a complete list of dBASE functions, refer to the dBASE documentation.

If you work with formula functions in a spreadsheet program such as Lotus 1-2-3, Excel, or Quattro Pro, you already know the format of a formula function in PC-File. A PC-File formula function consists of two parts: the function name and one or more arguments enclosed in parentheses. For example, UPPER(Last_Name) contains the function name UPPER, and Last_Name is the argument. In this case the argument is a field.

A more complex formula function may contain multiple arguments such as the field, starting position, field length, decimal places, condition, or a calculation. For example, STR(*field,length,decimal*) contains the function STR and three arguments. You enter a comma to separate the arguments and enclose the arguments in parentheses.

Understanding PC-File Formula Functions

The following is a description of PC-File functions:

CALC("*calculation*") uses a calculation in an index. Enter quotation marks around the calculation, and enclose the entire calculation in parentheses. Also, enclose in another set of parentheses any calculation that you want PC-File to perform first. An example is CALC("5*(3+8)").

DESCEND(*field*) converts numeric, date, or logical fields to a character string for indexing and indexes in descending order. This function operates like the TOSTR function, as described later in this section. An example is DESCEND(Renew_date).

IIF(*condition*, *field1*, *field2*) indexes a field based on the outcome of a comparison. The function tells PC-File to sort data in a particular field if a condition is true, but sort data in another field if the condition is false. For example,

   IIF(Company=" ",Last_Name,Company)

specifies that if the company field is blank, sort by last name; if the company field is not blank, sort by company.

LEFT(*field,length*) creates a partial field, starting with the first character in the field and continuing to the right according to the specified length. For example,

LEFT(Zip_code,5)

sorts only the first five digits of a 9-digit ZIP code. The LEFT function is the opposite of the RIGHT function.

RECNO() sorts records in record number order. PC-File assigns a record number to each record in the order you enter it into a database; RECNO() sorts all of the records by that record number. Enter nothing, not even a space, in the parentheses.

If you delete records, the record numbers do not change accordingly. You must either pack the database or make major changes to the database by using the Redefine command to change record numbers. Refer to Chapter 13, "Using Other PC-File Features," for information about packing a database. For information on changing a database by using the Redefine command, see Chapter 9,"Changing the Design of a Database."

RIGHT(*field,length*) creates a partial field, starting with the last character in the field and continuing to the left according to the specified length. For example, RIGHT(Phone,7) sorts only the last seven digits of a 10-digit phone number; thus, the area code is not included in the sort process. The RIGHT function is the opposite of the LEFT function, as described earlier in this section.

ROMAN(*field*) converts roman numerals to Arabic numbers before the sorting process begins. This is a PC-File function only, and not a dBASE function. For example, ROMAN(Chapter) converts chapter XV to 15 before sorting the chapter numbers.

SOUNDEX(*field*) sorts homonyms, words that sound the same but are spelled differently. For example, SOUNDEX(Last_Name) sorts names such as Miles and Myles together. This is a PC-File function only, and not a dBASE function.

STR(*field,length,decimal*) converts numeric values to a character string for indexing. You must specify the field length and the number of placeholders to the right of the decimal point. For example, STR(Salary,8,0) converts the numeric values in the salary field to a character string; the field length is 8 characters with no decimal places to the right of the decimal point. STR produces a much shorter character string than TOSTR and is recommended when you convert numeric values. TOSTR is also described here.

SUBSTR(*field,starting position,length*) defines a partial field for sorting, as described earlier in this chapter. You must specify the field name, starting position, and the length of the partial field. For example,

SUBSTR(Zip_code,1,5)

sorts the first five digits of a 9-digit ZIP code.

TOSTR(*field*) converts numeric, date, and logical fields to a character string for indexing and indexes in ascending order. Operates like the DESCEND function, as already described. This is a PC-File function only, and not a dBASE function. An example is

TOSTR(Claim_date).

UPPER(*field*) converts all characters to uppercase before performing the sort. This expression is case insensitive as it ignores the Case Sensitivity option that is usually turned off in the Utilities Configuration Case Sensitivity option.

VAL(*field*) converts a character string to a numeric value. This is useful for indexing numeric data in a character field when the data is of different lengths. For example, VAL(Acct_No) converts account numbers to numeric values for indexing. VAL is the opposite of TOSTR.

If you want to index more than one field at a time, you can perform a multilevel sort by using a Simple index or a Formula index, as described in the next section.

Performing a Multilevel Sort

PC-File lets you index more than one field at a time with a Simple index or a Formula index. With a Simple index, you can sort up to 10 fields simultaneously. With a Formula index, you can enter an index expression that sorts on multiple fields. For example,

UPPER(Last_Name + Company)

converts all characters to uppercase, sorts the primary field, LAST_NAME, then sorts the secondary field, COMPANY. You also can enter the index expression in a different way. For example,

UPPER(Last_Name) + UPPER(Company).

However, the first method for entering an expression is recommended because it is shorter than the second method.

The text box can accommodate 100 characters. Therefore, you can specify as many fields as you want, providing they fit in the 100-character window.

The following is an example of a long index expression:

UPPER(Last_Name + Company + Building + Floor + Department)

You also can index multiple fields that are not character fields, as described in the next section.

Indexing Multiple Noncharacter Fields

PC-File lets you index multiple fields in which some or all of the fields are non-character fields. To do this, you must convert all of the fields to characters strings.

You can index on a character and date field, and PC-File converts the date field to a character string. You also can index on a date and numeric field or any other combination of field types. However, you cannot index on memo fields.

To convert numeric fields to a character string, use the STR function. For example,

UPPER(Department) + STR(Acct_no,8,0)

converts the departments to uppercase and converts the account numbers to a character string before indexing.

To convert date and logical fields to character strings, you must use the TOSTR function. An example of converting a date field to a character string is

UPPER(Office) + TOSTR(Hire_Date)

PC-File sorts date fields as year, month, and day. For example, PC-File reads 08/15/91 as 91/08/15 so that it sorts properly.

If you want to index on two date fields, PC-File converts both of them to character strings. For example,

TOSTR(Claim_Date) + TOSTR(Claim_Dt2)

converts both claim dates to character strings.

If you want to convert numeric fields to character strings for indexing and you leave the data as numeric values, PC-File adds the data in each record before indexing. As a result, the index is in a different order than you get if you convert the numeric data to character strings. Thus, you must convert numeric fields to character strings before you index numeric data.

PC-File also lets you use the VAL function to index character fields that contain numeric data, as explained in the next section.

Indexing Character Fields Containing Numeric Data

Suppose that you have a character field that contains numeric data and you want to convert the character data to numeric values for sorting. PC-File reads the data in character fields flush left; if the numeric data is all the same length, you do not have to convert the numeric values to character strings. However, if the numeric data is of different lengths and you do not convert the data, PC-File gives you improper sorting results. For instance, PC-File sorts numeric values in a character field in the following order:

1, 12, 150, 2, 24

If you convert these numeric values to character strings before indexing, PC-File sorts them in the proper numeric order:

1, 2, 12, 24, 150.

To convert numeric values to character strings, you must use the VAL function; for example,

VAL(Employ_no)

If you want to sort records by record number, you can use the RECNO function, as explained in the next section.

Sorting by Record Number

When you add records to a database, PC-File assigns a record number to each record. The record number is a hidden numeric field, and therefore you do not see it on the screen. The number 1 is assigned to the first record, the number 2 is assigned to the second record, and so on. PC-File lets you sort data in the order it was entered by indexing on the record number with the RECNO function.

To sort only on the record number, you enter the expression RECNO( ) in the text box. Enter the parentheses but do not enter any character inside the parentheses. Do not even enter a space between the parentheses.

If you want to sort on the record number and on other fields in an index, you must convert the record number to a character string. For example,

UPPER(Contact + STR(RECNO( ),6,0)

converts contact names to uppercase and converts the record numbers to character strings before indexing.

If you delete records, and then add records later to replace the deleted records, the record numbers of the deleted records are assigned to the new records. In this case, the RECNO function may not give you the exact order in which the data was entered.

Using PC-File and dBASE Calculations

PC-File allows you to enter a calculation in an index expression. The calculation can contain an arithmetic operation that includes two or more numeric fields. For example, you can add the data in one field to another and index on the sum. You also can subtract the values in two or more fields.

To include a calculation in an expression, either use the CALC function or simply enter a calculation in the text box. CALC is useful when you want to abbreviate field names or perform date calculations. The CALC function is the only index function that lets you abbreviate field names.

When you enter a calculation in a CALC function, you enclose the calculation in quotation marks and parentheses. For example, CALC("Sales + Commission").

Using a sales database as an example, you can add the sales figures for each region together and then sort the total. You can shorten the field names to conserve space, but the names must remain unique within the database. The CALC function would look like this:

CALC("SALES_EAST + SALES_WEST + SALES_NORTH + SALES_SOUTH")

You need to be acquainted with several guidelines for Formula indexes when you define index expressions. These guidelines help you get the results you want when you use a Formula index, as explained in the next section.

Examining Guidelines for Formula Indexes

The following are some guidelines for creating index expressions in Formula indexes.

- You must enter complete field names in index expressions.

- You can enter up to 100 characters in an index expression.

- You can sort on fields that contain a maximum of 100 characters per field. For example, you cannot sort on two fields that each contain 70 characters. You must use partial fields for one field or both fields, as explained earlier in this chapter.

- You can mix field types in an expression by converting the fields to character strings using the TOSTR or STR functions. Information on functions is provided later in this chapter.

- You cannot use memo fields in Formula indexes.

- You must use the same number of left and right parentheses in an expression.

- When you use the CALC function in an expression, always enclose the calculation in quotation marks and parentheses; for instance, CALC("Sales*1.10").

- PC-File evaluates expressions from left to right, and evaluates calculations enclosed in parentheses first. For example, in the expression CALC("4*(3+2)"), PC-File adds 3+2 first, multiplies the result by 4, and arrives at the answer 20. If the expression is CALC("(3*2)+4"), PC-File multiplies 3 by 2, adds the result to 4, and arrives at the answer 10.

Attaching an Index to a Field

When you define a Simple or Formula index, you must attach an index to a field. Usually, an index is attached to the primary field, the first field you are sorting on. For example, if you are sorting on last name and company, attach the index to the LAST_NAME field.

Once you define a Simple index or enter a Formula index expression, PC-File prompts you to attach an index to a field. A list of field names appears in a dialog box (see figure 8.16). To select the field to which you want to attach an index, use the arrow keys to move to the field name and press Enter. With the mouse, you can click on the field name. For example, attach the last name index to the LAST_NAME field.

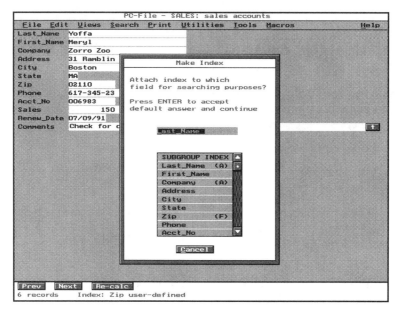

Fig. 8.16. *An index attached to a field.*

You need to be familiar with several guidelines when you attach an index to a field.

- Only one index can be attached to a field.

- In most cases, you can attach the index to the primary sort field.

- If you do not attach the index to the primary sort field, then attach it to a field that you may not want to search on.

There are three cases when you would not attach an index to a primary sort field.

You can specify two or more indexes with the same primary sort field, but use different secondary sort fields. Because PC-File lets you attach only one index to a particular field, you need to attach the index or indexes to another field that you use less often.

You can specify a calculation in an index that results in data that is different from the data in the primary sort field.

You can specify a RECNO function to sort on the record number in an index. Because PC-File does not evaluate the hidden record number field as a database field, you cannot attach the index to the record number field.

When you attach an index to a field, be sure to specify a field that you customarily do not search on. When you perform a search, PC-File looks for the data in the attached index file. If the search data does not match with the data in the primary sort field, PC-File does not retrieve any records.

For instance, if you attached the Formula index CALC("Total – Commission") to the Total field, PC-File automatically switches to the index attached to a search field before it begins the search. The data that results from the calculation, the sales figure, may be different than the data in the Total field. PC-File would only find the sales figures instead of finding the data in the Total field.

If you perform a search on an index field in which the data in the field might be different from the search criteria, you can force PC-File to use a different index. For example, if you perform a search on the index field TOTAL to find all of the records where the TOTAL field contains $1000, the data in the TOTAL index field may differ from the search criteria $1000. You can lock in a different index to find the records you want. To do this, press CTRL-I to switch to any index other than the TOTAL field, and press CTRL-X to lock in that index.

Then PC-File searches through the entire database file to retrieve the records you want. This method is slower, but you should get the results you want.

You must lock in a different index before you perform the search. To do this, press Ctrl-X and PC-File displays a list of indexes. To specify the index you want to use, use the arrow keys to highlight the index and press Enter. With the mouse, click the index you want. Then perform the search on the index field.

If you want to sort a selected group of records instead of attaching an index to a field, you can define a Subgroup index that is not attached to any field. For information on the Subgroup index feature, refer to the next section.

Assigning a Subgroup Index

With Subgroup indexes, you can redefine databases easily and quickly, and produce reports, letters, labels, and graphs, as explained later in the appropriate chapters. Subgroup indexes save you time because PC-File does not have to search through the entire database to search and index the records you want.

When you use the Subgroup index feature, PC-File lets you search on a group of selected records and sort only those selected records, rather than sorting all of the records in a database. This feature is useful particularly when you are working with a large database; you can assign a Subgroup index each time you want to use a small portion of the large database.

Suppose that you want to send a new product announcement to only those customers in Alaska. If 200 of your 1000 customers are in Alaska, you can create a separate ZIP code index called a Subgroup index for just those 200 Alaskan customers. That way, when you want to print mailing labels, PC-File uses the Subgroup index to find and print the labels for those 200 records. It does not have to search through the entire database to produce the mailing labels.

You do not have to name a Subgroup index or attach it to a field. A Subgroup index is a temporary file. The Subgroup index file name consists of the database file name and the file extension .NDS. For example, CLIENT.NDS represents a Subgroup index in the sample CLIENT database.

PC-File allows you to assign a Subgroup index to a Simple or Formula index. But you must create an index before you assign it as a Subgroup index. You define the index the same way you define a permanent index. You also can use the Pattern After button to copy an index instead of creating a new index, as described later in this chapter.

To define a Subgroup index, follow these steps:

1. Create a Simple or Formula index.

    PC-File displays a list of fields and prompts you to attach the index to a field. Note that Subgroup index is the first option in the field selection list (see figure 8.17).

2. Select Subgroup index from the list instead of selecting a field. Press Enter to select it or click Subgroup index with the mouse.

    PC-File displays the Search dialog box (see figure 8.18).

3. Select Simple or Formula search. Use the arrow keys to highlight the type of search you want and press Enter. With the mouse, click the appropriate search button.

    PC-File prompts you to enter search criteria.

4. Enter the search criteria. For example, with a Simple search, type *Boston* in the CITY field to search for all records that contain the city Boston (see figure 8.19). For information on entering search criteria for Simple or Formula searches, refer to Chapter 6.

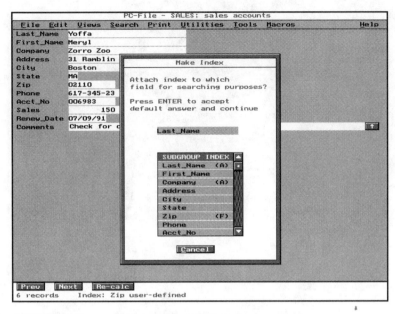

Fig. 8.17. *The Subgroup Index in the Attach Index.*

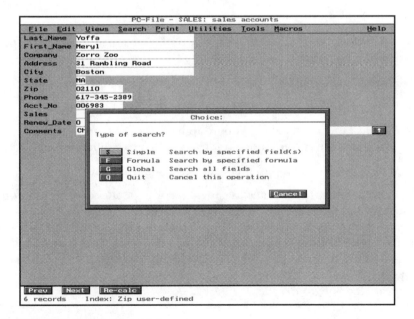

Fig. 8.18. *The Search dialog box.*

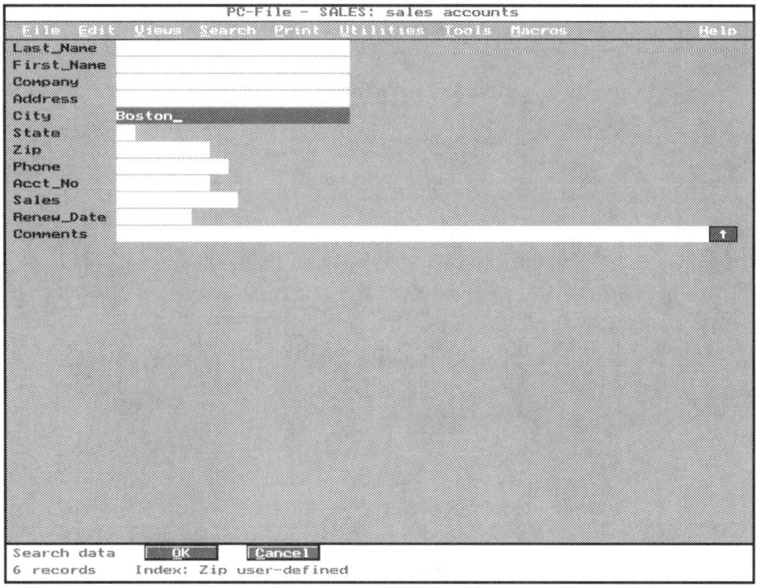

Fig. 8.19. *The search criteria.*

PC-File performs the search and defines the index.

A Subgroup index is the current index until you assign a new Subgroup index for a database.

When you want to use a Subgroup index, follow these steps:

1. Press Ctrl-I to switch indexes. PC-File displays a list of indexes.

2. Select the index named Subgroup from the list. The Subgroup index is the current index until you switch to a different index.

3. Perform the operation that requires a Subgroup index.

If you update records in a database, these records are added to the Subgroup index, even though they would not have been included initially. For instance, if you assigned the subgroup of records where State = CT, and you add or modify records in the database after you create the Subgroup index, PC-File adds these records to the Subgroup index, no matter what state you specify. Therefore, when you update records in a database, you must recreate the Subgroup index.

Naming Index Files

After you attach an index to a field or define a subgroup, PC-File prompts you to enter a name for the index. Each index has both a name and a file name. The index name is the name of the field to which you attach an index. The index file name is the name you assign to an index when PC-File prompts you to enter a name for the index.

An index file is a separate file from the database files. You must assign a file name to an index file, and PC-File automatically assigns the file extension .NDX. For instance, LASTNAME.NDX is an index file that sorts records by last name.

When PC-File prompts you to name an index file, it displays a default name that contains the first four characters of the database and the first four characters of the field name to which the index is attached. This way, the index names are unique within the current database and the directory that contains the database files.

You can press Enter to accept the default index file name or you can change it. For example, CLI_ZIP indicates a ZIP code index in the CLIENT database.

TIP

> To avoid duplication of index names, accept the default name that PC-File assigns. If you have two databases in a particular directory each having the same first four letters in the name, check your index file names to prevent conflicts in index names. If you have two fields in a database, each having the same first four letters in their names and you want to index on both of them, be sure to change the index file name for one of them.

The name of the current index appears on the status line at the bottom of the main screen.

If an index does not work the way you want it to, you can change it any time, as explained in the next section.

Modifying an Index Expression

Sometimes, an index does not work exactly the way you wanted. You can modify an index expression and run the index again at any time by using the Pattern After button in the Formula index dialog box.

To modify an index expression, follow these steps:

1. Select File from the menu bar.

2. Select Index from the File menu. PC-File displays the Index Operation dialog box.

3. Select Make a new index from the dialog box. PC-File displays the Make a New Index dialog box.

4. Select Formula index to specify the index type. PC-File displays a text box.

5. Click the Pattern After button in the Formula index dialog box. PC-File displays a list of indexes (see figure 8.20).

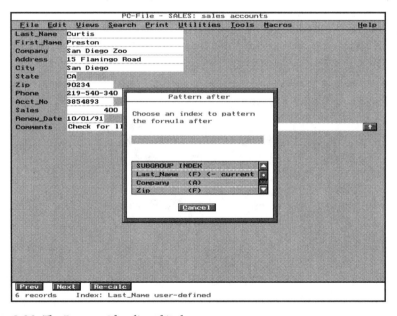

Fig. 8.20. The Pattern After list of indexes.

6. Select the index you want to use by pressing the arrow keys and Enter, or click on the index with the mouse.

   PC-File displays the index you want to use as a pattern; for example, UPPER(Last_Name) as shown in figure 8.21.

7. Change the expression to suit your needs and press Enter twice. For example, change it to UPPER(Last_Name + First_Name) by positioning the cursor on the right parenthesis and pressing the INS key. Then type the additional character.

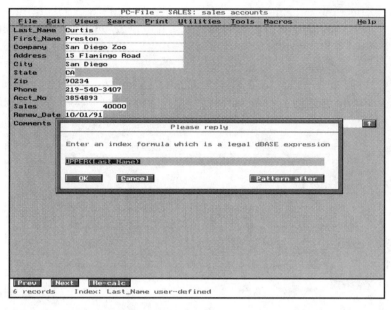

Fig. 8.21. *The index expression pattern.*

PC-File displays the Field Selection dialog box and prompts you to attach the index to a field (see figure 8.22).

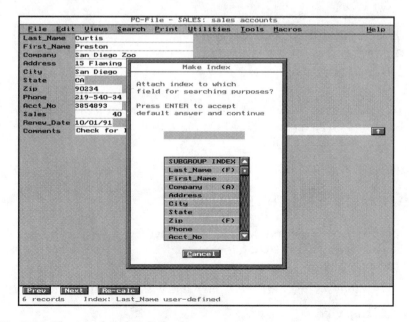

Fig. 8.22. *The Attach Index dialog box.*

8. Select the same field to which the field was attached. Use the arrow keys to highlight the field and press Enter, or, with the mouse, click the field name. PC-File displays the default index name and prompts you to enter an index file name.

9. Press Enter twice to accept the default index file name. You can change the name, if necessary, as explained earlier in this chapter. PC-File prompts you to overwrite the old index (see figure 8.23).

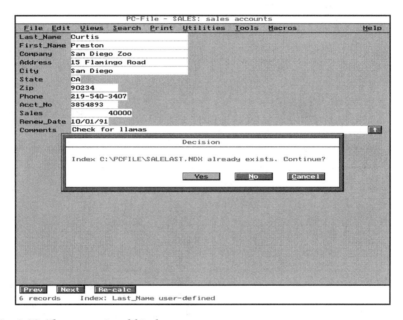

Fig. 8.23. *The overwrite old index prompt.*

10. Select Yes to overwrite the old index with the new index expression. PC-File replaces the old index with the new index. Now you can run the new index and see how it works.

Rebuilding Indexes

Suppose an index file gets damaged. You might have a bad index that PC-File will not let you run until it is recovered. A bad index can be the result of the following:

• Two indexes that have the same name within the current directory

• Corrupted data

- A corrupted index file

- A damaged disk

PC-File provides two ways to rebuild indexes. You can use the indexing operation called Rebuilding Indexes that recovers bad indexes. The second way to rebuild an index is when PC-File detects that there are two index files with the same name and you are prompted to rebuild the index. Then you respond to the prompt and PC-File rebuilds the indexes.

When you suspect a problem with any index, you should rebuild the indexes in the database. If, for example, you perform a search and do not receive the expected results, rebuilding the indexes in the database and performing the search again may solve the problem.

> PC-File does not rebuild Subgroup indexes. You must recreate a Subgroup index.

To rebuild all indexes, follow these steps:

1. Select File from the menu bar.

2. Select Index from the File menu. PC-File displays the Index Operation dialog box.

3. Select Rebuild all indexes from the dialog box.

   PC-File displays an information box and tells you that it will rebuild all indexes except Subgroup indexes (see figure 8.24).

4. Click the OK button.

   PC-File rebuilds all of the indexes in the database.

If PC-File finds a bad index when you open a database, it displays a Bad Index dialog box. At this point, you can choose how to handle a bad index. You can either rebuild the index, delete the index, or ignore the warning. Usually, a bad index is the result of two indexes with the same name in the same directory. One index might run successfully for the database it was created for, but the index in the other database is a bad index that you cannot run.

If you select Rebuild the index, PC-File recreates the index for the database it was created for. The index in the other database becomes a bad index. Then you can select Delete the index to delete the bad index in the other database. For information on deleting indexes, refer to the next section.

If you want to cancel the Rebuild index operation, select Ignore this warning or click the Cancel button.

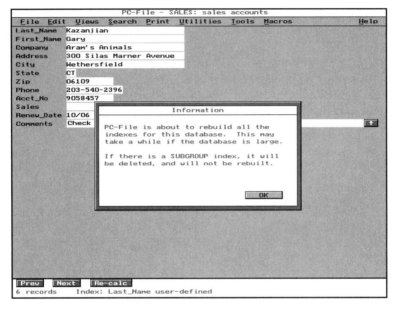

Fig. 8.24. *The Rebuild Index information box.*

To rebuild an index when you are prompted, follow these steps:

1. When PC-File detects a bad index, it prompts you to rebuild the index.

2. Select Yes to rebuild the index.

PC-File rebuilds the index.

Another way to recover a bad index is to copy your files to another directory. You also can use the DOS CHKDSK/F command to find damaged files. For information on using the DOS CHKDSK/F command, refer to your DOS documentation.

> If you use the DOS CHKDSK/F command to find damaged files, be sure to exit from all programs and applications before running it. Also, do not use the Drop to DOS command to run the CHKDSK/F command. If you are running Windows, make sure you exit from Windows and return to the DOS prompt before running the command. Otherwise, the File Allocation Table on your hard disk may be damaged.

Deleting Indexes

Occasionally, you may not use all of the databases you have created. When you no longer want an index, you can delete it by using the File Index Delete operation.

Indexed fields take up space; the more indexed fields in a database, the slower PC-File executes operations. When you add, modify, or delete data in a database, PC-File must update each index, which can be time consuming if you have many indexes.

> Keep only those indexes you need for sorting and searching. If you do not use an index, delete it. You can always redefine an index if you need it in the future.

TIP

Because every PC-File database must have at least one index attached to a field, PC-File does not allow you to delete an index if it is the only permanent index in the database.

To delete an index, follow these steps:

1. Select File from the menu bar.

2. Select Index from the File menu. PC-File displays the Index Operation dialog box.

3. Select Delete an existing index from the dialog box. PC-File displays a list of indexes.

4. Select the index you want to delete.

PC-File deletes the index and the .NDX index file from the database.

> Do not delete an index file with the DOS DELETE command because the reference to the index in the HDB database header file is not deleted. Thus, PC-File displays a warning message that the index may be damaged the next time you open the database.

CAUTION

Summary

In this chapter you saw how easy it is to work with PC-File's indexing operations. You learned how to switch, create, rebuild, and delete indexes. You also learned how to create many indexes from beginning to end.

You have now learned how to create a database from start to finish. As you work with your database more and more, you might find that you want to make some changes to the design of your database. Chapter 9 explains how to change the design of a database.

9

Changing the Design of a Database

In this chapter you learn how to change the design of your database using the File Redefine command. You examine how to copy, rename, and delete database files. And you discover how to export and import data to and from PC-File.

Using the File Redefine Command

You can change the design of your database any time. PC-File lets you make both minor and major changes. You can even create a subset of your original database, limiting the records in the new database.

Generally, the design of a database is not changed often. The adjustments are usually in response to changes in your business environment that require adding, changing, or deleting fields in your database. PC-File's redefine capability helps you fine-tune the database, even after you have entered data in the fields.

The File Redefine command lets you make the following minor changes to the design of your database without having to define and name a new database. The minor changes include:

- Changing field names

- Changing field labels

- Changing field characteristics

- Changing lines and boxes

The File Redefine command also allows you to make major changes in the design of your database; however, these modifications do require that you define and name a new database. When you define and name the new database, PC-File automatically transfers your records from the old database to the new one. The major changes include:

- Changing field length

- Changing decimal placement

- Changing field types

- Adding and deleting fields

- Changing the order of the fields

Whether you use the Fast or Paint method to create a database, the process for changing the design of the database is the same. You make some changes in an edit window that looks just like the Paint edit window and other changes in a series of dialog boxes.

Changing the design of your database requires the following general steps:

1. To open the database file you want to redefine, select File from the menu bar.

2. Select Open from the File menu. PC-File displays the File Selection dialog box.

3. Select the file you want to open.

4. Select OK. PC-File opens the database and displays the first record on your screen.

5. To redefine your database, select File from the menu bar.

6. Select Redefine from the File menu.

   PC-File displays the edit window that contains the current design of your database. The data entry screen in the edit window for re-defining the design of your database looks just like the data entry screen for creating the database by using the Paint method (see figure 9.1).

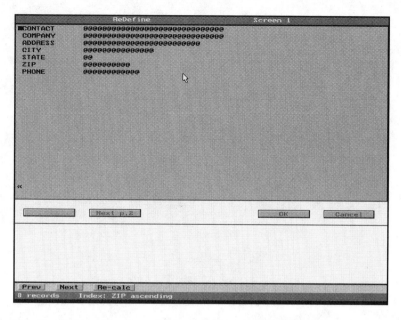

Fig. 9.1. The data entry screen in the redefine edit window.

7. Make the changes.

   You can make some changes directly in the data entry screen in the
   edit window (see the section Changing the Data Entry Screens).
   These changes include moving fields, text, and lines and boxes.
   You also can add, modify, and delete fields and field labels as well
   as change field lengths and the order of fields by using the field
   buttons after you finish making changes in the edit window.

8. After you finish making the changes in the edit window, select OK.
   PC-File displays field buttons at the beginning of each field (see
   figure 9.2).

   There are two types of field buttons: required and optional. Required field buttons display a question mark (?). You must select a
   required field button because PC-File needs additional information
   about a change you made to a field in the edit window.

9. Select the field button for each field you want to change (see the
   section Choosing Field Buttons). You can select the data source
   from the old database to transfer data to the new database by
   selecting the required field button (see figure 9.3). You also can
   change field names and characteristics, such as performing a calculation and changing the access order of the fields by selecting an
   optional field button.

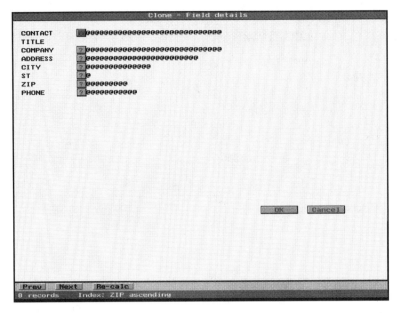

Fig. 9.2. *The Field buttons.*

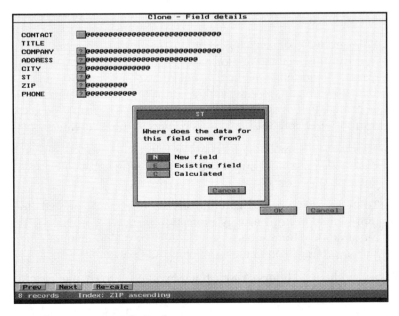

Fig. 9.3. *The Data Source dialog box.*

10. After you make changes using the field buttons, select OK. PC-File prompts you to change the access order of the fields. Refer to the section Changing Access Order (see figure 9.4).

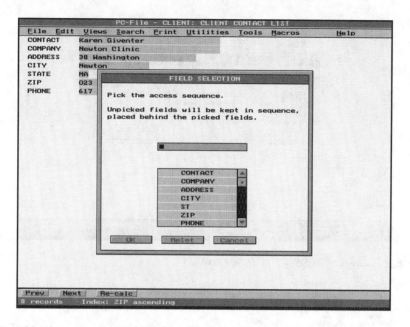

Fig. 9.4. Changing the field access order.

11. If you want to change the access order of the fields, select the fields in the order you want by using the arrow keys and pressing or clicking each field name with the mouse. The fields you do not select are accessed after the selected fields. Changing the access order is optional. Select OK to continue. PC-File prompts you to transfer records to the new database (see figure 9.5).

12. If you want to transfer all records, select All records in the database. If you want to transfer some records, select Some (selected) records. Then perform a search, as explained in Chapter 6, "Searching for Records." If you do not want to transfer any records, select None. The new database will be empty. PC-File prompts you to name the new database and displays a File Selection dialog box (see figure 9.6).

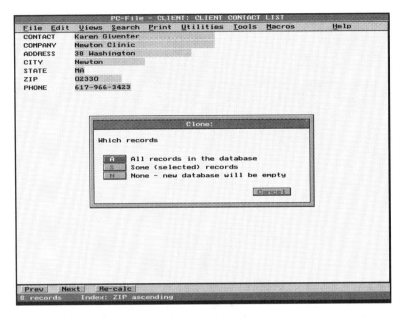

Fig. 9.5. The Record Selection dialog box.

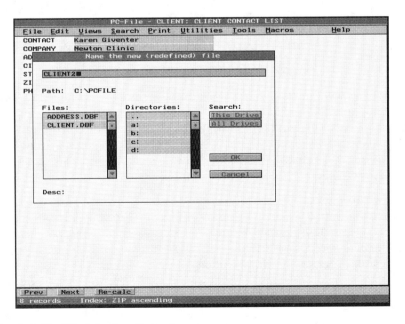

Fig. 9.6. The File Selection dialog box.

13. If you made only minor changes to the design of your database, you can keep the original database file with the same name, but you must store the database in a different directory or on a different drive. To do this, type the path in the text box. For example, type *c:\pcfile\zoo\telemkt.dbf.* Be sure the subdirectory exists. If it does not, create a new subdirectory at the DOS prompt with the DOS MD command. For information on creating directories, refer to your DOS documentation. PC-File automatically updates the current database.

14. If you make major changes to the design of your database, you must create a new database file. Type the new file in the text box and click OK or press Enter. If you create a new database, PC-File prompts you to output the records to the new database (see figure 9.7).

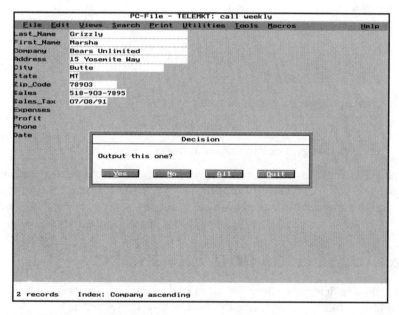

Fig. 9.7. *The Output Records dialog box.*

15. If you want to output one record at a time, select Yes. Select No to skip the records you do not want to transfer to the new database. Select All to transfer all of the records at one time. PC-File prompts you to enter a file description.

16. You can use the current file description, if there is one, or you can enter a new one. Then select OK. PC-File displays a status box that shows the number of records transferred. You also see an information box that tells you the redefine process is complete. When you click OK, you are presented with the first record of your database.

Making Changes in the Data Entry Screen

The data entry screen in the edit window displays fields, field labels, and miscellaneous text as well as lines and boxes.

You can make the following changes in the edit window:

- Add fields and field labels
- Delete fields and field labels
- Change field lengths
- Change field labels
- Change the order of fields on the screen
- Add, change, and delete miscellaneous text
- Add, change, and delete lines and boxes

To make changes to your data entry screens in the edit window, use the same guidelines and procedures you followed when you created the database using the Paint method, as explained in Chapter 4.

Adding Fields and Field Labels

You can add fields anywhere you want in the data entry screen. If you want a new field to appear on a line by itself, follow these steps:

1. Move the cursor to where you want to add a field. You can use the Home key to move the cursor quickly to the beginning of a field.

   A cursor appears on the screen. The cursor indicates that PC-File is in Insert mode, which allows you to add characters in the edit window. Be sure the cursor is on the first character of the field label when you want to add a new field on a line by itself at the beginning of a row.

2. Press the Enter key to insert a blank row for the new field. The other fields shift down to accommodate the blank row.

3. Type the new field label.

4. Press the space bar to insert spaces between the field label and the first field marker you want to enter.

5. Type the appropriate field markers.

If you want a new field to appear between other fields, follow these steps:

1. Use the arrow keys to place the cursor where you want to add the field.

2. Type the new field label. PC-File shifts the other fields to the right to accommodate the new field label.

3. Enter the field markers.

When you finish making the changes to the data entry screen, select OK to display the field buttons as shown in figure 9.8.

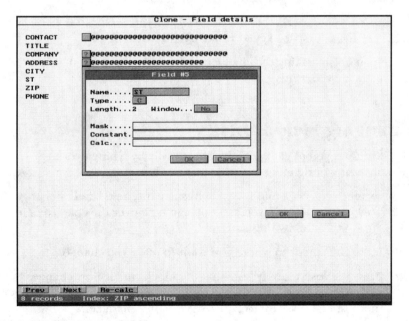

Fig. 9.8. Adding a new field.

Deleting Fields and Field Labels

PC-File lets you delete any fields in the data entry screen. To delete a field, you must delete the field label, the field markers, and any extra spaces you no longer need.

To delete a field, press the Home key to move the cursor to the beginning of the field label you want to delete. Hold down the Delete key to delete the field label, the field markers, and any extra spaces. PC-File adjusts the other fields accordingly by closing up the space between fields.

When you finish making the changes to the data entry screen, select OK to display the field buttons.

Changing Field Lengths

You can change field lengths in the edit window by adding or deleting field markers. To lengthen a field, press the End key to move the cursor to the end of the field. Then type the additional field markers.

To shorten a field, press the End key to move the cursor to the end of the field. Use the Backspace key to remove field markers.

When you finish making the changes to the data entry screen, select OK to display the field buttons.

Changing Field Labels

PC-File allows you to change field labels easily by typing over the existing field, inserting or deleting characters as needed.

If you want to correct a minor typing mistake in a field label or change the field label to upper- or lowercase, you can type over the characters in the label. To do this, follow these steps:

1. Move the cursor to where you want to make the change.

2. Press the Insert key. Notice that the block cursor now changes to an underline cursor. This change indicates that PC-File is in Typeover mode and allows you to type over existing characters.

3. Type the new characters.

4. Press the Insert key again to exit Typeover mode and to return to Insert mode.

If you want to add characters to a field label, follow these steps:

1. Move the cursor to where you want to insert the characters in the field label.

2. Type the characters.

If you want to delete characters in a field label, follow these steps:

1. Move the cursor to where you want to delete characters in the field label.

2. Use the Backspace or Delete key to remove the characters. The Backspace key removes characters to the left of the cursor. The Delete key removes characters to the right of the cursor.

When you finish making the changes to the data entry screen, select OK to display the field buttons.

Changing the Order of Fields on the Screen

You can change the order of the fields on the screen in the edit window. To move a field, follow these steps:

1. Highlight the field you want to move with the mouse. To do this, click and drag through the field name and the field markers. PC-File highlights the line, as shown in figure 9.9.

2. Press Shift-Delete to cut the line. The information is temporarily stored in the buffer memory.

3. Move the cursor to the new location.

4. Press Shift-Insert. PC-File moves the field to the new location, and the other fields adjust accordingly.

When you finish making the changes to the data entry screen, select OK to display the field buttons.

Changing Miscellaneous Text

You can add, change, and delete miscellaneous text such as headings or titles at the top of the data entry screen or any notes you may have entered for other people who use the database and enter data.

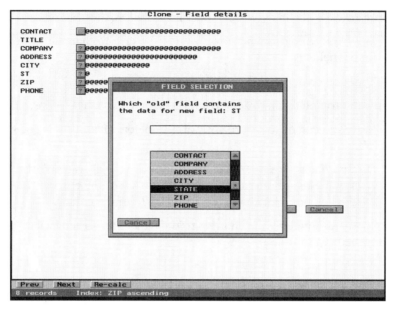

Fig. 9.9. Moving a field.

If you want to add characters to text, follow these steps:

1. Move the cursor to where you want to make the change.

2. Type the characters.

You can type over the text to correct minor typing errors or change the text to upper- or lowercase. To do this, follow these steps:

1. Move the cursor to where you want to make the change.

2. Press the Insert key. Notice that the block cursor now changes to an underline cursor. This change indicates that PC-File is in Typeover mode and allows you to type over existing characters.

3. Type the new characters.

4. Press the Insert key again to exit Typeover mode and to return to Insert mode.

If you want to delete text, follow these steps:

1. Move the cursor to where you want to delete the text.

2. Use the Backspace or Delete key to remove the characters. The Backspace key removes characters to the left of the cursor; the Delete key removes characters to the right of the cursor.

When you finish making the changes to the data entry screen, select OK to display the field buttons.

Adding and Deleting Lines and Boxes

You can add, change, and delete lines and boxes. If you want to add lines and boxes to text, follow these steps:

1. Move the cursor to where you want to insert the characters.

2. Type the ASCII characters that represent the line and box characters. To do this, type the decimal value for the ASCII character, and then release the Alt key. You must repeat this process for each line and box character you want to draw on the screen. (To determine the appropriate ASCII characters, refer to the ASCII character chart in your PC-File documentation.)

   To create an upper-left corner in a box, hold down the Alt key, type 218 using the numeric keypad, then release the Alt key. The ┌ appears on the screen.

If you want to delete the line and box characters, follow these steps:

1. Move the cursor to the first line or box characters you want to delete.

2. Use the Backspace or Delete key to remove the character. The Backspace key removes characters to the left of the cursor; the Delete key removes characters to the right of the cursor. Continue deleting each individual character.

When you finish making the changes to the data entry screen, select OK to display the field buttons.

Choosing Field Buttons

After you indicate that you are finished making the changes to the data entry screen, PC-File displays field buttons at the beginning of each field, just as it does when you define a new database using the Paint method.

In the PC-File redefine edit window, there are two kinds of field buttons: required and optional. If you make a change to the field, a required field button marked with a question mark (?) appears, indicating that you made a change to the field. PC-File requires additional information when you select a required field button. An optional field button is not marked with a question mark and does not require additional information.

Required Buttons

You must select each required field button and enter additional information when it is requested by PC-File. You must enter all of the required field buttons; otherwise, PC-File will not let you continue beyond the file edit window.

To answer required field buttons, follow these steps:

1. Click on the required field button with the mouse, or use the arrow keys to move the cursor to the button and then press Enter. PC-File displays the Data Source dialog box you saw in figure 9.3.

2. Tell PC-File where to find the data you are transferring to a new field. For example, the Data Source can be a New field, an Existing field, or a Calculated field. To select a data source, press the appropriate letter that appears to the left of the data source menu item or click the appropriate button. For example, press E or click the E button to delete an Existing field.

   When you have finished selecting a data source, PC-File displays the Field Characteristics dialog box.

3. If you select Existing field in Step 2, PC-File displays a Field selection dialog box. Tell PC-File which existing field contains the data for the new field. To do this, use the arrow keys and press Enter to select the field or click the field name with the mouse.

PC-File displays the Field Characteristics dialog box.

4. At this point, you can enter a mask, a constant, or a calculation if you wish. To do so, simply type the appropriate information in the text box. For example, type AZ in the Mask text box to indicate restricting all letters to uppercase. For information on entering masks, constants, and calculations, refer to Chapter 4, "Creating a Database." If you do not want to enter any additional information, click OK or press Alt-O.

You can select the field buttons in any order. Select one field button at a time, answer all of the questions, and enter the appropriate information in each dialog box. After you respond to a prompt or make changes to a field, PC-File displays a check mark on the button field.

When you're done, select OK. PC-File continues redesigning the database by asking you to identify the access order of the fields, as described later in this chapter.

Optional Buttons

An optional field button is not marked with a question mark and does not require you to enter additional information. However, if you want to change a field name or any field characteristics, you can select the optional field button for a particular field. When you choose an optional field button, PC-File displays the Field Characteristics dialog box. You can change the field name, an indexed field, a mask, a constant, or a calculation. Then select OK to continue redesigning the database. PC-File displays the Access Order dialog box.

Identifying the Data Source

If you change one or more fields in your database, PC-File transfers data from the old database to a new one. But first, you must define the data source for each field you change. Then PC-File knows where the data is transferred from.

For example, if you add a field called TITLE to your database, PC-File asks you to identify the data source (or field). In this case, you select New field. PC-File then knows there is no existing data or calculated field from which to transfer data.

After you choose a required field button, PC-File prompts you with the Data Source dialog box to select from three data sources: a new field, an existing field, or a calculated field. Figure 9.10 shows the Data Source dialog box.

If you select New field, PC-File creates a new field and leaves that field blank when you finish redefining your database. Then PC-File prompts you to define the field characteristics. Refer to Defining Field Characteristics later in this chapter. To enter data in the new field, you can either type the data or import the data from another database. For more information on importing data, see the section Importing Data later in this chapter.

If you select Existing field, PC-File transfers the data from an existing field in the current database to the new field you defined in the new database. For more information on the Existing field option, read the next section, Choosing an Existing Field.

Choosing an Existing Field

When you choose the Existing field option, PC-File displays a list of fields in the current database in the Field Selection dialog box (see figure 9.11).

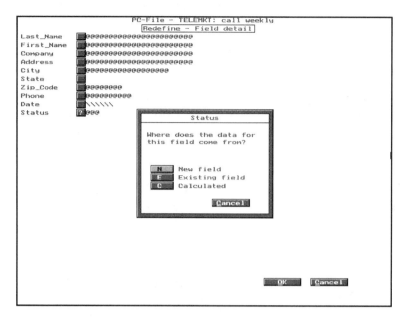

Fig. 9.10. *The Data Source dialog box.*

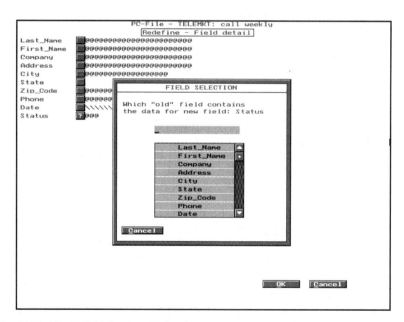

Fig. 9.11. *The Field Selection dialog box.*

You can choose only one field from an existing database that contains the data you want to transfer to the new field you have defined. PC-File allows you to transfer all or part of the data within a field.

To specify transferring part of the data, enter the field name, starting position, and length of the partial field in the text box at the top of the dialog box. The starting position is the first character you want from the field. The number of positions is the total number of characters you want from the partial field, including the first character. You must enter commas between each part of the command, and you cannot use any spaces.

Suppose that you want to transfer only the first five spaces of a 9-digit ZIP CODE field. You would type *ZIP_CODE,1,5* in the text box.

Changing Field Characteristics

You can change the database field name, but PC-File does not change the field label. You also can change a field type such as @ (at) for character and # for numeric fields, as explained in Chapter Four, "Creating a Database."

When you choose a field button in the edit window, PC-File displays the Field Characterization dialog box. It looks just like the dialog box that displays for each field when you define a database by using the Paint method, as noted in Chapter 4, "Creating a Database."

When you are finished changing the field characteristics, select OK to return to the Redefine edit window.

Performing a Calculation

To determine the values to enter in a particular field, you need to perform a calculation. Begin by selecting Calculated from the Data Source dialog box. When you choose Calculated for a data source, PC-File displays a dialog box where you can enter a calculation as shown in figure 9.12. Type the calculation in the text box labeled Calc. For more information on how to enter a calculation, refer to Chapter 4, "Creating a Database."

When you are finished redefining the database, PC-File performs the calculation and determines the values to enter in the specified field.

For example, to calculate profit, enter *Sales - Expenses* in the CALC text box. To calculate sales tax, enter *Price * SalesTax*. Another example of a calculation is Yr-Salary/12 which calculates your monthly salary.

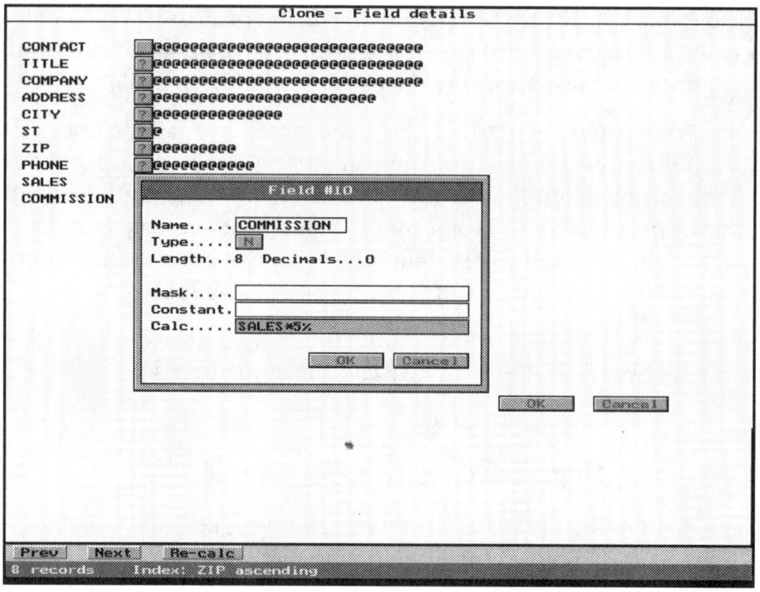

```
              Clone - Field details
 CONTACT      @@@@@@@@@@@@@@@@@@@@@@@@@@@@@
 TITLE        @@@@@@@@@@@@@@@@@@@@@@@@@@@@@
 COMPANY      @@@@@@@@@@@@@@@@@@@@@@@@@@@@@
 ADDRESS      @@@@@@@@@@@@@@@@@@@@@@@@@
 CITY         @@@@@@@@@@@@@@@
 ST           @
 ZIP          @@@@@@@@@
 PHONE        @@@@@@@@@@
 SALES
 COMMISSION            Field #10

             Name..... COMMISSION
             Type..... N
             Length...8  Decimals...0

             Mask.....
             Constant.
             Calc..... SALES*5%

                       OK    Cancel

                              OK    Cancel


 Prev   Next   Re-calc
 8 records    Index: ZIP ascending
```

Fig. 9.12. *The Calculation text box.*

Changing Access Order

The access order is the order in which fields normally are accessed in the database. It determines the order in which fields are highlighted when you enter data in your database. In Table View, the access order is the order in which fields are positioned across the screen.

When you add or modify records, PC-File moves the cursor in the order that you entered the fields, from left to right and top to bottom. If you use the Paint method to create your database, you can change the access order. If you want the cursor to move through the fields in a different order, you can tell PC-File to do just that. You cannot change the access order when you use the Fast method to create a database, however.

You might want to layout your data entry screen to look like a paper form, for example, but place the fields that rarely contain data at the end of the access order. After you change the access order, the appearance of your data entry screen does not change, but the cursor now moves to each of the fields in the order you have specified. If you have no data to enter in the fields at the end of the access order, you can skip quickly to the next record.

After you have finished redefining your database by using the field buttons and specifying the data source, PC-File asks whether you want to change the order in which the fields are accessed. The order in which the fields appear in the Field Selection dialog box is the current access order (see figure 9.13). To number the fields in the Field Selection dialog box, follow these steps:

1. Use the arrow keys to highlight the field you want to renumber and press Enter. PC-File assigns that field the next sequential number (1,2,3,...) and continues until all fields are numbered.

   With the mouse, you can simply click on each field in the order (1,2,3,...) you want each to be accessed.

   As you highlight the fields, PC-File displays a check mark and a number next to each field name in the list box. The fields you do not renumber are placed in sequence behind the last field you renumbered. The numbered fields remain in their preceding order.

2. To move from field to field by using the keyboard, press the up- and down-arrow keys.

3. When you are finished renumbering the fields, select OK. PC-File displays the Record Selection dialog box.

Fig. 9.13. Fields appear in their current access order.

Transferring Records

When you finish renumbering the fields, PC-File displays the Record Selection dialog box. At this point, you must specify which records you want to transfer to the new database. Figure 9.14 shows the Record Selection dialog box.

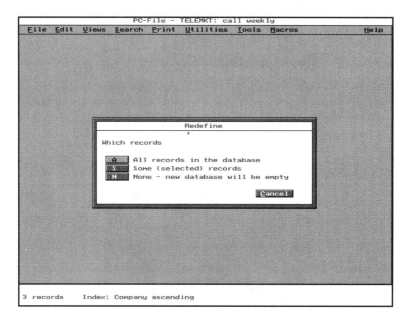

Fig. 9.14. The Record Selection dialog box.

PC-File gives you three options for transferring records: All, Some, or None.

If you choose All from the Record Selection dialog box, PC-File transfers all the records or selects the records randomly. Selecting the records randomly means that you can view each record on the screen and choose to select it or skip over it. Follow these steps for All:

1. Select All from the Record Selection dialog box. PC-File prompts you to enter a name for the new database.

2. Type the filename and press Enter. PC-File asks you if you want to output the current record. Outputting a record is the same as transferring a record to the new database. The current record is the first record in the original database that appears on the screen.

3. If you want to output the current record, select Yes from the Output Record dialog box (see figure 9.15). PC-File outputs the current record and prompts you again to output the next record. To continue selecting records randomly, select Yes. If you do not want to output the current record, select No. To output all of the records at one time, select All. You can select All at any time, when prompted to output the first record or any subsequent record.

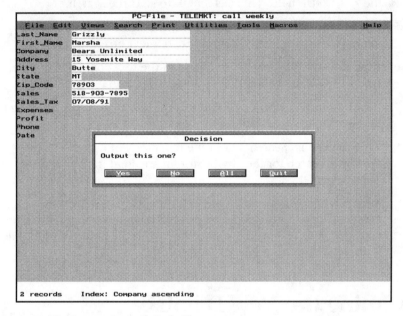

Fig. 9.15. The Output Record dialog box.

If you choose Some records from the Output Record dialog box, you perform a search to select the records you want to transfer. You must enter the search criteria. For example, to select only the employees from one department, enter the name of that department in the DEPARTMENT field. This creates a new database for that department. For more information on the Search command, refer to Chapter 6, "Searching for Records."

To select some of the records, follow these steps:

1. Select Some from the Record Selection dialog box. PC-File displays the Search dialog box. You can choose from three types of search modes: Simple, Formula, or Global.

2. If you want to perform a Simple search, select Simple by pressing **S**. PC-File displays a blank record from the current database.

3. Use the arrow keys to move the cursor to the field where you want to enter search criteria.

4. Enter the search criteria. For example, if you want to search for all the records that contain a particular ZIP code, type that ZIP code in the ZIP_CODE field. Then select OK to start the search.

5. If you want to perform a Formula search, select Formula by pressing **F**. PC-File displays a Formula Search text box.

6. Type the Formula Search command in the text box. For example, type ZIP_CODE < 50000. Then select OK.

7. If you want to perform a Global search, select Global by pressing G. PC-File displays a Global Search text box.

8. Type the Global Search text in the text box. For example, type *Boston* to search for the city Boston in any field in the database. Then select OK.

   After you enter the Search criteria for any type of search and select OK, PC-File searches for the records according to the search criteria you specified. Then you are presented with the first record PC-File finds and the Output Record dialog box.

Naming the New Database

If you make any changes to your database, as explained in this chapter, you must name the new database as one of the final steps in redefining your database.

If you choose to create a new database, PC-File displays a File Selection dialog box (see figure 9.16). Enter the new name for the database either within the current directory or in a different directory. If you want to move the database to a different directory, you can use the same name or give the file a new name.

To change directories, follow these steps:

1. To select the directory you want, press the Tab or right-arrow key to move to the Directories List box.

2. Use the arrow keys to move to the directory you want and press Enter.

3. Type the name of the file you want to store in the directory specified.

4. Press Enter. PC-File stores your database in the directory specified.

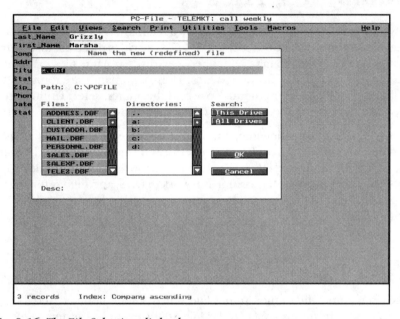

Fig. 9.16. *The File Selection dialog box.*

Changing the File Description

After you name a new PC-File database, you are prompted to enter an optional description, as explained in Chapter 4, "Creating a Database." If you enter a description for the database you currently are redefining, it appears next to the new filename. You can use the same description by selecting OK to accept the current description that appears in the text box. Or you can enter a new description in the text box just by typing your description in the displayed dialog box. A description can contain a maximum of 50 characters.

Whether you keep the same file description or enter a new one, select OK. PC-File tells you that the redefine process is complete. Select OK to remove the Information box and return to the first record in the original database.

Managing Files

As you create more and more of your own database files with PC-File, you need to do some disk housekeeping. PC-File provides three useful features that let you copy your database files between disks, rename files in memory and on disk, and delete unwanted files. These commands are found in the Utilities File Management menu. To access this menu, select Utilities from the menu bar and then select File Management from the Utilities menu.

Using PC-File's Copy, Rename, and Delete document commands is easier and more convenient than having to perform these tasks in DOS by using the COPY, RENAME, and DELETE commands. However, you can exit PC-File with the Tools Drop to DOS command, work in DOS, and then return to the program. Refer to the next section for instructions on how to work in DOS from PC-File.

Copying a File

The Copy command in the Utilities File Management menu is used to copy or duplicate any file created with PC-File. In the event of a system failure or power outage, you might lose the information on your hard disk. To avoid losing your work, you need to back up or copy your file every time you finish working on it. You can store it on disk to save it for future use.

To copy a file with PC-File's Copy option, follow these steps:

1. Select Utilities from the menu bar.

2. Select File Management from the Utilities menu. PC-File displays the File Management dialog box as shown in figure 9.17.

3. Select Copy from the File Management dialog box. PC-File displays the File Type dialog box as shown in figure 9.18. The types of files include a database file, a profile that contains the configuration set-up for PC-File, a macro file, a letter, a report, and a graph.

4. Select the file you want to copy. PC-File displays the Copy "From" File Selection dialog box.

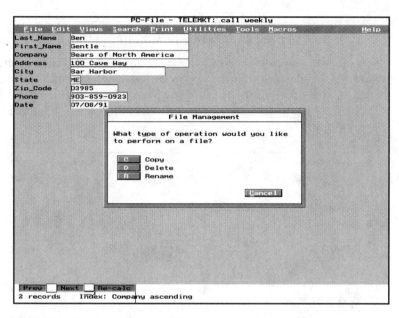

Fig. 9.17. The File Management dialog box.

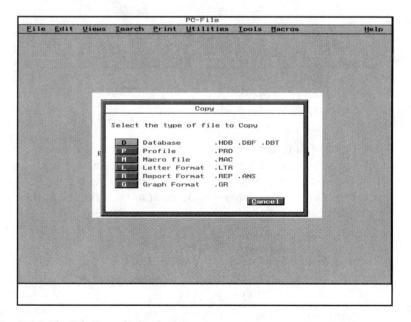

Fig. 9.18. The File Type dialog box.

5. Select the file you want to copy from and press Enter. PC-File displays the Copy to File Selection dialog box.

6. To copy to a floppy disk, type the drive name, a backslash, and the name of the file you want to copy in the text box. Because you are copying to a different drive, you can give the file the same name. Figure 9.19 shows the drive letter and filename when saving a file on a floppy disk.

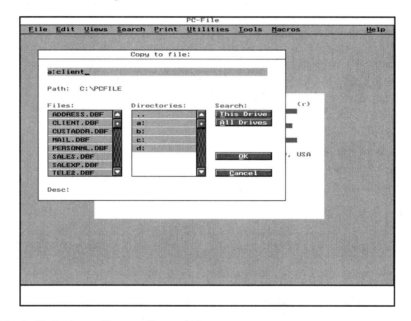

Fig. 9.19. *Saving a file on a floppy disk.*

To copy to a different directory, type *c:\pcfile* followed by a subdirectory name and the filename you want to assign to the copy. Because you are copying to a different directory, you can give the database file the same name. If you want to copy the file to the same drive and path, you give the file a new name.

7. Press Enter or select OK.

PC-File saves an exact copy of your file. The database file remains on the hard disk, and a copy of the database file is on the floppy disk or in the other directory.

When the copy is completed, PC-File displays Successful.

8. Select OK. PC-File displays the File Management dialog box again. If you are finished using the File Management operations, select Cancel. Otherwise repeat Steps 3 through 7.

Backing Up Database Files

As a rule, you back up your databases often. It's worth the few minutes it takes to back up your files at the end of a work session, because you never know when a database might be damaged. You could accidentally erase data, your hard disk could crash, or you might experience a power outage. If you do not back up your database and it is accidentally damaged or erased, you must design your database again and retype all the data.

You can save your database on a floppy disk rather than on the hard disk. But your database probably takes up more space than is available on one floppy disk. If you want to save a large database on several floppy disks, you use the DOS BACKUP command or other backup utilities software. You also can copy a database file from one directory to another directory on the hard disk with the DOS COPY command.

There are three file extensions associated with a database: DBF, DBT, and HDB. DBF stands for *database file* and contains all the field names, field types, and field order for a database. DBT stands for *database text* and contains the memo text stored in the memo fields in a database. HDB represents a header file and contains the *location* of the fields on the screen, the calculations, the masks, and the next available unique number. If you create a database called CLIENT, for example, you need to backup three files: CLIENT.DBF, CLIENT.DBT, and CLIENT.HDB.

See your DOS manual for information on the BACKUP and RESTORE commands.

Renaming a File

The Utilities File Management Rename command is used to change a database file's name. For instance, if you're working with an older version of a database file and you want to update the name, or if you're working with a practice database file and you want to make it the final working version, you can rename the file.

Another situation in which you might use Rename is when two versions of the same database file, stored on the same disk, have similar names. Renaming one file may lessen the confusion between the two files. Or, for another example, a coworker may give you a database file he or she created with PC-File that has the same filename as one of your own database files. You easily can rename the new database file with PC-File's Rename command.

To rename a database file, follow these steps:

1. Select Utilities from the menu bar.

2. Select File Management from the Utilities menu. PC-File displays the File Management dialog box.

3. Select Rename from the File Management dialog box. PC-File displays the File Type dialog box.

4. Select Database from the File Type dialog box.

5. Select the database file you want to rename.

6. Type a new filename. Figure 9.20 shows renaming a file.

7. Press Enter.

The database file is renamed.

Deleting a File

When you no longer want a database file, you can delete it from PC-File and free the disk space. PC-File's Utilities File Management Delete command lets you remove a database file with its index files. You can delete a database that is currently open or one that is not open.

Because deleting a file is serious business, PC-File's Delete command is the safest way to delete a database file. With this command, you can change your mind and back out of the command if you decide you don't want to get rid of a file. PC-File asks you to confirm deletion of the file before you complete the procedure, thereby giving you a last chance to back out.

If you find you are about to destroy a file in error and have not yet pressed the Enter key after selecting the filename, you can select Cancel to exit the Delete command. If you want to continue with the deletion, select Yes. PC-File then deletes your file from whatever disk and drive you specified.

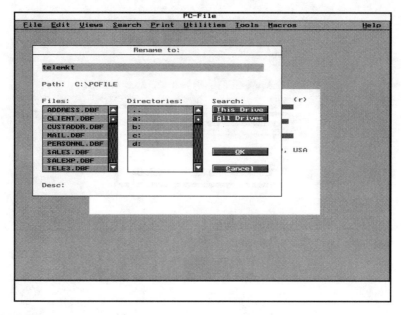

Fig. 9.20. *Renaming a file.*

To delete a database file, follow these steps:

1. Select Utilities from the menu bar.

2. Select File Management from the Utilities menu. PC-File displays the File Management dialog box.

3. Select Delete from the File Management dialog box. PC-File displays the File Type dialog box.

4. Select Database from the File Type dialog box.

5. Select the database file you want to delete. If you want to delete a file on the hard disk, specify drive C and the path name. If you want to delete a file on a floppy disk, specify drive A.

    PC-File asks you to confirm deletion of the file (see figure 9.21).

6. Select Yes to confirm deletion of the database file. If you do not want to delete the database file, select No.

    After you select Yes, PC-File deletes the database file from disk, including the DBF, DBT, and HDB files. The index files, however, are not deleted. You must delete the index (NDX) files with the DOS DELETE command.

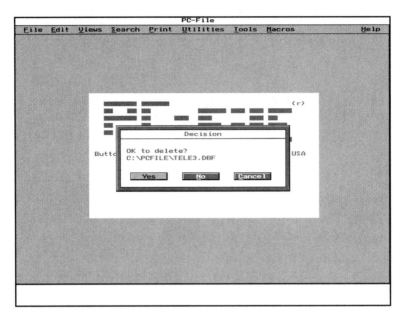

Fig. 9.21. *Deleting a database file.*

Using the Drop to DOS Feature

Normally, you exit PC-File to perform DOS commands or run another program; however, exiting and reloading the program is time-consuming and requires more keystrokes. Instead, you can temporarily exit PC-File to DOS or another program, perform a task, and then return to PC-File and continue where you left off.

PC-File provides a Drop to DOS command that enables you to exit PC-File temporarily to perform DOS commands and run other programs. For example, you can exit to DOS and copy multiple database files to another directory or run Lotus 1-2-3 to look at a spreadsheet file from which you want to import data.

What is nice about PC-File's Drop to DOS feature is that you do not have to make sure your computer has enough memory to run other programs while PC-File is still in memory. You can free up memory by simply selecting Yes when PC-File prompts you to free up memory. PC-File frees up approximately 10K of memory by creating a temporary file on disk. The temporary file stores the actions you have taken in PC-File so that you can return to where you left off.

To issue a single DOS command, follow these steps:

1. Save the file you are currently working on before using the Drop to DOS command, just in case you run out of memory and have to reboot your computer.

2. Select Tools from the menu bar.

3. Select Drop to DOS from the Tools menu. PC-File displays the Drop to DOS dialog box (see figure 9.22).

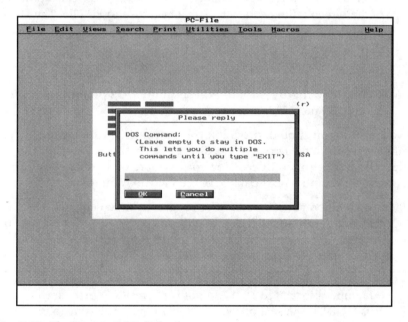

Fig. 9.22. *The Drop to DOS dialog box.*

4. Type the DOS command in the text box and press Enter. PC-File asks you if you want to free up memory.

5. If you are only processing DOS commands, select No. If you want to run another program, select Yes. In some cases, if your computer has a lot of memory, you usually can select No. In other cases, if your computer has a minimum of memory, select Yes.

6. When DOS completes the command, press any key to return to PC-File.

If you want to process multiple DOS commands, follow these steps:

1. Save the file you are currently working on before using the Drop to DOS command, just in case you run out of memory and have to reboot your computer.

2. Select Tools from the menu bar.

3. Select Drop to DOS from the Tools menu. PC-File displays the Drop to DOS dialog box you saw in figure 9.22.

4. Select OK. The screen goes blank, and a message appears at the top of the screen telling you to type exit to return to PC-File. The DOS prompt appears.

5. At the DOS prompt, enter any DOS commands or run another program.

6. When you want to return to PC-File, at the DOS prompt type *exit* and press Enter. This returns you to PC-File.

If you want to run another program, you can type the name of the file you want to execute in the Drop to DOS dialog box and press Enter. Or you can select OK in the Drop to DOS dialog box to exit temporarily to DOS. Then, at the DOS prompt, type the name of the file you want to execute.

When you temporarily exit to another program, the screen goes blank and the other program starts. When you quit this program, you return to the DOS prompt. Type *exit* and press Enter to return to PC-File. You are returned to the same place where you left off.

CAUTION

If you temporarily exit to DOS, do not run a resident program such as MODE because a portion of this program will remain in memory. Also, be sure you do not delete the temporary file created by PC-File. An example of a temporary file is TEMPxxxx.PCF, where the x's represent any combination of letters.

If you want to exchange data between PC-File and other programs, read the next two sections on exporting and importing data.

Exporting Data

You may want to use the data from a PC-File database in another program or format. This is referred to as exporting data. You can export all of the data in the database or only the records you want. You also can export selected fields.

For example, you can export names and addresses from a PC-File customer database into a sales announcement form letter created in WordPerfect. In this case, you select only the name and address fields and leave out other fields such as the phone numbers. You also could select only the customers who are located in a specific geographic area.

PC-File provides several exchange formats for transferring data between files. They include DIF, Fixed length, Lotus PRN, Mail merge, Peachtext, Text editor, User-defined, and WordPerfect.

DIF stands for *data interchange format* and is used by Lotus 1-2-3 and Microsoft Excel. Fixed length is used by many programs that create random files where the end of each record is not marked with a carriage return. Lotus PRN is used to export PC-File data into Lotus 1-2-3 using the File Import Numbers command in Lotus 1-2-3.

Mail merge is used by WordStar, Microsoft Word, and BASIC programs. Peachtext is used by Peachtext software and places each field on a separate line in Line Delimited format. The Text Editor format, which has the SDF file extension, can be used to import a Lotus 1-2-3 PRN file into PC-File.

User-defined lets you exchange data with programs that do not use one of the standard formats. You can specify your own delimiter for exporting and importing data. A delimiter is used as a separator between each field and between each record. In PC-File, the default delimiter is the backslash (\), but you can change it to the appropriate character.

WordPerfect is used to transfer data to or from WordPerfect secondary merge files and document files. You can use WordPerfect 4.2, 5.0, or 5.1.

PC-File also supports files in ASCII format such as fixed length, mail merge, line delimited, text editor, and Lotus PRN.

The Utilities Export command is used to transfer data from PC-File into other programs.

To export data, follow these steps:

1. Check the available space on the target disk or drive. Be sure there is enough to hold the data you want to export. The fixed length and text editor format take up more disk space than .DBF database files.

2. Use the File Open command to open the database from which you want to export data. You cannot export data from a closed database.

3. Select Utilities from the menu bar.

4. Select Export from the Utilities menu. PC-File displays the Export Format dialog box (see figure 9.23).

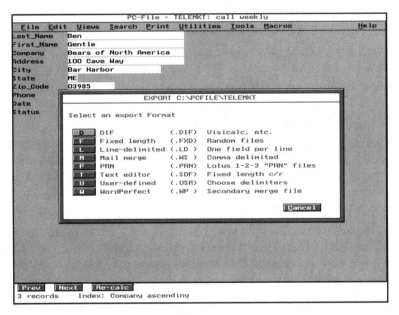

Fig. 9.23. *The Export Format dialog box.*

5. Select the format type you want for your exported file. PC-File displays the File Selection dialog box.

6. Select the directory you want to save the exported data to. To do this, press the Tab key to move the highlight to the directory list box. Use the arrow keys to select the directory.

7. Use the Tab key to move to the text box at the top of the File Selection dialog box.

8. Type the filename you want to save the exported data to.

9. If you select the mail merge format, PC-File asks you if the first record of the exported file should contain the field names. If you are using Microsoft Word, which requires the field names in the first record, select Yes. If the field names are not required, select No. To determine whether your word processing program requires field names in the first record, read the documentation for the word processing program you are using.

10. PC-File then asks you if you want quotation marks around every field. If the program you are exporting to requires quotation marks around every field, even when the field does not contain a command, select Yes. Otherwise, select No.

11. If you select user-defined format, enter the field delimiter. You can use the backslash, which is the default field delimiter. Or you can select one of the options to enter a different character. To determine which field delimiter your word processing program requires to separate fields, read the documentation for the word processing program you are using.

    Other possible field delimiter options include the ASCII decimal values for keys such as the Tab key that are not represented by a character. You also can choose from actual characters as represented on the keyboard, the carriage return/line-feed, or no delimiter at all.

12. Enter the record delimiter. You can choose from the same options as the field delimiter, as already mentioned.

    PC-File then asks you if the first record of the exported file should contain the field names.

13. If you are using Microsoft Word, select Yes. If the field names are not required, select No.

    The user-defined export format requires that you provide delimiter information. The other export types do not require you to enter anything when you export them.

14. If the data contains a tilde (~) and you want to flip the output, select Yes. Otherwise, select No. (Flipping the output pertains to the mail merge format; it flips first and last names. In other words,

if the LAST_NAME field is followed by the FIRST_NAME field in the PC-File database, you can flip the names around when you export the data to the word processing program. The first names then appear before the last names in the word processing file.)

15. To select the fields you want to export, choose All or Some fields. If you choose All, PC-File exports all the fields in the database. If you choose Some, PC-File displays the database fields in a Field Selection dialog box as shown in figure 9.24. Select each field you want to export by using the arrow keys to highlight the field you want and pressing Enter. Or, with the mouse, you can simply click on each field you want. As you select the fields, PC-File displays a check mark and a number next to each field name in the list box.

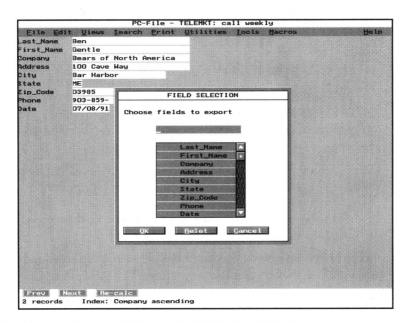

Fig. 9.24. The database fields in a Field Selection dialog box.

If you want to export a portion of a field—for example, the first five digits of a nine-digit ZIP code—you can do this as well. At the top of the Field Selection dialog box is a text box where you type the field name, the starting position, and the number of positions for the partial field.

The starting position is the first character you want to choose from the field. The number of positions is the total number of characters in the partial field, including the first character. You must enter commas between each part of the command and cannot use any spaces. To export just the first five digits of a nine-digit ZIP code field called ZIP, for example, you specify a partial field of only the first five characters, and type *ZIP,1,5* in the text box.

16. Select OK. PC-File displays the Export Records Selection dialog box.

17. To select the records you want to export, choose either All or Some records.

If you choose All, PC-File exports all the records in the database or lets you choose the records as they are exported. PC-File asks you if you want to export the current record and displays the Export Output dialog box shown in figure 9.25. If you want to export the current record, select Yes. PC-File exports the current record and prompts you again to export the next record. To continue selecting records randomly, select Yes. If you want to export the current record and all of the remaining selected records without being prompted again, select All. If you do not want to export the current record, select No. If you want to cancel the operation, select Quit.

If you choose Some, PC-File asks you if you want to perform a Simple or Formula search for the records. Select the Search mode and enter the search criteria, as explained in Chapter 6, "Searching for Records." Once you enter the search criteria, select OK. PC-File exports the data based on the search criteria you specified.

Importing Data

You may want to transfer data created with another program to PC-File. This is called importing data. You can import data from a dBASE database file into a PC-File database file, for example. Or you can import data from one PC-File database to another.

The Utilities Import command is used to transfer data from other programs into PC-File. An existing file in PC-File must be open in order to transfer the data into it. Or you can create a database to which the data will be imported. The files you import can have any file extension, with two exceptions: dBASE files must have a DBF extension, and DIF files must have a DIF extension.

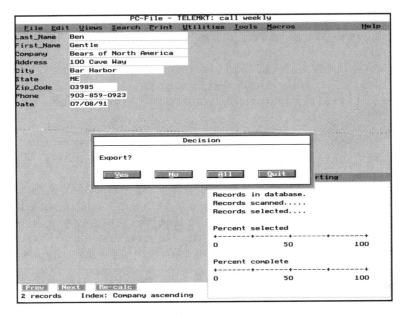

Fig. 9.25. The Export Output dialog box.

Before you import data, you need to be acquainted with the following import file requirements:

Text editor (SDF) or fixed length file: The database must be identical to the import file. Define the database with the fields in the same sequence, number, and lengths as they appear in the import file.

Another PC-File or dBASE file: The database must have the same database or field sequence and field lengths as the import file, but it is not required to have the same number of fields.

Line delimited file: The database must have the same sequence and number of fields as the import file. The field lengths should be at least as long as those in the import file to prevent the data from being truncated.

Any other format: The database must have the same field sequence as the import file, but it is not required to have the same number of fields or matching field lengths.

If the import file has more fields than the database, the extra fields are ignored. If the import file has fewer fields than the database, the fields at the end of the record in the database are left blank. If the import file contains fields longer than those set up in the database, the data in those fields are truncated to the database field length. If the import file contains fields shorter than the database fields, the extra spaces are filled with blanks.

You must define or redefine your PC-File database according to the requirements of the file to be imported. For all file formats, the sequence of the fields must be identical. In some cases, however, the database number of fields and length of fields can be different from those of the import file.

In those cases in which the number of files can vary, the extra fields are ignored if the import file has more fields than the database. If the import file has fewer fields than the database, the fields at the end of the record in the database are left blank.

When the import file and the database file can have different field lengths, you need to make the database fields at least as long as those in the import file. Otherwise, if the import file contains fields longer than those set up in the database, the data in those fields are truncated to the database field length. If the import file contains fields shorter than the database fields, the extra spaces are filled with blanks.

To import data, follow these steps:

1. Use the File Open command to open the database to which you want to import data. You cannot import data into a closed database.

2. Select Utilities from the menu bar.

3. Select Import from the Utilities menu. PC-File displays the Import Format dialog box (see figure 9.26).

4. Select the format of the import file. If you select a field type other than User-defined, continue with Step 6.

5. If you select User-defined, you are prompted to enter the field delimiter. Type the field delimiter in the text box and select OK. For example, type $ (dollar sign). To determine which field delimiter you need to enter, read the documentation for the software used to create the data you are importing. The record delimiter default is set to a carriage return/line-feed. After you enter the field delimiter, PC-File displays the File Selection dialog box.

6. Select the path and type the filename of the import file. Select OK. PC-File displays the Import Append and Overwrite dialog box, as shown in figure 9.27.

7. If you want to add records to the current database and sequence them according to the current index, select the Append option. If you want to delete the current records and add the new records starting at record 1, select the Overwrite option.

8. To select the records you want to import, choose All or Some records.

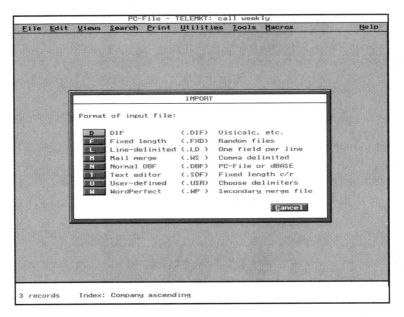

Fig. 9.26. The Import Format dialog box.

If you choose All, PC-File imports all the records in the database or lets you choose the records as they are imported. PC-File asks you if you want to import the current record and displays the Import Output dialog box, as shown in figure 9.28. If you want to import the current record, select Yes. If you do not want to import the current record, select No. PC-File imports the current record and prompts you again to import the next record. To continue selecting records randomly, select Yes. If you want to import the current record and all the remaining selected records without being prompted again, select All. If you want to cancel the operation, select Quit.

If you choose Some, PC-File asks you if you want to perform a Simple or Formula search for the records. Select the Search mode and enter the search criteria, as explained in Chapter 6, "Searching for Records." Then select OK. PC-File displays the Import Output dialog box. To import the data, follow the steps in the previous paragraph.

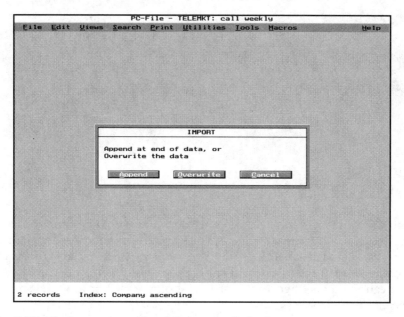

Fig. 9.27. *The Import Append and Overwrite dialog box.*

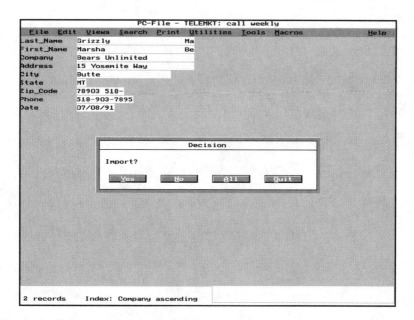

Fig. 9.28. *The Import Output dialog box.*

TIP

Select Yes to import the first few records to see if the records are being imported properly. If they are not, select Quit to cancel the operation. Examine the current database and import file and make sure that they match according to the requirements, as explained earlier in this chapter. Make the necessary changes and process the Import command again.

Summary

You saw the many ways you can refine your database to fine-tune and tailor the design according to your needs. You learned techniques for maintaining your PC-File database files as they grow in size. And you also looked at techniques for using PC-File with other programs. Finally, you learned how you can share data between PC-File and other word processors, spreadsheets, and database programs.

In the next chapter, you find out how to generate reports using the data from your database.

Part IV

Working with Other PC-File Features

Includes

Generating Reports

Producing Form Letters and Mailing Labels

Creating Graphs

Using Other PC-File Features

10

Generating Reports

To get the most mileage from your database, you need to master PC-File's report generator. You can design varying types of reports based on the information from your databases. When the records are updated, you can generate a customized report.

PC-File lets you create reports with various formats by combining information from one or more databases. The program comes with several fonts for communicating any kind of message in your reports. With PC-File's other sophisticated report features, you can add headers and footers, number pages automatically, insert breaks on columns with subtotals and totals, and use formulas to perform calculations on fields.

You can preview your report to see exactly how it looks before it is printed. That way, you can make changes to the report before you print it, if necessary. Then you can produce first-class output from 9- to 24-pin dot-matrix or laser printers.

In PC-File, you can use the powerful Language format to generate customized reports. The Language format is an advanced feature and is not covered in this book. If you are an experienced database user and have some programming experience, you might want to learn about the Language format. Refer to your PC-File documentation for more information on the Language format.

You can create some of the following professional-quality reports in PC-file.

- Mailing labels
- Phone lists
- Inventory lists
- Customer lists

- Invoices
- Checks
- Quarterly sales reports
- Fortune 1000 reports
- Contact lists
- Current projects reports
- Medical reports
- Insurance reports
- Personnel reports
- Quality assurance reports
- Marketing reports
- Advertising reports

This chapter assumes that you already know how to create database files by using PC-File or dBASE. If this is not the case, work through the Quick Start lesson in Chapter 2 or read Chapters 4, 5, and 6 before you continue with this chapter.

Step-by-step instructions for creating professional-quality reports are provided in this chapter, in formats ranging from simple to complex. PC-File provides five report formats: Page, Row, Mail Label, Free Form, and Language. You learn how to create a Page report, a Row report, a Mail Label report, and a Free Form report. You explore how to modify reports and create customized reports with PC-File's Free Form format.

The next section gives you deeper insight into what constitutes a well-designed report and explains how to communicate your ideas effectively by using PC-File.

Planning and Designing Reports

There are several concepts to think about when creating a report. A professional-quality report requires some planning before you actually create the report.

1. Decide on the purpose of the report. What do you want to accomplish with the report? Do you want weekly, monthly, or quarterly sales figures? Do you want to show sales commissions and bonuses on this report, or use separate reports? Jot down the information you want to generate with the report.

2. Understand PC-File terminology such as section heads, database fields, system fields, calculations, date arithmetic, IF commands, print masks, and buckets. How does PC-File solve your business problem? To produce a sales report that contains both text and numbers, for example, you can use the Row format to create a report with calculations to add the columns of sales figures.

3. Design the report. If the report contains complex formatting (many tabular columns), first make a sketch of it with paper and pencil. Change it as many times as necessary. You also can use an existing report.

4. Plan the layout. What do you want the finished report to look like? What do you want for a title? Do you want the date to appear at the top of the report? How do you want the field labels to be aligned over the columns? Should they be lined up flush left or flush right? Do you want to include lines to separate sections?

5. Make a list of the fields you want to use in the report. Decide in what order you want the fields to appear in the report.

6. Decide what totals to include. Do you want to include subtotals with a final total? How do you want the subtotals to break? Decide on the number of decimal places you want on the left side of the decimal point when PC-File calculates your records and gives you a final total.

7. Aim for simplicity. Determine the number of important points that must be communicated. Organize your report to include these key points.

8. Make the report as professional as possible. Select PC-File fonts and a report format that create a clear and legible appearance. Important ideas or titles should be made of larger type size than the remainder of the information in the report. Use a limited number of fonts to avoid inconsistency. To add emphasis to text, use PC-File's enhancements such as boldface, underline, lines, and boxes.

9. Stay within the 1-inch border of a report. One inch is equivalent to 6 lines; specify 1 inch for the top, bottom, left, and right margins in PC-File. If you have to, leave more top and bottom margin than right and left margin.

To select a report format that suits your needs, refer to the next section.

Selecting a Report Format

There are five report format options you can choose from when you define a report.

- Page

- Row

- Mail Label

- Free Form

- Language

If you are a beginner when it comes to creating reports, use any of the first three format options. PC-File steps you through creating a Page, Row, and Mail Label report. These report formats are simpler to use and generally faster than the Free Form and Language formats, but not as flexible.

If you have experience with creating reports, use the report format that fits your experience. The Free Form and Language formats are flexible and allow you to be as creative as you want. With these, you can create myriad types of reports.

When you define a report with any of the report formats, you can modify the report with either the Free Form or Language formats. For example, you could define a report quickly with the Mail Label format and then use the Free Form or Language format to make changes in the report to get the results you want.

With the exception of the Language format, each report format is covered in detail in the next few sections. Refer to your PC-File documentation for information on how to use the Language format.

Creating a Page Report

The Page format, the fastest and easiest of the report formats, is useful for printing all or some of the records in your database. The Page format prints one record per page; each record in the report looks just like the record you see on the Paint method data entry screen. PC-File uses all the fields in the database and prints all the records. Figure 10.1 shows a sample PC-File report created by using the Page format.

```
     Last_Name   Fuhlbruck

    First_Name   Carole

       Company   Care Center

       Address   200 Main Street

          City   Kalamazoo

         State   MA

           Zip   02107

         Phone   508-344-2345

       Acct_No   0056239

         Sales   300000

    Renew_Date   07/10/91

      Comments   Check for alligator in pool


     Last_Name   Yoffa

    First_Name   Meryl

       Company   Zorro Zoo

       Address   31 Rambling Road

          City   Boston

         State   MA

           Zip   02110

         Phone   617-345-2389

       Acct_No   006983

         Sales   150000

    Renew_Date   07/09/91

      Comments   Check for crocodiles in lake
```

Fig. 10.1. A report using the Page format.

To create a report by using the Page format, follow these steps:

1. Select Print from the menu bar. PC-File displays the Print menu shown in figure 10.2.

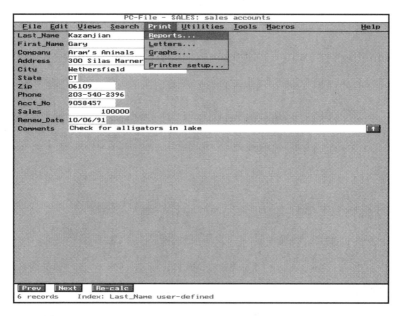

Fig. 10.2. *The Print menu.*

2. Select Reports from the Print menu. PC-File displays the Reports Operations dialog box, as you can see in figure 10.3.

3. Select New from the Reports Operations dialog box. PC-File displays the Report Format dialog box as shown in figure 10.4.

4. Select Page from the Report Format dialog box. PC-File creates the report and then prompts you to save the report, as shown in figure 10.5.

5. If you want to save the report so that you can view or print it in the future, select Yes. If you want to create a quick, temporary report that you do not need to save, select No. If you select No, you can view or print the report only once.

   If you select Yes, PC-File prompts you to enter a description of the report. The report description is optional, but it is useful when you want to know the contents of the report at a later date. The description can have up to 50 characters.

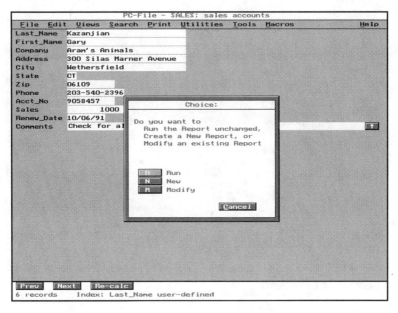

Fig. 10.3. *The Reports Operations dialog box.*

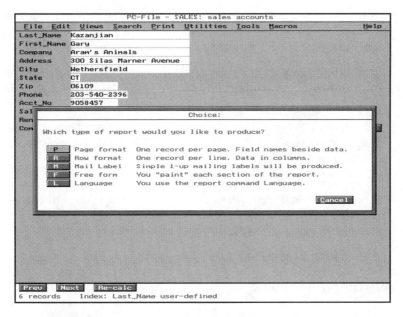

Fig. 10.4. *The Report Format dialog box.*

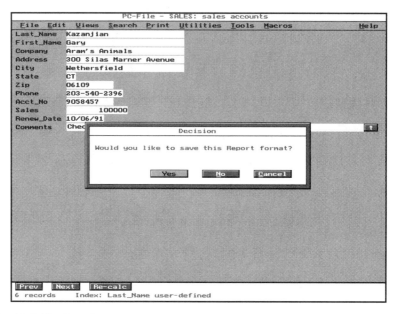

Fig. 10.5. The Save Report prompt.

6. If you want to enter a report description, type the description. An example might be *sales call report* (see figure 10.6). Then click the OK button; PC-File prompts you to enter a report name.

   If you do not want to enter a report description, leave the text box blank and click the OK button. PC-File prompts you to enter a report name.

   If you select No in Step 5, PC-File displays the Print Options dialog box. For information on printing reports, refer to the section on Printing Reports later in this chapter.

7. Type the report name and click the OK button. A report name can have up to 8 characters, both letters and numbers. PC-File assigns the file extension REP to a report name. An example of a report name with extension is SALECALL.REP (see figure 10.7).

Once you enter the report name, PC-File displays the Print Options dialog box. For information on printing reports, refer to the section on Printing Reports later in this chapter.

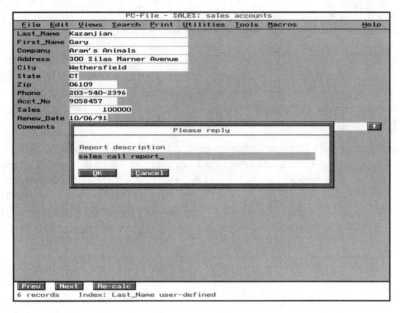

Fig. 10.6. *A report description.*

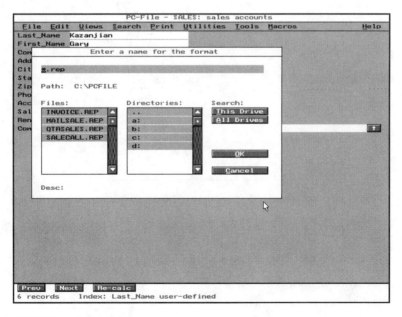

Fig. 10.7. *The report name.*

Creating a Row Report

The Row format report is useful for creating customized reports because you can restrict the number of fields in the report. You can specify the fields and the order of the fields you want. The data in the Row format appears in columns, and the field names appear as field headings across the top of each column. You also can enter a title for the report.

Thus, you can select a few fields instead of all of the fields to include the key points in a report. You can generate a contact list using the same database and selecting only the CONTACT and PHONE fields. In the CLIENT database example, you can select four fields, COMPANY, CITY, STATE, and ZIP CODE to see the geographic location of customers. Figure 10.8 illustrates this example with a sample report created by PC-File by using the Row format.

```
                    Quarterly Sales
    September 25, 1991 at 11:33 a.m.              Page   1

    Company                    Acct_No    Sales
    _____             _____   _____

    San Diego Zoo              3854893    40000

    Rover Ranch                0947596    65000

    Care Center                005627     300000

    Aram's Animals             9058457    100000

    Zorro Zoo                  006983     150000

    Zorro Zoo                  007893     200000

    _____

    TOTALS:     Sales                855,000

    Printed 6 of the 6 records.

    PRIMARY SORT FIELD: Last_Name

    All records

    SELECTION CRITERIA:

    All Records
```

Fig. 10.8. A report using the Row format.

The fields are arranged in rows for each record. Each row contains a record, and each column corresponds to a field in the record. One space appears between each column. PC-File automatically totals and subtotals the numbers in the numeric fields.

You can view a report on the screen and look at the first 79 characters of each row of the report. However, you cannot view the entire width of the report on the screen if the report contains more than 79 characters per row.

When you print a row report on the printer, one record or a part of a record prints on each line of the report. If the width of the report is larger than your printer can print on one line, PC-File wraps the contents of the record and prints them on multiple lines. To prevent PC-File from splitting the records on multiple lines, use condensed type, as explained later in this chapter.

Subtotals and totals appear in each column where appropriate.

In a Row report, PC-File prints only the display length of character and memo fields; that is, the characters in the field that display on the screen. You can print all of the characters in a character or memo field by editing the field with the Free Form format option, as explained in the Modifying a Report by Using Free Form section of this chapter.

The following steps demonstrate how you can create a simple row report that shows the sales figures for all the customers in a sample database called SALES.

1. Select Print from the menu bar. PC-File displays the Print menu.

2. Select Reports from the Print menu. PC-File displays the Reports Operations dialog box.

3. Select New from the Reports Operations dialog box. PC-File displays the Report Format dialog box.

4. Select Row from the Report Format dialog box. PC-File displays a check-off dialog box with a list of the fields in your database.

5. Select the fields you want to use and specify the order in which you want the fields to appear in the Row report. Use the arrow keys and press Enter to select each field. With the mouse, click the field you want. For example, select COMPANY and SALES to show the sales figures for the customers in the SALES database.

    PC-File displays a check mark and a number next to each field you select. The fields you do not want to include in the report should be left blank (see figure 10.9).

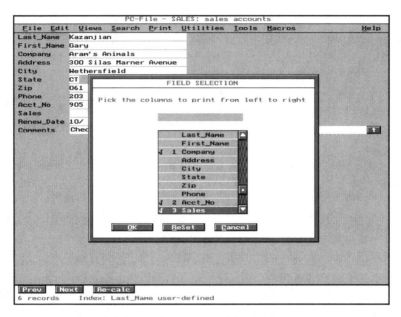

Fig. 10.9. *The selected fields and the order of the fields.*

6. Enter the permanent title for the report in the text box. For example, type *Quarterly Sales* and press Enter (see figure 10.10). Each time you print the report, the permanent title appears at the top of the report. This title is useful when you do not expect the title to change each time you print the report. A permanent title can have a maximum of 65 characters.

   If you want to create a quick, temporary report without storing a permanent title for the report, you can leave the text box blank. Each time you print the report, PC-File prompts you to enter a temporary title. A temporary title appears at the top of the report just as the permanent title does, but the temporary title can have no more than 35 characters. This title is useful when you know the title is going to change each time you print the report.

   For example, suppose you print a sales report for each quarter's sales figures. A temporary title for the first sales report would be 1991 1st Quarter Sales. An appropriate temporary title for the second quarter sales report would be 1991 2nd Quarter Sales, and so on.

7. When you finish selecting the fields and entering a title for the report, click the OK button. PC-File prompts you to save the report.

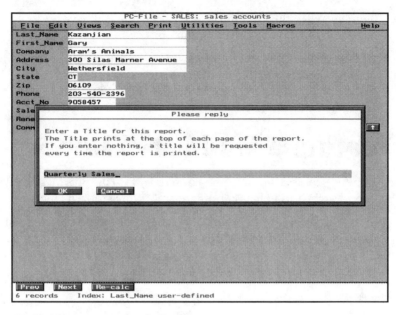

Fig. 10.10. *The permanent title for the row report.*

8. If you want to save the report so that you can view or print it in the future, select Yes. If you want to create a quick, temporary report and not save the report, select No. If you select No, you can view or print the report only once.

   If you select Yes in Step 8, PC-File prompts you to enter a description of the report. The report description is optional, but it is useful when you want to know the contents of the report at a later date. The description can have up to 50 characters.

9. If you want to enter a report description, type the description and click the OK button. For example, type *1991 4th Quarter Sales*. PC-File prompts you to enter a report name.

   If you do not want to enter a report description, leave the text box blank and click the OK button. PC-File prompts you to enter a report name.

   If you select No in Step 8, PC-File displays the Print Options dialog box. For information on printing reports, refer to the section on Printing Reports later in this chapter.

10. Type the report name, *sales*, for example. Do not type a file extension. PC-File automatically adds the file extension REP to a report

file. Then click the OK button. A report name can have up to 8 characters, both letters and numbers.

PC-File displays the Print Options dialog box. For information on printing reports, refer to the section on Printing Reports later in this chapter.

Creating a Mail Label Report

For business people who are time-conscious, PC-File provides the Mail Label report format to help you prepare and print standard labels.

The Mail Label format produces mailing labels in a single column. This is useful when you want to print only a handful of labels. Figure 10.11 shows a PC-File mailing label created by using the Mail Label format.

```
Preston Curtis
San Diego Zoo
15 Flamingo Road
San Diego CA 90234


Terri Digiro
Rover Ranch
35 Milkbone Avenue
Stowe MA 02546


Carole Fuhlbruck
Care Center
200 Main Street
Kalamazoo MA 02107


Gary Kazanjian
Aram's Animals
300 Silas Marner Avenue
Wethersfield CT 06109


Meryl Yoffa
Zorro Zoo
31 Rambling Road
Boston MA 02110
```

Fig. 10.11. Mailing labels using the Mail Label format.

You also can generate snapshot labels with this format, as explained in Chapter 11, "Producing Form Letters and Mailing Labels."

If you want to produce hundreds of labels at a time, you can print multiple column mailing labels. To do this, you must use PC-File's mailing label program called PC-Label, as explained in Chapter 11. PC-Label lets you print three or four labels across a standard sheet of computer labels.

When you use the Mail Label format to print mailing labels, you first must determine the number of lines you want to print on a label. These lines are called print lines, and they include the total number of lines from the top of one label to the top of the next label. Print lines contain the name and address plus the blank lines above and below the name and address.

Typically, a one-inch label can have six lines. If your labels are a different size, they may have a different number of lines. The font size also determines the print lines on a label. The font size is the height of the characters that print. The larger the font size, the fewer print lines on a label. With a smaller font size, you can fit more print lines on a label, as explained in the section on Printing Reports in this chapter.

Some labels have two, three, four, or even five printed lines. If one of the fields is blank, PC-File closes up the label—the field below the blank field is printed on this line. If the COMPANY field is blank, for example, the ADDRESS field is printed on the COMPANY line, and the CITY, STATE, and ZIP_CODE are printed on the ADDRESS line.

If there is more than one field on a line, PC-File inserts one space between the fields. One space appears between the city and the state and the state and the zip code, for example. If you want to enter commas or other punctuation between fields, you can do this in either of two ways.

You can enter the punctuation when you enter the data in a field, or you can enter the punctuation when you edit the report with the Free Form format.

To create mailing labels on one-inch labels by using the Mail Label format, follow these steps:

1. Select Print from the menu bar. PC-File displays the Print menu.

2. Select Reports from the Print menu. PC-File displays the Reports Operations dialog box.

3. Select New from the Reports Operations dialog box. PC-File displays the Report Format dialog box.

4. Select Mail Label from the Report Format dialog box. PC-File displays a check-off dialog box with a list of the fields in your database.

5. Enter the number of print lines for each label. To do this, first count the total number of lines from the top of one label to the top of the next label. Include the name and address plus the blank lines above and below the name and address. Then type the number of print lines in the text box. Notice the default is 6 lines. For example, type *4* to specify a 4-line address. Then click the OK button or press Enter twice.

6. Select the fields you want on the first line of the label and specify the order in which you want the fields to appear on the label. Use the arrow keys and press Enter to select each field. With the mouse, click the field you want. For example, select FIRST_NAME as the first field and LAST_NAME as the second field to appear on the first line of the label. Notice the 1 that appears next to FIRST_NAME and the 2 next to LAST_NAME. Then click the OK button to move to the next line.

    If you want to space down from the top of a label and leave the first line blank, select OK to skip the first line. The cursor moves to the second line. Now you can start the name on the second line. Select the fields you want to appear on the second line of the label.

7. Repeat Step 6 to select the fields you want to appear on rest of the lines in the label. For example, select COMPANY for the second line, ADDRESS for the third line, and CITY, STATE, and ZIP for the fourth line.

    When you select fields for each line, the numbering scheme starts over. For instance, the number 1 appears next to COMPANY on the second line as well as next to ADDRESS on the third line. After you number the fields for each line or skip lines, click the OK button or use the Tab key to move to the OK button and press Enter. Figure 10.12 shows the selected field for the mail label.

8. When you finish selecting the fields for the mail label, click the OK button. PC-File prompts you to save the report.

9. If you want to save the label format so that you can view or print it in the future, select Yes. If you want to create quick, temporary labels and not save the labels, select No. If you select No, you can view or print the labels only once.

    If you select Yes, PC-File prompts you to enter a description of the report. The report description is optional, but it is useful when you want to know the contents of the report at a later date. The description can have up to 50 characters.

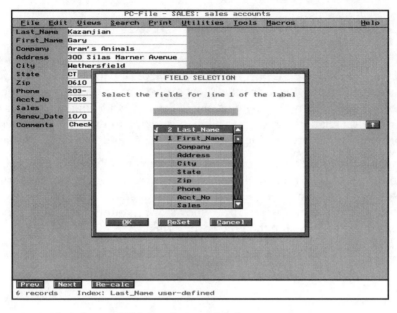

Fig. 10.12. The selected fields for the mail label.

10. If you want to enter a report description, type the description and select OK. For example, type *sales labels*. PC-File prompts you to enter a report name.

    If you do not want to enter a report description, leave the text box blank and select OK. PC-File prompts you to enter a report name.

    If you select No in Step 9, PC-File displays the Print Options dialog box. For information on printing reports, refer to the section on Printing Reports in this chapter.

11. Type the report name *label*, for example. Do not type a file extension. PC-File automatically adds the file extension REP to a report file. Then select OK. A report name can have up to 8 characters, both letters and numbers.

    PC-File displays the Print Options dialog box. For information on printing reports, refer to the section on Printing Reports in this chapter.

Creating a Free Form Report

With the Free Form format, you can paint the report on the screen exactly the way you want the report to look on a piece of paper. PC-File lets you position titles, headings, and fields where you want them. You also can subtotal and total numeric fields, enter the data and time automatically, perform calculations, enter miscellaneous text, and draw lines. The Free Form format is more flexible than the Page, Row, and Mail Label formats.

By using the Free Form report format, you can create virtually any type of report you want. For example, you can create your own personnel forms, insurance forms, invoices, medical forms, membership reports, advertising reports, and so on. Figure 10.13 shows an accounts receivable report created by PC-File using the Free Form format.

```
                    Accounts Receivable
      Company              Account No.              Cost


      San Diego Zoo          3854893                40000

      Rover Ranch            0947596                65000

      Care Center             005627               300000

      Aram's Animals         9058457               100000

      Zorro Zoo               006983               150000

      Zorro Zoo               007893               200000


                               Total $855000.000000
```

Fig. 10.13. *An accounts receivable report created by PC-File using the Free Form format.*

PC-File displays a Free Form edit window. You draw the report on the screen, and you can see exactly what your report looks like.

The File, Data, and Help commands appear in a menu bar at the top of the edit window. The File commands are used for creating, opening, and saving reports. The Data commands are used to enter fields automatically. The

Help command provides information on creating a Free Form report. These commands are covered in detail in the section on Examining Free Form Menus in this chapter.

The fields are represented by field markers just like the field markers you use in the Paint method when you create a database. The field markers indicate the five field types: character, number, date, logical, and memo.

You can build the report in sections. The Free Form edit window has six sections: Cover, Heading, Detail, Subtotal, Total, and Footing. These sections are covered in detail in the section on Defining the Report Sections in this chapter.

PC-File enters fields automatically, just as it does when creating a database with the Paint method. The report fields can extract data from fields in one or more databases, system fields such as the computer's date and time, calculations, and field totals.

You also can use an existing report that you created with any format as a pattern for your new report. To do this, first you create a quick report using Page, Row, or Label. Then you can edit the report with the Free Form format until it suits your needs. You also can use the Free Form format to modify existing reports that you created with any of the formats. For information on modifying a report, refer to the section on Modifying a Report Using Free Form later in this chapter.

The steps for creating a Free Form report are provided in the next section.

Setting Up a Free Form Report

The following general steps show you how to set up a report by using the Free Form format. For more information on each step, refer to the appropriate sections later in this chapter.

1. Select Print from the menu bar. PC-File displays the Print menu.

2. Select Reports from the Print menu. PC-File displays the Reports Operations dialog box.

3. Select New from the Reports Operations dialog box. PC-File displays the Report Format dialog box.

4. Select Free Form from the Report Format dialog box. PC-File displays the Free Form edit window (see figure 10.14). This is where you paint the report.

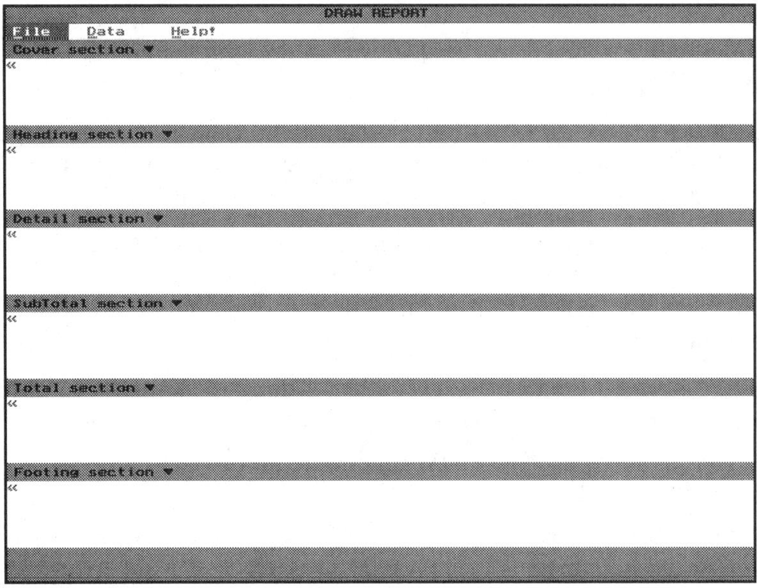

Fig. 10.14. *The Free Form edit window.*

5. Draw the report in the Free Form edit window. Press the Tab key to move down and the Shift-Tab key to move up through the sections. For example, type a title in the Cover section, enter field headings in the Heading section, enter fields in the Detail section, and draw lines and boxes in any section. Information on how to enter data in these sections is covered in detail later in this chapter.

6. When you finish drawing the report, select OK. PC-File prompts you to save the report.

7. If you want to save the report so that you can view or print it in the future, select Yes. If you want to create a quick, temporary report and not save the report, select No. If you select No, you can view or print the report only once.

   If you select Yes, PC-File prompts you to enter a description of the report. The report description is optional, but it is useful when you want to know the contents of the report at a later date. The description can have up to 50 characters.

8. If you want to enter a report description, type the description, for example, *1st quarter accts pay*. Then select OK, and PC-File prompts you to enter a report name.

If you do not want to enter a report description, leave the text box blank and select OK. PC-File prompts you to enter a report name.

If you select No in Step 7, PC-File displays the Print Options dialog box. For information on printing reports, refer to the section on Printing Reports in this chapter.

9. Type the report name and select OK. A report name can have up to eight characters, both letters and numbers. PC-File assigns the file extension REP to the report name. An example of a report name with extension is ACCTPAY.REP.

    PC-File displays the Print Options dialog box. For information on printing reports, refer to the section on Printing Reports later in this chapter.

Some rules you should know about when you create a report using the Free Form format are explained in the next section.

Examining Free Form Guidelines

Follow these guidelines when you use the edit window to create a Free Form report:

Sections: When entering data in Free Form sections, enter only the essential information. Leave blank the sections you do not want to use in the report. PC-File inserts an end marker (<<) in the first line of a section to indicate a blank line.

Formatting Commands: If you want to force a new page, remove blank lines, or enter printer codes, you can use PC-File's formatting commands. A formatting command begins with a period followed by one or more characters. For example, .=25 tabs to column 25. A list of the formatting commands is provided later in this chapter.

Blank Lines: A blank line is represented by an end marker (<<) in the first line of a section. A blank line is saved and appears in the printed report as a blank line. Be sure you enter blank lines only when you want them.

Lines and Boxes: PC-File provides three ways to draw lines and boxes in any section of a report. (1) You can use hyphens to draw lines. (2) You can use the underscore to draw lines. (3) You can use ASCII characters to draw lines and boxes, as explained in Chapter 4, "Creating a Database."

Text: The field markers and the form feed formatting commands (as explained later in this chapter) are not considered as text in the edit window. The text that prints in the report appears the way you enter it on the screen. For example, PC-File prints upper and lowercase letters just as they are entered.

For more information on the Free Form window, refer to the next section.

Exploring the Free Form Window

The Free Form edit window is the same edit window that PC-File uses in other locations. It resembles, for example, the Paint method window you use to define a database. The exception is that the Free Form edit window is divided into six sections. Each section is used to build a Free Form report.

The first step toward working in the Free Form window is learning to move around the window. In this section, you learn how to move between sections, how to expand and contract each section for easier viewing and use, and how to display the current location of the cursor.

Moving around the Window

If you want to move quickly from section to section and within a section, do one of the following:

Press the Tab key to move down and the Shift-Tab key to move up through the sections.

With the mouse, click the section in which you want to work. The active section of the window appears in a darker shade than the rest of the window.

To move the cursor within a section, use the arrow keys. With the mouse, click the location you want within the section.

Using Expanded and Contracted View

There are two ways you can view the sections in the window: contracted and expanded. When you open the Free Form edit window, the sections appear in contracted view and the menu bar displays. The contracted view only lets you enter information and view two or three lines at a time. Use the up and down arrow keys to move from one line to another within a section.

PC-File makes it easier for you to define and format a section by letting you expand each section. That way, you can easily visualize the report as you are creating it. In the expanded view, the menu bar is unavailable.

To expand a section, follow these steps:

1. Position the cursor in the section you want to expand.

2. Press Ctrl-E. PC-File expands the section to a window (see figure 10.15).

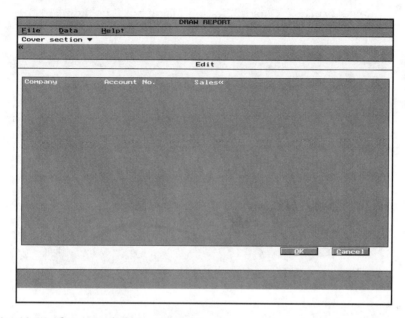

Fig. 10.15. The expanded view of a section.

3. Draw your report in the section by using the expanded view.

4. Select OK.

5. PC-File shrinks the window and returns you to the contracted size for the section.

Displaying the Cursor Location

The field headings in the Heading section and the field markers in the Detail section display in separate sections. Therefore, if you can see the current cursor location, you can easily see if the fields line up with their respective field headings.

PC-File lets you display the current cursor location in the edit window in either expanded or contacted view. Thus, you can see the current row and column location of the cursor.

To display the current cursor location, follow these steps:

1. Position the cursor where you want to see the current cursor location.

2. Press Ctrl-W.

   PC-File displays a Cursor Location dialog box (see figure 10.16). For example, it can display row 1, column 18.

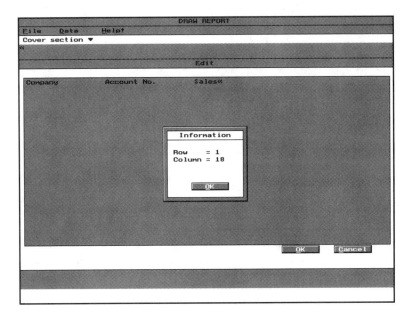

Fig. 10.16. The Cursor Location dialog box.

3. Click the OK button to return to the edit window.

Defining the Report Sections

A report that you create or modify in the Free Form window has six sections: Cover, Heading, Detail, Subtotal, Total, and Footing. Each section handles a particular part of a report. PC-File prints the report with only those sections that you define in the Free Form window.

The following section describes each section in the Free Form window.

The Cover section: Prints text only once at the beginning of a report. It defines a separate cover or title page, or prints a title at the top of the first page of the report. You must enter the Form Feed formatting command (.FF) after the title to create a separate title page, as explained in the section Using Formatting Commands later in this chapter.

The Heading section: Prints titles, page numbers, field headings, and lines at the top of each page.

The Detail section: Prints the information once for each record you select. You must define this section to print the data from the records.

The Subtotal section: Prints text, subtotals of numeric fields, and blank lines. You must specify a subtotal break at print time to print the subtotal section.

The Total section: Prints totals for numeric fields, the number of records printed, and any search criteria used for selecting records. This information prints at the end of the report.

The Footing section: Prints page numbers, blank lines, and text at the bottom of each page. This section determines the bottom margin on each page.

Now that you can define the report sections, you need to know more about the menus in the Free Form edit window, as explained in the next section.

Examining the Free Form Menus

At the top of the Free Form window is a menu bar that displays three commands: File, Data, and Help. In the sections that follow, you further examine these commands.

Using the File Menu

The commands in the File menu are used primarily to create, open, and save reports. When you select File from the menu bar, PC-File displays the Free Form File menu that contains five commands (see figure 10.17). Table 10.1 lists the Free Form File commands and briefly explains the function of each command.

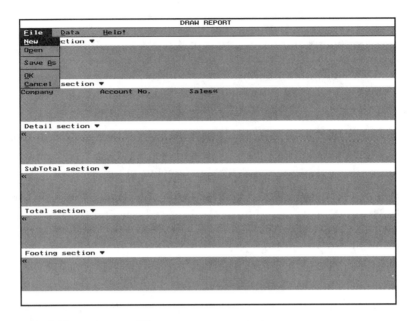

Fig. 10.17. The Free Form File menu.

Table 10.1
Free Form File Commands

Command	Function
New	Clears the existing report from the edit window
Open	Displays an existing report
Save As	Saves the current report with a new name or different directory
OK	Exits the Free Form edit window and saves the current report with the same name
Cancel	Exits the Free Form edit window

Using the Data Menu

The commands in the Data menu are used to enter fields in a Free Form report automatically. When you select Data from the menu bar, PC-File displays the Free Form Data menu, which contains four commands (see figure 10.18).

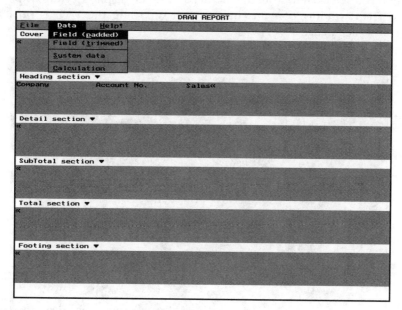

Fig. 10.18. *The Free Form Data menu.*

The Field (padded) command: Displays a Field Selection dialog box. Select a field from the dialog box, and PC-File enters the data without removing the spaces that occur in a field. If a report field is 10 characters long, PC-File prints 10 characters, even if some of them are spaces.

The Field (trimmed) command: Displays a Field Selection dialog box. Select a field from the dialog box, and PC-File enters the data and removes the trailing spaces that follow the data in a field. If a CITY report field is 25 characters long, PC-File prints only the characters in that field—for example, Boston—and ignores the spaces that follow the data.

Trimmed fields are useful for mailing labels.

The System Data command: Displays a list of system field options. PC-File automatically enters data that is generated by your computer in a Free Form report. Examples of generated data are your computer's date and time, page numbers, and a record count. For a complete list of system field options, refer to the section on Defining the Fields later in this chapter.

The Calculation command: Displays a text box for entering a calculation. PC-File generates data from the calculation.

Using Help

When you select Help from the menu bar, PC-File displays a Help window. The Help window contains information on using the Free Form edit window (see figure 10.19).

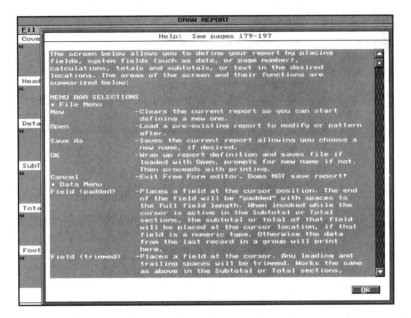

Fig. 10.19. The Free Form Help window.

To close the Help window, select OK. You are returned to the Free Form edit window.

Information on entering text in the Free Form window is explained in the next section.

Entering Text

The text you enter in the Free Form window includes titles, field headings and labels, lines and boxes, and miscellaneous descriptions or information.

To enter text in a Free Form report, first position the cursor where you want the text to appear. Then type the text. You can use upper- and lowercase letters. PC-File prints the text in the report just the way the text appears on the screen.

When you enter text in the Free Form window, make sure you type the text in the correct section. If you want the report title to print only on the cover or title page, be sure you enter the title in the Cover section. If you want the report title to print on every page, enter the title in the Heading section.

In most cases, the fields should be identified with either labels, headings, or a description. You can enter this text next to the field or above it. Some fields do not need a descriptive label, for instance, the current date or time at the top of a report.

If your report contains columns of data, enter field headings above each column in the Heading section (see figure 10.20). The headings are printed on every page of the report so that the columns of data are identified clearly. Thus, the reader does not have to go back to the first page to see the field headings.

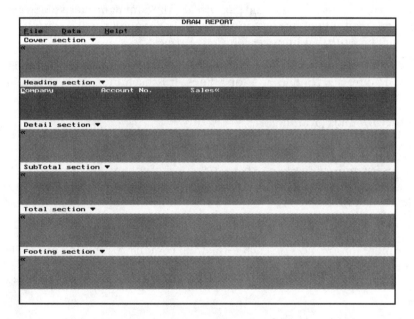

Fig. 10.20. The field headings in the Heading section.

You can enter a single or double line below the field headings to separate the headings from the data in the first row of the report. To create a single line, use the hyphen. To create a double, broken line use the equal sign. To print solid lines, use the ASCII line characters, as explained in the section on Drawing Lines and Boxes in Chapter 4, "Creating a Database."

For information on locating fields in a Free Form report, refer to the next section.

Using Formatting Commands

In PC-File, there are nine formatting commands you can use to control how your report is printed. You can enter a formatting command in any section of the report. The following section lists the formatting commands and describes each command:

=nn represents horizontal tab, such as Tab to column *nn*. For example, =15 tabs to column 15.

/n represents line feed and inserts *n* lines. For example, /2 inserts 2 lines.

.FF represents Form feed and starts a new page. For example, .FF after the title in the Cover section prints the title on the cover page only and enters a page break to start printing the first page of the report.

.CP n represents a conditional page break. The command starts a new page if fewer than *n* lines are left on the page. For example, .CP 3 starts a new page if fewer than 3 lines are left on the page.

.GROUP compresses lines within a grouping and removes the blank lines when addresses contain 3, 4, or 5 lines. It is useful for address lists and mailing labels.

.EGROUP ends grouping.

.EGROUP R ends grouping and replaces lines at end.

.X inserts printer markers where *X* is a print enhancement or style. For example, .BOLD starts bold, .ITALIC starts italic, and .NORMAL returns to the default font.

.A nn,nn inserts printer control codes.

For more information on each formatting command, refer to your PC-File documentation.

Locating Fields

The purpose of locating fields in a Free Form report is to generate data from any of four places.

- Database fields
- Calculated fields
- System fields
- A summation of other fields

PC-File lets you locate fields in any of the six sections of a report. However, in some sections of a Free Form report only certain fields that you locate are valid. Table 10.2 lists the sections and the valid fields.

Table 10.2
Valid Fields for Locating Fields in a Free Form Report

Section	Valid Field
Cover	System fields
Heading, Detail, and Footing	System fields, database fields, and calculated fields
Subtotal and Total	System fields and summations of other fields

To locate fields, you enter field markers to designate the field and the field length. These are the same field markers you use when you create a database with the Paint method. PC-File displays the markers on the Free Form report screen, but does not print the field markers in the report.

For database fields, the field marker is determined by the field type. For calculated fields, system fields, and a summation of other fields, the field marker is determined by the kind of data that you may enter in those fields. Table 10.3 lists the field markers and field types you can enter.

Table 10.3
Field Markers and Field Types

Field Marker	Field Types
At (@)	Character database fields and system fields
Pound (#)	Numeric database fields, calculations, and summations
Backslash (\)	Date database fields
Pipe (|)	Logical database fields
Tilde (~)	Memo database fields

PC-File provides two ways to enter the field markers for most fields. You can select options from the Data menu, or you can type the characters directly from the keyboard, as explained in the section on Entering Fields in a Free Form report later in this chapter.

You can follow several guidelines when locating and defining fields in a Free Form report, as explained in the next section.

Examining Guidelines for Locating Fields

The following guidelines should make it easier for you to locate and define fields in a Free Form report:

Spacing: At least one space between each report field and at least one space between a report field and any text. Numeric report fields can include commas and decimal points. For example, ###,###.## prints 350000.25 as 350,000.25, and 539 prints as 539.00

Field length: The number of field markers you enter and the number of characters that appear in a report field. For example, @@@@@@@@ prints eight characters for a character field.

Make your report fields long enough to accommodate the data that comes from a database, system, calculated, or summation field. When the field in a report is shorter than the database field, PC-File truncates the extra data in the report.

Wrapping fields: You can enter a maximum of 65 field markers in a report field. Any field marker beyond the 65th marker is ignored by PC-File. With character and memo fields longer than 65 characters, you can either print only the first 65 characters of the field, or you can wrap the data on two or more lines within a field. There are two methods for wrapping data within a field.

To wrap data, you can enter a single set of field markers in your Free Form report. Then edit the report using the Language format. To do this, use a print mask to restrict the field to a specific length, as explained later in this chapter. Change the at symbols (@) to Ws; for example, WWWWWWWWWWWWWW wraps all of the data on two or more lines within a field.

Another way to wrap data within a field is to enter as many sets of at symbols (@) as are necessary to print all of the data. Then define partial fields for each set of field markers. Suppose you have a 100-character field called Movietitle.

You could define two 50-character partial fields, for example,

[Movietitle,1,50].

[Movietitle,51,50]

The first line specifies the starting position of 1 for the first 50 characters; 51 specifies the starting position for the second 50 characters.

PC-File prints the first 50 characters of data in the first Movietitle report field and the second 50 characters of data in the second Movietitle report field. For information on partial fields, refer to the section on Choosing an Existing Field in Chapter 9, "Changing the Design of a Database."

Field markers: Use the correct field markers in a report field to indicate the field type and help you interpret the report format more clearly. For example, use the at symbol (@) for character fields and pound (#) for numeric fields. Using the wrong field markers, the pound (#) for a character field, for example, does not affect the report.

To enter fields in a Free Form report, refer to the next section.

Entering Fields

PC-File gives you two ways to enter fields in a Free Form report. You can enter fields from the Data menu or from the keyboard.

In PC-File, you can enter database, calculated, and system fields from the Free Form Data menu. However, you cannot enter summation fields from the Data menu. You must enter them from the keyboard in either the Subtotal or Total sections of the report.

To enter fields from the Data menu, follow these steps:

1. Position the cursor where you want the field to appear.

2. Select Data from the menu bar. PC-File displays the Data menu (see figure 10.21).

3. Select an option from the Data menu. If you select Field (padded) or Field (trimmed), PC-File displays a Field Selection dialog box. Select a field from the dialog box. If you select System data, PC-File lists 10 system field options in a dialog box. Select a system field option. The system field options are explained later in this chapter. If you select Calculation fields, PC-File prompts you to enter a calculation. Enter the expression in the text box.

   PC-File enters the field marks in the report.

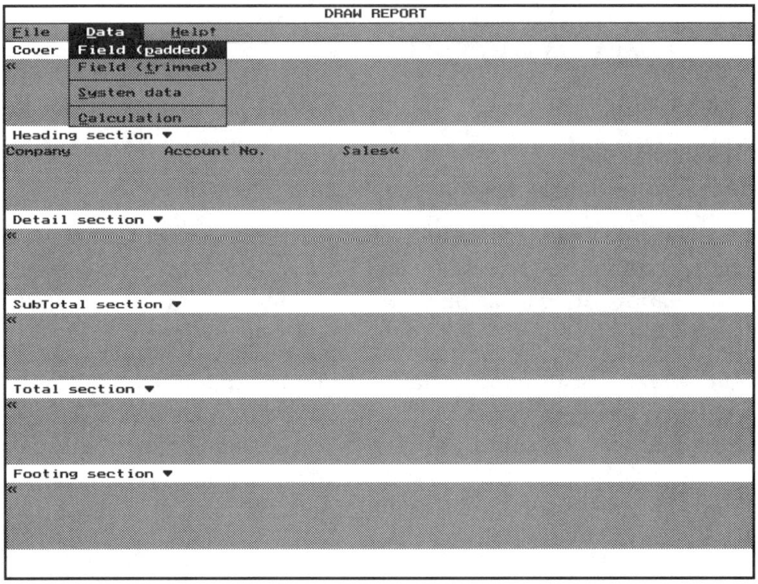

```
                         DRAW REPORT
 File   Data     Help↑
 Cover  Field (padded)
  «      Field (trimmed)
         System data
         Calculation
 Heading section ▼
 Company           Account No.        Sales«




 Detail section ▼
 «




 SubTotal section ▼
 «




 Total section ▼
 «




 Footing section ▼
 «



```

Fig. 10.21. The Data menu.

Suppose that you enter a character field from the Data menu that is too long. For example, you define a 10-character field and you know that all the data in that field consist of 8 characters or less. PC-File lets you change the length of the field in the report. To do this, move the cursor to any field marker for the field you want to shorten, and use the Backspace or Delete key to remove the extra field markers.

Instead of entering fields from the Data menu, you can enter any type of field into the appropriate section of a report in the edit window. With this method, be sure you enter the correct field marker and the correct number of characters for the field length. For example, for a date field enter eight backslashes (\). The field marker characters are listed earlier in this chapter.

To enter a field from the keyboard, follow these steps:

1. Position the cursor where you want the field to appear.

2. Type the field markers. The number of field markers you enter designates the field length. To determine which field marker you should enter, think about how you will define the data source for the field.

3. Repeat Step 2 to enter the fields for the entire report.

4. Select File from the menu. PC-File displays the File menu.

5. Select Save from the File menu. Enter a name for the report and click the OK button. PC-File prompts you to enter the data source. Figure 10.22 shows a data source prompt.

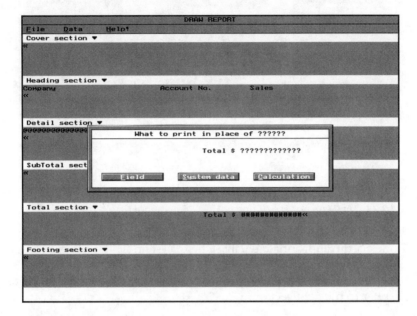

Fig. 10.22. *A data source prompt.*

If you entered any fields from the Data menu, PC-File skips over these fields because it already knows the data source.

6. Click the appropriate data source button. If you select Field (padded) to enter the data and retain the spaces that follow the data in a field—or if you select Field (trimmed) to enter the data and remove the spaces that follow the data in a field—PC-File prompts you to select a database field.

If you select System data, PC-File prompts you to select a system field option. If you select Calculation, PC-File prompts you to enter an expression.

PC-File displays a Data Source dialog box for the first field you entered from the keyboard (see figure. 10.23).

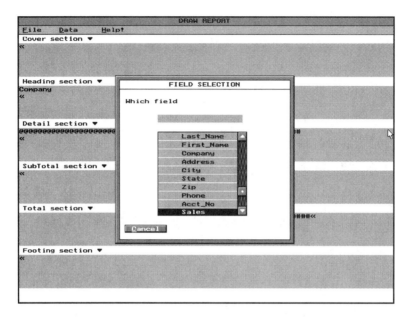

Fig. 10.23. *The Data Source dialog box.*

7. Select the appropriate database field, system field option, or enter an expression. PC-File displays a Data Source dialog box for the next field. For more information defining the data source for fields, refer to the next section.

8. Repeat Steps 6 and 7 to define the data source for the rest of the fields you entered from the keyboard.

Defining the Data Source

Depending on which method you use to enter fields, PC-File asks you to define the data source in different ways. If you use the Data menu method for entering fields, you define the data source as you enter the fields. If you enter fields directly from the keyboard, you define the data source for the fields after you finish drawing the entire report.

There are four data sources: data fields, system fields, summations, and calculations. These data sources are covered in detail in the next few sections.

Using Data Fields

There are two types of data fields: padded and trimmed. In a padded field, PC-File enters the data without removing the spaces that occur in a field. For example, if a report field is 10 characters long, PC-File prints 10 characters, even if some of them are spaces.

In a trimmed field, PC-File enters the data and removes the trailing spaces that follow the data in a field. If a CITY report field is 25 characters long, PC-File prints only the characters in that field—for example, Boston—and ignores the spaces that follow the data.

Trimmed fields are useful for mailing labels. For example, @@@@@@@@@@@@@@@, @@ @@@@@ designates a 15-character CITY field, a 2-character STATE field, and a 5-character ZIP_CODE field. If you define these fields as trimmed fields on a mailing label, PC-File removes the trailing spaces from the CITY field when a city name is less than 15 characters long. PC-File adjusts the data in the STATE and ZIP_CODE fields according to the length of the data in the CITY field as the city names change in each record. As a result, PC-File would print an address as follows:

Boston, MA 02110

If you use the first method for entering fields in a report, that is, from the Data menu, you can define either padded or trimmed fields. If you use the second method, entering fields from the keyboard, PC-File assumes the fields are padded.

Using System Fields

You can use system fields in any section of the report. A system field automatically enters in a report data that is generated by your computer, the program, the database, or the operator. For example, you can have PC-File automatically enter the date and time in a report.

You select a system field when you select System data from the Data menu or when PC-File prompts you to define the data source after you enter fields directly from the keyboard. PC-File displays 10 system fields in a dialog box. The following section describes each system field:

Date now: Enters the computer's current date.

Time now: Enters the computer's current time.

Page number: Enters the current page number and considers the first page in the report as page 1.

Records in database: Enters the current number of records in the database.

Selection criteria: Enters any search criteria you specify to select records you want to print in the report. For instance, ST = IN prints reports with Indiana addresses only.

Index field: Invokes the current index to sort the records when you print the report.

Qty in Subtotal group: Enters the number of records in the current subtotal.

Field name of Subtotal group: Enters the name of the field you selected to subtotal.

Count of records printed: Enters the total number of records printed.

Operator input: Prompts you for input.

Using Summations

If you want to specify a summation in your report, you must enter it from the keyboard. You cannot enter a summation using the Data menu. PC-File enters subtotals in the Subtotal section and enters totals in the Total section in the report.

Defining a subtotal involves two steps:

1. Define the field you want to sum into subtotals.

2. Define the subtotal break field. A subtotal break lets you group together records that you want to subtotal.

What if you want to subtotal sales volume by month or by region? The SALES field would be the field you sum and MONTH or REGION would be the subtotal break field.

To define the field you want to sum into subtotals, you enter the appropriate field markers in the Subtotal section of your report (see figure 10.24).

You define the subtotal break field when you print the report, as explained later in this chapter.

To define the field you want to sum into totals, you enter the appropriate field markers in the Total section of your report (see figure 10.25). PC-File prints totals only at the end of a report.

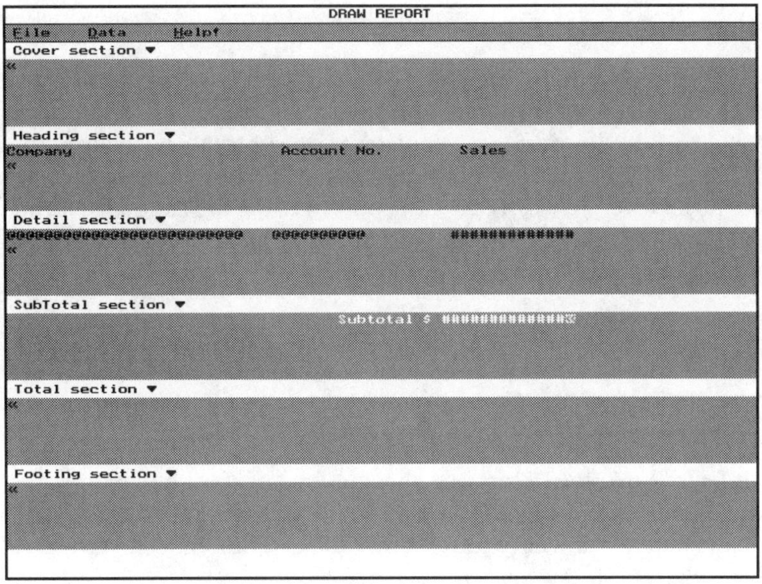

Fig. 10.24. *A subtotal field.*

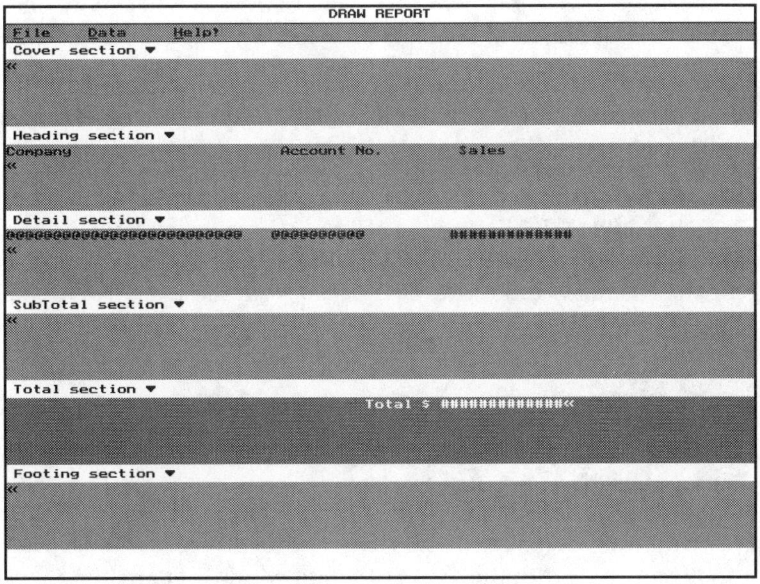

Fig. 10.25. *A total field.*

Using Calculations

PC-File lets you enter calculations in the Detail, Heading, and Footing sections of a report. You can use any of the calculations supported by PC-File. You cannot perform calculations on subtotals or totals in the Free Form format. For instance, you cannot calculate a bonus based on a subtotal of sales. However, you can edit the report by using the Language format and adding the bonus calculation to the Subtotal section. For information on using the Language format, refer to your PC-File documentation.

There are five types of calculation you can enter in a report. The following section describes each of the types of calculations PC-File can perform:

Mathematical calculations: Add, subtract, multiply, divide, exponentiate, and find the modulo. For example, (SALES-EXPENSES).

Date calculations: Determine the number of days between dates or a future date. For example, ((@TODAY#) - (EXP-date (@DAY#,mdy))) determines how many days have passed since the expiration date. MDY stands for the month, day, and year format.

Conditional calculations: Make decisions based on the contents of a field. For example, (((CheckFee = "y") + ((CheckFee = "N")*qty)) calculates a check fee of 10 cents per check if the CHECKFEE field contains Y for Yes. If the CHECKFEE field contains an N for No, there is no check fee.

Random number calculations: Create random numbers and use them in subsequent calculations. For example, (@RANDOM#) calculates a random number between 0 and 1.

Relational lookups: Retrieve data from other databases. For example, (@EMP_NO,EMPLOYEE,EMP_NO,LAST_NAME) uses the EMP_NO field in the current database to go to the EMPLOYEE database, finds the same data in the EMP_NO field, and retrieves the data from the LAST_NAME field.

Modifying a Report by Using Free Form

Suppose you want to make changes to a report you created in PC-File. You can modify any report in the Free Form edit window at any time.

An easy way to modify a report is to first create a quick report with the Page, Row, or Mail Label format, and then edit the report in the Free Form edit window.

You also can use the Free Form edit feature to use an existing report that you created with any format as a pattern for your new report. To do this, first you create a quick report using Page, Row, or Mail Label. Then you can edit the report in the Free Form edit window until it suits your needs. When you save the report, you give it a new name.

To modify a report in the Free Form edit window, follow these steps:

1. Select Print from the menu bar. PC-File displays the Print menu.

2. Select Reports from the Print menu. PC-File displays the Reports Operations dialog box.

3. Select Modify from the Reports Operations dialog box. PC-File displays the Report Format dialog box.

4. Select Free Form Paint from the Report Format dialog box. PC-File displays the Free Form edit window. This is where you modify the report.

5. Select File from the menu bar. PC-File displays the File menu.

6. Select Open from the File menu. PC-File displays the File Selection dialog box.

7. Select the report you want to modify. Use the arrow keys and press Enter, or use the mouse to click on the file you want. You are presented with the report in the Free Form edit window (see fig-ure 10.26).

   PC-File displays the report in the appropriate sections in the Free Form edit window.

8. Make the modifications to the report. Press the Tab key to move down and the Shift-Tab key to move up through the sections. To add information, press Insert; the cursor changes from an under-score to a block. Type the characters; PC-File adjusts the existing data. Press the Insert key again to exit Insert mode. To delete infor-mation, use the Backspace or Delete key. Highlight the text with the mouse by clicking and dragging through the data you want to delete, then press the Delete key.

   To type over information, just type the new information. To select fields automatically, use commands in the Data menu, as explained earlier in this chapter.

9. When you finish modifying the report, select File from the menu bar. Then select OK from the File menu. PC-File prompts you to save the report. Click the OK button to update the report with the

changes. PC-File saves the report with the same name and exits the Free Form edit window.

If you want to save the report with a different name, select the File Save As command. Type a new name for the report and click the OK button. The original report remains intact.

When you finish naming the report, PC-File prompts you to enter a description of the report.

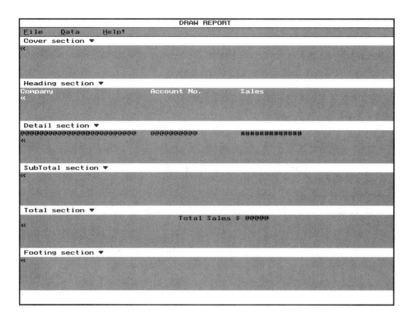

Fig. 10.26. The report in the Free Form edit window.

10. Enter a new description or leave the current description. Then click the OK button. PC-File displays the Print Options dialog box. For information on printing reports, refer to the next section.

Printing Reports

Printing your report is probably one of the most rewarding tasks in PC-File. After creating, editing, and formatting reports, you feel a special sense of achievement when you finally print your reports on paper. This section shows you how to print any report in PC-File.

When working with any computer and a printer, you must become familiar with the type of printer you are using. PC-File is set up to use all the features of your printer; however, you must know your printer's limitations. Refer to your printer manual and determine what the printer can do.

Before you print a report, you can change several print options to customize your printout. You discover how easily you can specify such print options as printing all or some records, subtotals, continuously, one page at a time, specific pages, multiple copies, flip data, condensed type, line spacing, margins, and page length.

When you have tailored the print options, you are ready to print your report. You can send the report directly to the printer, to the screen, or to a file. If you select the printer file, your report can be printed any time.

If you change your mind about printing the report, PC-File also lets you cancel the print request.

After you create your report, you can choose from various print options to change the way your report prints out. PC-File displays a Print Options dialog box just before you print your report (see figure 10.27).

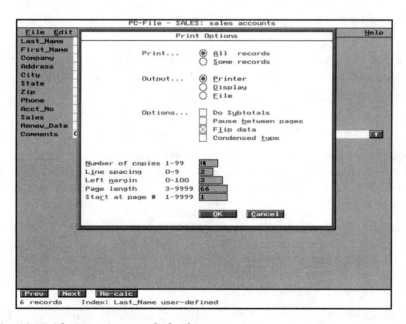

Fig. 10.27. The Print Options dialog box.

The Print Options dialog box gives you fourteen print options from which to choose. In the top half of the dialog box are nine print options that contain option buttons and check-off boxes. PC-File gives you three ways to select these print options. You can press the underlined letter of the printing option or press the Tab key to highlight the option. For example, press S to select Some records. Or you can use the mouse to click the print option button or check-off box you want.

The bottom half of the dialog box has five print options. To select a print option, use the Tab key. Then type a number in the text box.

The following section describes PC-File's print options:

Print All records: Prints all of the records in your database. This is the default for printing records.

Print Some records: Prints some of the records in your database by searching for the specified records you want to print, as explained in Chapter 6, "Searching for Records."

Output Printer: Prints the report directly to the printer set up for PC-File. This is the default for the output device.

Output Display: Prints the report directly to the screen so that you can preview your report before printing it.

Output File: Prints the report directly to a printer file on disk as an ASCII file. Enter the drive, path, and file name; for example, type *c:\pcfile\print\sales.txt*.

Options Do Subtotals: Prints the subtotals in a report. The default is off, and a check mark does not display in the check-off box.

Options Pause: Prints one page at a time. If you do not select Pause between pages, PC-File prints the entire report automatically on continuous-form paper. The default is off, and a check mark does not display in the check-off box.

Options Flip data: Flips the data in a field that contains the flip character, the tilde (~), as explained in Chapter 5, "Adding Records." For example, LAST_NAME~FIRST_NAME prints the first name first and the last name second when the Flip data option is turned on. The default is on, and a check mark displays in the check-off box.

Options Condensed type: Prints smaller characters so that you can print more characters on each line of your report. If your report is more than 80 characters wide, select the Condensed type option. The default is off, and a check mark does not display in the check-off box.

Number of copies: Prints multiple copies. Enter a number between 1 and 99. The default is 1.

Line spacing: Prints a single-space or double-space report. Enter 1 for single space and 2 for double space. The default is 1. When you want to print only the subtotal or total information, you can prevent the Detail section from printing in a report by entering 0 for the Line spacing option.

Left margin: Adds extra spaces to the left side of your report, beyond the normal left margin. The default is 0. This is useful for narrow reports that you want to center on the page horizontally. For example, if you want to print a contact list that contains only names and phone numbers, you can increase the left margin to center the two columns of information.

Page length: Adjusts the length of your report to conform to the size of the paper and the type of printer you are printing on. The default is 66 lines. For dot-matrix and daisywheel printers, enter 66 lines for 8 1/2 X 11 standard-size paper. With laser printers, the page length is usually 60 lines in portrait mode and 45 lines in landscape mode. For legal-size paper, enter 78 lines for laser printers and 84 lines for other printers.

To determine the number of lines per page for your report, multiply the page length in inches times the number of lines per inch. For example, if you want to print on paper that measures 7 (times) 9, multiply a page length of 9 inches times 6 lines per inch. The resulting page length is 54 lines. Also, if a page in your report prints higher on the page than did the previous page, increase the page length. If it prints lower, decrease the page length.

Start at page #: Restarts printing your report on a specific page. The default is page 1. If, for example, you already have printed 5 pages out of your 10-page report and the paper jams in the printer, you can specify starting at page number 6.

When you print a report the print options are stored in a file. The file name consists of the name of the report, to which PC-File assigns the file extension ANS. For example, a typical file with extension is SALES.ANS. Each time you print the report, PC-File uses the print parameters in the ANS file to print the report.

The stored print settings are now the default print options. However, you can change the parameters at any time by selecting different print options the next time you print the report. Once you print the report again, PC-File uses the new settings as the default print options.

Follow these steps to print a report in PC-File:

1. Select Print from the menu bar. PC-File displays the Print menu.

2. Select Report from the Print menu. PC-File displays the Print Report dialog box.

3. Select Run to print the report.

4. Select the report you want to print. PC-File displays the Print Options dialog box you saw in figure 10.27.

5. Select the options you want. Refer to the section earlier in this chapter for an explanation of the print options.

   If you select print Some records, PC-File prompts you to perform a search to retrieve the records you want to print in the report, as explained in Chapter 6, "Searching for Records."

   If you select Output Display, you can view your report on the screen before you print it. PC-File prompts you to view the final totals. Click the OK button. PC-File displays the totals (see figure 10.28).

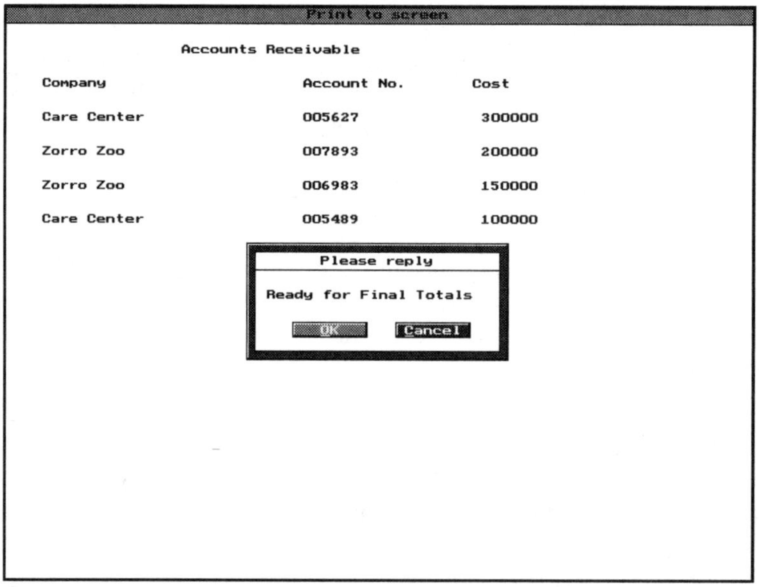

Fig. 10.28. The Output Display screen.

When you finish looking at your report, click the OK button to exit the Output Display screen. You are returned to the main PC-File screen.

If you select Output File to print the report to a file on disk, PC-File prompts you to enter a path and file name; for example, type *c:\pcfile\print\sales.txt*.

If you select Do Subtotals, PC-File prompts you to enter a field or calculation that generates the subtotal.

If you select printing to a printer or to a file, PC-File displays the first record on the screen. You are prompted to make a choice about printing the current record (see figure 10.29).

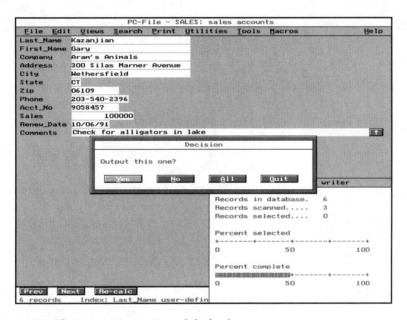

Fig. 10.29. *The Print Current Record dialog box.*

If you want to print the current record and display the next record, select Yes. If you do not want to print the current record and you want to display the next record, select No. If you want to print the current record and all the rest of the records that meet the search criteria without being prompted again, select All. If you want to stop printing the report, select Quit.

Summary

In this chapter you learned how to create professional-quality reports in formats ranging from simple to complex. You were given several guidelines for planning and designing a professional and effective report. You learned how to select report formats.

You also learned how to create a Page report, a Row report, a Mail Label report, and a Free Form report from start to finish. You explored how to modify a report and to create new, customized reports using PC-File's Free Form format.

The next chapter shows you how to create form letters using the Mail Merge feature as well as produce labels using PC-File's PC-Label program.

11

Producing Form Letters and Mailing Labels

In an instant, you can produce form letters and mailing labels from a PC-File database. This chapter shows you how to produce form letters using PC-File's letter-writing feature and print mailing labels quickly by using PC-File's snapshot label feature.

You find out how to use mail merge commands to automate creating form letters. And you learn how to modify an existing PC-File letter and how to use the PC-Label program to print labels on label stock.

The letter-writing feature is used to create personalized form letters for mass mailings, product announcements, reports, invitations, and contribution solicitations. You also can merge a list of names and addresses to generate invoices and mailing labels and to fill in standard forms.

The advanced mail merge commands give you ultimate control over the merging process and the output. PC-File lets you choose from a wide variety of mailing labels and then lets you print the labels on gummed label sheets or continuous forms.

Figure 11.1 shows a form letter created by PC-File.

```
PCF:dB;70,                    .<DATE*>


.GROUP
.<First_Name>.<Last_Name>
.<Company>
.<Address>
.<City>,.<State> .<Zip>
.EGROUP

Dear .<First_Name>,

Many local supermarkets are now recycling plastic bags.
The major issue with this is that many people are bringing
perfectly reusable plastic bags to be recycled instead of
using them again.

This is not in line with ecological preservation and is
contradictory to the goals of a healthy recycling program.

.FORMFEED
```

Fig. 11.1. *A form letter created by PC-File.*

Creating Form Letters

Generating form letters involves three major steps:

1. Create the letter.

2. Enter mail merge commands.

3. Print the form letters.

To generate a form letter, PC-File combines or merges a letter that contains the mail merge commands with information in the database. Completed letters are stored in a separate file that you can print.

Creating a New Letter

This section steps you through creating a new letter using PC-File's letter-writing feature. Entering mail merge commands and printing form letters are covered later in this chapter.

Keep the following guidelines in mind as you type a letter using the letter-writing feature.

Top Margin

To insert blank lines at the top of your letter, enter the appropriate number of Returns. With dot-matrix and daisywheel printers, allow six Returns for each inch at the top of the letter to provide a typical top margin. With laser printers, PC-File inserts three Returns automatically. You can insert additional returns if you want a top margin larger than three lines.

Side Margin

To adjust the left and right margins, increase or decrease the column width. The left margin always should start in column 1; the column width of the letter can be from 10 to 78 characters wide.

If your letter prints too far to the left or right on the paper, first try shifting the paper in the printer. If your letter still prints too far to the left, you can increase the number in the Left margin parameter in the Print Options dialog box, shifting the letter on the paper to the right.

Bottom Margin

To determine whether you have enough space for a bottom margin or you need to extend a long letter to two pages, count the number of lines in the letter, including the top margin. Then subtract the result from the total page length. For example, if you add six lines in the top margin to 40 lines in the letter, the total is 46 lines. An 8 1/2-by-11-inch sheet of paper has 66 lines. Subtract 46 from the total page length of 66 lines. This gives you 20 blank lines at the bottom of the letter. Therefore, you can enter a Form Feed (.FF) command on line 60 to specify a 1-inch bottom margin, or 6 lines from the bottom of the letter.

To eject the letter from the printer, enter a Form Feed (.FF) command at the top of the letter on a line by itself. The Form Feed command also starts each letter on a new page.

If you need to extend a letter to more than one page, enter a Form Feed (.FF) formatting command at the bottom of each page, including the last page. Then PC-File starts each following page one line below the Form Feed command on the previous page. You can have up to five pages in a letter.

Cursor Location

To line up fields and see how many lines you have used in the letter, you can display the cursor location in the letter writing window. To do this, press Ctrl-W. PC-File displays an Information box (see figure 11.2). The current row and column cursor location appears in the Cursor Location Information box. Click the OK button to return to the letter writing window.

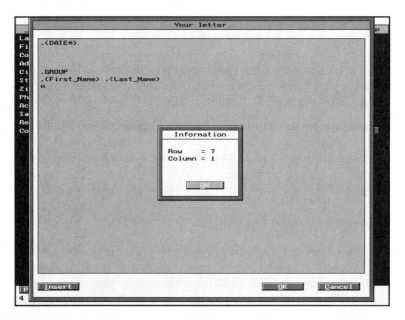

Fig. 11.2. *The current Cursor Location Information box.*

Letter Contents

To determine which information you want to extract from the database and where you want the information to appear in the letter, first plan the contents of the letter on paper.

If you want to extract data from more than one database, determine which is your primary database. (The primary database contains most of the data you want to include in the letter.) Open the primary database and create the letter. PC-File lets you use relational lookup to extract data from the secondary databases, as explained later in this chapter.

PC-File uses files from two programs to perform a merge: the letter file and the database file. The letter-writing feature lets you create a letter file that contains the basic letter, form, or invitation. Any information that remains constant is included in the letter, such as the salutation "Dear" and the letter closing, "Sincerely."

Any information that changes is specified in the letter with a mail merge command. The mail merge command indicates where information from the database file—such as the inside address, data, time, or place—is to be inserted. Figure 11.3 shows the PC-File form letter format.

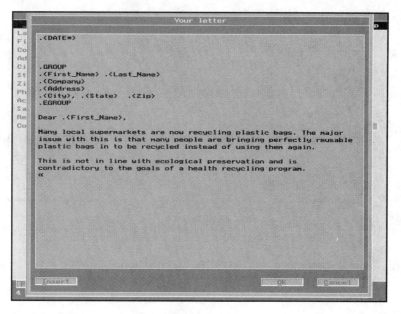

Fig. 11.3. *The PC-File form letter format.*

Typing a letter in PC-File is just like typing a letter with any word processor. PC-File displays a letter-writing window, and you type the letter in that window. The text wraps automatically as you type.

To create a new letter, follow these general steps:

1. Use the File Open command to open the database for which you want to create a form letter. PC-File displays the first record of the database in the window.

   If want to extract data from more than one database, open the primary database, the database that contains most of the data you want to include in the letter.

2. Select Print from the menu bar. PC-File displays the Print menu (see figure 11.4).

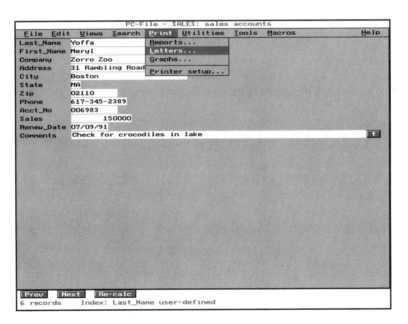

Fig. 11.4. The Print menu.

3. Select Letters from the Print menu. PC-File displays the Letter Operations dialog box (see figure 11.5).

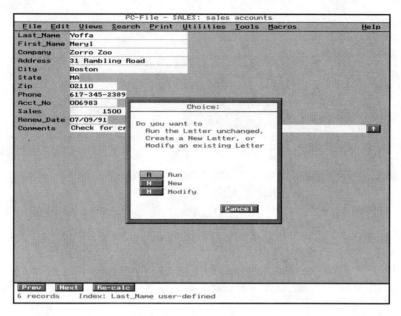

Fig. 11.5. The Letter Operations dialog box.

4. Select New from the Letter Operations dialog box. PC-File displays the default column width of 70 characters for the letter (see figure 11.6).

   PC-File assumes you are using 8 1/2-by-11-inch paper and normal type. The left and right margins are each set at 3/4 inch. You can increase these margins by decreasing the number of characters for the column width. The minimum column width is 10, and the maximum column width is 78. If you want 1-inch margins, for example, change the column width to 60 by typing *60* and pressing Enter.

5. Type the letter and enter the merge commands that specify the data you want and where you want to include that data from the database. You can enter the merge commands in two ways:

   Type the appropriate merge commands or click the Insert button to tell PC-File to enter the merge command. For information on this step, refer to the section on Using Mail Merge commands in the next section.

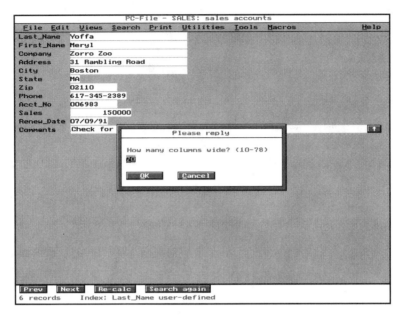

Fig. 11.6. *The default column width.*

6. When you finish typing the letter and entering the merge commands, click the OK button. PC-File prompts you to save the letter.

7. If you want to use the letter again, save the letter by selecting Yes. If you want to use the letter only once and not save it, select No.

   If you select Yes in Step 7, PC-File prompts you to enter a name for the letter.

8. Type a file name for the letter. You can use letters, numbers, or both up to 8 characters. PC-File automatically assigns the file extension LTR to a letter file, for example, ANNOUNCE.LTR. Then click the OK button.

   PC-File prompts you to enter an optional description for the letter.

9. Enter a description or leave it blank. Then click the OK button. PC-File displays the Print Options dialog box. Printing form letters is explained in the appropriate section later in this chapter.

Using Mail Merge Commands

PC-File gives you two methods for entering mail merge commands. You can type the commands, or you can click the Insert button and select the commands from a dialog box. Several types of commands are available.

If you want to type the mail merge commands, you need to follow the rules for entering the commands and formatting the letter, as explained in the next section.

Examining Merge Commands

PC-File provides five major types of mail merge commands. Table 11.1 lists the types of mail merge commands and describes each type.

Table 11.1
Mail Merge Command Types

Command Type	Description
Data field	Inserts data from database fields.
System field	Prompts you to enter data and inserts current date.
Formatting	Specifies the format and layout of the letter.
Calculation	Inserts the results of a calculation.
IF	Includes or excludes text based on a comparison.

You can type the command or use the Insert Button. When you select the Insert button to have PC-File enter the merge commands, those commands appear in the Insert dialog box (see figure 11.7). The Insert dialog box contains six merge commands: Data, Current Date, Keyed data, Group..Egroup, If..Else..Endif, and Form Feed.

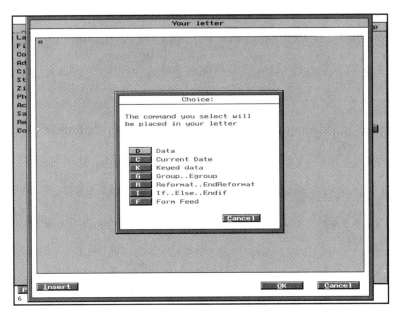

Fig. 11.7. The merge commands in the Insert dialog box.

Typing Merge Commands

Before you type mail merge commands in your letter, you need to be familiar with three guidelines.

- All mail merge commands must start with a period (.). For example, .FF represents the Form Feed command.

- All command words must be entered in uppercase letters. The only exceptions to this are database field names, calculations, and any messages you want to include with a KEYIN command, as explained later in this chapter.

- All formatting and IF commands must be on a line by themselves. Always start these commands in column 1 in the letter. You do not count the lines that contain the commands as part of the line count for the letter. PC-File interprets the commands but ignores the lines that contain the commands.

To type a mail merge command, first move the cursor to where you want to enter the command. Then type the command by using the appropriate format. Most users find it much easier to use the Insert button and have PC-File enter most of the mail merge commands, as explained in the next section.

Using the Insert Button

The following steps demonstrate how you can use the Insert button to enter mail merge commands quickly and easily.

1. Position the cursor where you want to insert a merge command.

2. To select the Insert button, either click it or press Alt-I. PC-File memorizes the cursor's previous location in the edit window when you move the cursor to select the Insert button. The Insert dialog box appears (see figure 11.8).

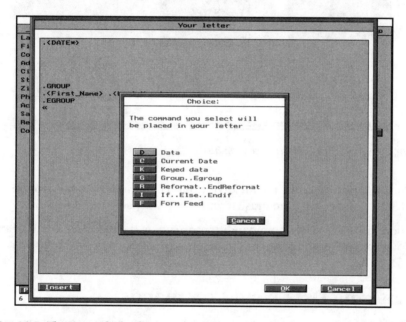

***Fig. 11.8.** The Insert dialog box.*

3. Select the option you want such as Data, for example. PC-File displays the Field Selection dialog box (see figure 11.9). Select a field from the dialog box. You are returned to the edit window, and PC-File displays the field name at the cursor location in the letter. The format of the field name is a trimmed field.

If you select Keyed data, PC-File prompts you for additional information before it displays the merge command on the screen. With the Keyed data option, you must enter a prompt for the operator in the text box.

The rest of the Insert data options enter merge commands directly to the screen, as explained earlier in this chapter. If you select If..Else..Endif, be sure to enclose the IF expression in parentheses.

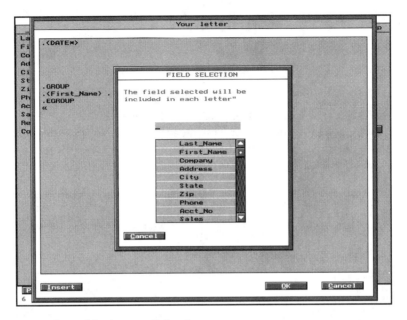

Fig. 11.9. The Field Selection dialog box.

The ELSE portion of the command is optional. If you do not want to use the ELSE command, you can erase it with the Backspace or Delete key.

There are other merge commands that are not in the Insert data dialog box. You can type these commands yourself, as explained in the next section.

Entering Data Field Commands

The data field commands are the most commonly used merge commands in PC-File. These commands insert data directly into your letter from the fields in your database. For example, contact, company, address, city, state, and zip code are data commands that come from the respective fields in the database.

You can enter data field commands in upper- or lowercase letters. PC-File recognizes these commands in two formats: trimmed and padded (as explained in Chapter 10, "Generating Reports").

Trimmed Fields

Trimmed fields are most commonly used for addresses in letters. When you select Data from the Insert dialog box to enter a field, the field is formatted as a trimmed field.

In a trimmed field, PC-File enters the specified data in the field and removes the trailing spaces that follow. From a 25-character CITY field, for example, PC-File prints only Boston and ignores the spaces that follow that data.

To enter a trimmed field, you must enclose the field name in angle brackets: .<*ADDRESS*>. An example of trimmed fields for an inside address in a letter follows:

    .<FIRST_NAME> .<LAST_NAME>

    .<COMPANY>

    .<ADDRESS>

    .<CITY>, .<ST> .<ZIP>

The example shows the spaces and punctuation you must enter when using trimmed fields. You enter one space between the first and last name, a comma and a space between the city and state fields, and two spaces between the state and zip code. PC-File does not consider the brackets and periods as spaces.

The address in the example prints as follows:

    Samantha Simmons

    The Designer's Forum

    1500 Thames Avenue

    Newport, MA 02110

> **NOTE**
> You can enter an abbreviation for a field name when using the trimmed format. Use enough characters in the field name so that it is unique in the database. For example, you can use FNAME for FIRST_NAME and LNAME for LAST_NAME.

Padded Fields

In a padded field, PC-File enters the data without removing the spaces that occur in a field. For example, if a field is 10 characters long, PC-File prints 10 characters, even if some of them are spaces. This is useful for setting up columns of data in a letter.

The field length you define in the letter does not have to be the same length as the data field from the database. However, if you define a shorter field length in the letter, PC-File truncates the extra characters from the database data inserted in the letter.

To enter a padded field, you enclose the field name in square brackets: *.[Minerals]*. Here is an example of padded fields for columns of data in a letter:

.[Vitamins   ]   .[Minerals   ]

The example shows the spaces and punctuation you must enter when using padded fields. You enter spaces after the field name to pad the field command. For example, if the field name in the letter is 8 characters long and the field in the database is 15 characters long, you must enter 7 spaces after the field name to specify the correct spacing for the data.

You must also enter spaces between the right bracket of the first padded field and the period (.) that specifies the beginning of the next padded field. These spaces represent the amount of space between the brackets.

If you select Data from the Insert dialog box to enter a field, the field is formatted as a trimmed field. To change a trimmed field to a padded field, use the Backspace or Delete key to delete the angle brackets and enter square brackets.

NOTE

You can enter an abbreviation for a field name when using the padded format. Use enough characters in the field name so that it is unique in the database. For example, you can use Vitam for Vitamins and Miner for Minerals.

Using System Field Commands

The system field commands automatically enter data in a letter. PC-File provides two types of system field commands: Current Date and Keyed data. The Current Date is generated by the computer, and the Keyed Data is generated by the person using PC-File.

The Current Date command automatically enters the date and time in each letter. The date comes from your computer or network. This feature is especially useful when you want to use the letter again but do not want to update the current data each time you print it.

To use the Current date command, you can either type *.<DATE*>* or select Current date from the Insert dialog box. If you type the Current date command, make sure you enter the asterisk (*) after the word DATE. If you do not enter the asterisk, PC-File translates the command as a data field command and looks for a field called DATE in your database.

The Keyed data command lets you define a field that prompts a user to enter information for each record. As the printer is printing your letters, PC-File pauses the printer and displays the prompt message you entered as part of the command. When you finish entering the information, press Enter to continue printing the rest of the letter.

To use the Keyed data command, you can type both the command and the message. For example, the following command displays "Enter the policy number here" in the letter:

.<KEYIN*Enter the policy number here>

Be sure to enter the asterisk (*) following the KEYIN command. You can enter a maximum of 40 characters for each message. With angle brackets, you do not have to specify the field length of the information the user enters. You can enter a maximum of 65 characters in response to a prompt. If you want to indicate a specific length for the possible input, you can type a print mark following the KEYIN command. If you wanted the user to enter only two characters in response to a prompt, the KEYIN command would look like this:

[KEYIN*Enter state]:@@

This command prompts the user to enter only two letters for the state. Each @ (at) symbol represents the character that you allow to be entered in response to the prompt. For instance, if you want to allow 5 characters, you would type :@@@@@: following the KEYIN command. The square brackets are used to indicate a specific length for possible input.

Using Formatting Commands

PC-File's formatting commands specify the format and layout of a letter. You can use the formatting commands to do the following:

- Skip to a new page with the Form Feed command.

- Force a new page with the Conditional Page command.

- Remove blank lines with the Line Compression command.

- Prevent an extremely uneven right margin with the Reformat command.

- Print bold and italic characters by entering printer codes.

To enter the Form Feed and Conditional Page commands, you either type them where you want them to appear in the letter, or you select them from the Insert dialog box, as explained earlier in this chapter. You must type the printer codes in the letter. They are not included in the Insert dialog box.

A formatting command begins with a period (.) and contains uppercase letters only.

Using the Form Feed Command

The Form Feed command (.FF) starts a new page. The .FF tells PC-File to enter a page break and start printing the next page of the letter. You must enter the .FF command at the bottom of a one-page letter; otherwise, PC-File does not eject the page from the printer unless it is printing on the last line of the paper. For multiple page letters, you enter the .FF at the bottom of each page.

Enter the Form Feed command on a line by itself and start it in the left margin.

Using the Conditional Page Command

The Conditional Page command (.CP) starts a new page if fewer than a specified number of lines are left on the current page. For example, .CP 3 starts a new page when there are fewer than 3 lines left on the current page. The .CP command is handy when you want to prevent a section of a letter from being split on two pages.

Enter the Conditional Page command on a line by itself and start it in the left margin.

Using the Line Compression Command

Suppose that you have 3- and 4-line addresses that contain blank lines as a result of empty fields. You can remove the unwanted blank lines with the Line Compression commands .GROUP, .EGROUP, and .EGROUP R.

Enter the .GROUP command *before* the group of text that contains the unwanted blank lines you want to remove. Enter the .EGROUP command *after* the group of text that contains the blank lines. The following example compresses lines in a five-line address:

```
.GROUP

.<CONTACT>

.<COMPANY>

.<ADDRESS1>

.<ADDRESS2>

.<CITY>, .<ST>  .<ZIP>

.EGROUP
```

If the ADDRESS2 field is empty and displays as a blank line, PC-File removes the unwanted blank line in the address.

To enter the Line Compression commands, you can either type them where you want the address in the letter or select the commands from the Insert dialog box, as explained earlier in this chapter.

If you want to maintain the line spacing in the letter, you can move the blank lines to the end of the group of text with the .EGROUP R relocate command. That way, the blank lines are not removed from the letter. The lines are moved to the end of the letter where they are kept in the letter. Instead of entering the .EGROUP command after the group text, enter the .EGROUP R command. To enter .EGROUP R from the Insert dialog box, select the .EGROUP command, press the Spacebar to insert a space, and type *R*.

Enter the Line Compression commands on lines by themselves and start them in the left margin.

Using the Reformat Command

If you enter a merge field command in the middle of a line of text within a merge letter, the information that PC-File inserts for that field may differ in length. As a result, the line of text may spill over and beyond the right margin or contain a large gap. To prevent this, you can use the .REFORMAT and .ENDREFORMAT commands.

Enter the .REFORMAT command before the paragraph you want to reformat automatically. Enter the .ENDREFORMAT command after the paragraph you want to reformat. The following example reformats a paragraph that contains a merge field command in the middle of a line of text.

```
.REFORMAT

The trustee meeting will be held at <hotel> on <date> at 7:00 p.m.

.ENDREFORMAT
```

If the hotel field contains a hotel name that is very long, for example, The Norwich Spa and Conference Center, PC-File would insert the entire name at the end of the first line of text, even if the name extends beyond the right margin. With the .REFORMAT command, part of the long name will wrap automatically to the next line.

Using Printer Codes

You can enhance your letter with bold, italics, or underline fonts by using the PC-File printer codes called printer markers. These codes are not available in the Insert dialog box; you must type the printer codes where you want to change a font or type style in your letter. To stop the special font, type the printer marker again where you want to change back to the original font.

For example, you might want to use bold for important words in your letter to emphasize a concept. For bold text, you type

.BOLDThe Wizard of Id.NORMAL is playing at the Schubert Theater this month.

There are no spaces between the marker and the text. In the same way, you can underline words or sentences to draw attention to them. You also can use condensed type to fit a letter on one page.

Before you use printer codes in your letter, you must know your printer's capabilities. Refer to your printer manual and determine what the printer can do. Table 11.2 lists the printer markers and describes each marker.

Table 11.2
Printer Markers

Printer Marker	Description
.NORMAL	Normal text; default type style
.CONDENSED	Small text
.BOLD	Darker text
.ITALIC	Italics
.UNDERLINE	Underline text

.PORTRAIT	Upright vertical printout
.LANDSCAPE	Horizontal printout
.PROPORTIONAL	Proportional space type style
.DOUBLEWIDE	Double wide text
.USERn	User defined; set up in PC-File

The .PORTRAIT and LANDSCAPE printer markers specify the print orientation for a letter. For example, if you want to print a letter upright on standard 8 1/2-by-11-inch paper, enter the .PORTRAIT marker at the top of the letter. If you want to print a form to be filled in horizontally on 11-by-8 1/2-inch paper, enter the .LANDSCAPE marker at the top of the letter.

The proportional and doublewide printer markers specify a particular typestyle. The .PROPORTIONAL marker prints proportionally spaced characters. The .DOUBLEWIDE marker prints very wide characters.

The .USERn marker is a printer marker that you can define and specify in the Configuration profile, as explained in Appendix A. Use this for setting up a print enhancement you use frequently.

Using Calculation Commands

If you have used calculations in your PC-File reports as explained in Chapter 10, "Generating Reports," you are already familiar with the way you use calculations in letters. You specify where you want the results of the calculation to appear in each letter.

A calculation must be enclosed in parentheses and angle brackets, as in this example:

.<(@Acct_No,Sales,Acct_No,Price) :$$,$##.##:>

This calculation is a relational lookup that extracts data from the PRICE field in the Sales database. The ACCT_NO field is common to both the Telemarket and Sales database.

You also can use print masks with calculations to specify the formatting, as explained in Chapter 10, "Generating Reports." The print mask in the example inserts a dollar sign, commas, and a decimal point in the data that results from the calculation.

Examining IF Commands

PC-File's IF commands include or exclude information based on a comparison. An IF command can include a middle initial in a name when the MID_INIT field contains data; it can exclude the MID_INIT field when the field is empty and close up the space for the empty field. If you want to use an IF command in your letter for including or excluding the middle initial, the beginning of the letter would look like this:

```
.IF(MID_INIT=" ")
.<FIRST_NAME> .<LAST_NAME>
.ELSE
.<FIRST=NAME> .<MID_INIT> .<LAST_NAME>
.ENDIF
.ADDRESS>
.<CITY> .<ST> .<ZIP_CODE>
```

If you are experienced with IF statements or programming, you will have no problem understanding IF commands in PC-File's letter writing feature. If you are not familiar with IF commands, however, you might want to practice by using the Language format when creating reports in PC-File. Refer to your PC-File documentation for information on using the Language format.

This gives you a foundation for understanding the basics of programming techniques in PC-File. For more information on using IF commands in a letter, refer to the PC-File documentation.

Printing Letters

After you have created, edited, and formatted a letter, seeing the form letters on paper provides a special sense of accomplishment. If you have printed reports in PC-File as explained in Chapter 10, "Generating Reports," you already know how to print letters in PC-File.

When working with any computer and a printer, you must be familiar with the type of printer you are using. PC-File is set up to use all the features of your printer; however, you must know your printer's limitations. Refer to your printer manual and determine what the printer can do.

Before you print a report, you can customize your printout with several print options. For information on these print options, refer to the section on Printing Reports in Chapter 10, "Generating Reports."

Once you customize the print options, you are ready to print your report. You can send the letters directly to the printer, to the screen, or to a file. If you select a file, the letters can be printed any time. If you change your mind and want to cancel the print request, PC-File also lets you do that.

To print form letters in PC-File, follow these steps:

1. Select Print from the menu bar. PC-File displays the Print menu.

2. Select Letter from the Print menu. PC-File displays the Letter Options dialog box.

3. Select Run to print the letters. PC-File displays the File Selection dialog box (see figure 11.10).

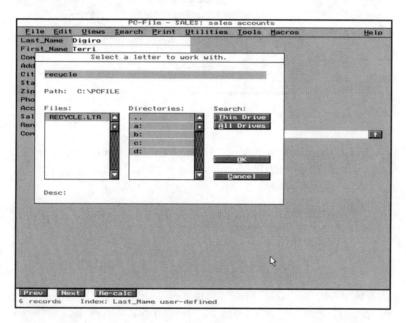

Fig. 11.10. *The File Selection dialog box.*

4. Select the letter you want to print. Report files contain the file extension REP. PC-File displays the Print Options dialog box (see figure 11.11).

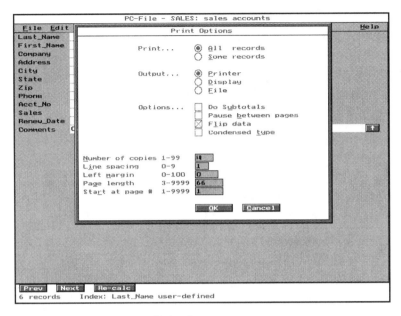

Fig. 11.11. *The Print Options dialog box.*

5. Select the options you want. Refer to the section on Printing Reports in Chapter 10, "Generating Reports," for an explanation of the print options.

> If you change the print settings, PC-File uses those print settings only for the current printout. The next time you print the letter, PC-File returns the settings to the default print settings.

If you select print Some records, PC-File prompts you to perform a search to retrieve the records you want to print in the letters, as explained in Chapter 6, "Searching and Retrieving Records."

If you select Output display, you can view your letters on the screen before you print them (see figure 11.12). When you finish looking at your letters, click the OK button to exit the Output display screen. You are returned to the main PC-File screen.

If you select Output file to print the letters to a file on disk, PC-File prompts you to enter a path and file name. For example, type *c:\pcfile\print \announce.txt*.

If you select printing to a printer or to a file, PC-File displays the first record on the screen. You are prompted to make a choice about printing the current record (see figure 11.13).

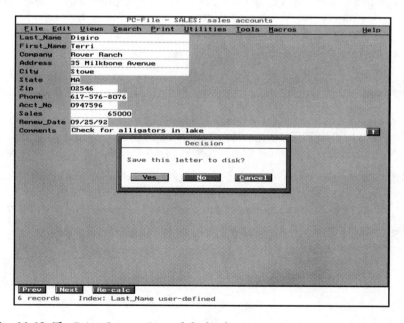

Fig. 11.12. The Output display screen.

```
                        PC-File - SALES: sales accounts
    File  Edit  Views  Search  Print  Utilities  Tools  Macros              Help
Last_Name   Digiro
First_Name  Terri
Company     Rover Ranch
Address     35 Milkbone Avenue
City        Stowe
State       MA
Zip         02546
Phone       617-576-8076
Acct_No     0947596
Sales             65000
Renew_Date  09/25/92
Comments    Check for alligators in lake

                        ┌──────────── Decision ────────────┐
                        │                                   │
                        │   Save this letter to disk?       │
                        │                                   │
                        │   [ Yes ]    [ No ]   [ Cancel ]  │
                        └───────────────────────────────────┘






 Prev    Next    Re-calc
6 records     Index: Last_Name user-defined
```

Fig. 11.13. The Print Current Record dialog box.

If you want to print a letter for the current record and display the next record, select Yes. If you do not want to print a letter for the current record and want to display the next record, select No. If you want to print a letter for the current record and all the rest of the records that meet the search criteria without being prompted again, select All. If you want to stop printing the letters, select Quit.

Modifying a Letter

With PC-File's flexible letter-writing feature, you can modify an existing letter any time. Just follow these steps:

1. Use the File Open command to open the database containing the form letter you want to modify. PC-File displays the first record of the database in the window.

2. Select Print from the menu bar. PC-File displays the Print menu.

3. Select Letters from the Print menu. PC-File displays the Letter Operations dialog box.

4. Select Modify from the dialog box. PC-File displays the 70 character default column width of the letter. You can change the width, if necessary, by typing a new column width.

5. Make the changes in the letter.

6. When you finish making the changes to the letter, click the OK button. PC-File prompts you to save the letter (see figure 11.14).

7. Select Yes to save the letter. If you want to keep the same file name for the letter, select the file name. When PC-File prompts you to overwrite the existing file, select Yes to do so.

8. If you want to change the file name, type the new name in the text box and press Enter. PC-File prompts you to accept the current description for the letter or enter a new one.

9. Enter a description or leave it blank. Then click the OK button. PC-File saves the letter.

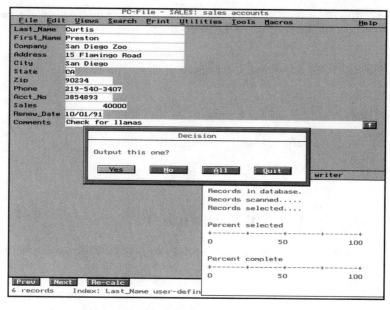

Fig. 11.14. The Save Letter dialog box.

Printing Snapshot Labels

In PC-File, you can print mailing labels one at a time quickly by using the Snapshot feature. With the Snapshot feature, you can print a single mailing label for each record that PC-File displays on the screen. This is handy for anyone who wants to print labels one at a time, especially people who take phone orders.

If your printer is not set up for printing single labels, you might want to print the snapshot labels to a file and then print all of them at once at a later time.

You also can use the Snapshot feature to set up a phone log by quietly printing the names of the people you talk with on the phone so that you can remember who you called. PC-File lets you format envelopes with both a mailing and return address by using the Free Form Report format. You can quickly create a COD label, print an invoice, or even print snapshot letters using the Snapshot feature.

This section shows you how to print snapshot labels. Once you get the basic idea, you should be able to use the Snapshot feature to create a wide variety of your own snapshot applications.

"Snapping" a snapshot label involves four simple procedures:

1. Define the label.

2. Assign the label to a snapshot.

3. Define the output, usually a printer or a file on disk.

4. Take a snapshot of the label.

Defining the Snapshot Label

The first step toward creating snapshot labels is to define the structure of the snapshot label. You can use the Mail Label Report format, as explained in the section on Creating a Mail Label Report in Chapter 10, "Generating Reports."

Assigning the Label to a Snapshot

The second procedure is to assign the mail label report to a snapshot number. Follow these steps:

1. Select Utilities from the menu bar. PC-File displays the Utilities menu (see figure 11.15).

2. Select Configuration from the Utilities menu. PC-File displays the Configuration screen. The Snapshot button appears in the lower left portion of the screen.

3. Click the Snapshot button with the mouse, or press the Tab key until the Snapshot button is highlighted and press Enter. PC-File displays the Snapshot Number dialog box (see figure 11.16).

   There are five Snapshot buttons. You can define up to five snapshot label reports for each database.

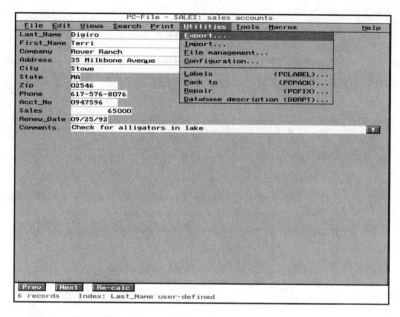

Fig. 11.15. *The Utilities menu.*

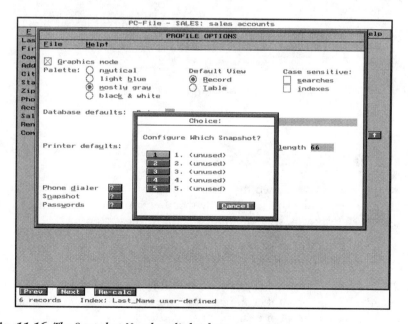

Fig. 11.16. *The Snapshot Number dialog box.*

4. Select the snapshot number button to which you want to assign the label. PC-File displays the File Selection dialog box.

5. Select the report that contains the snapshot label you defined; for example, select LABEL.REP. PC-File displays the Snapshot Labels Output dialog box as shown in figure 11.17. See the next section.

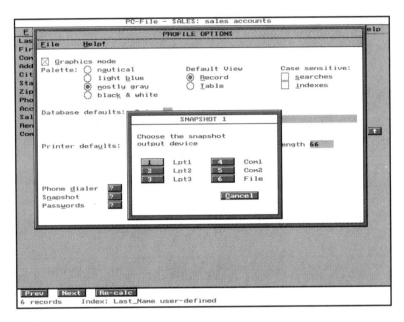

Fig. 11.17. The Snapshot Labels Output dialog box.

Defining the Output

Now that you have assigned the label to a snapshot, the next procedure is to define the output. This tells PC-File whether you want to send the labels directly to a printer or to a file on disk. Follow these steps:

1. If you want to send the snapshot labels directly to the printer, select the Printer port.

2. If you want to print all of the snapshot labels at a later time, select File. PC-File prompts you to enter a file name. Type the file name and press Enter. For example, type *LABEL.TXT*.

3. Select File from the menu bar. PC-File displays the File Configuration menu.

4. Select Exit from the File Configuration menu. PC-File prompts you to save the changes you made to the configuration file.

5. Select Yes to save the changes.

The type of output you select is stored in your configuration file.

Taking a Snapshot of the Label

The final procedure is to take a snapshot of the label and print the label instantly. Complete the following steps:

1. Display a record on the screen in Record or Table View, as explained in Chapter 7, "Modifying Records." To do this, select Views Table or Views Record from the menu bar. In Table View, PC-File highlights the current record. In Record View, PC-File displays a record on the screen.

2. To take the snapshot, select Tools from the menu bar. PC-File displays the Tools menu (see figure 11.18).

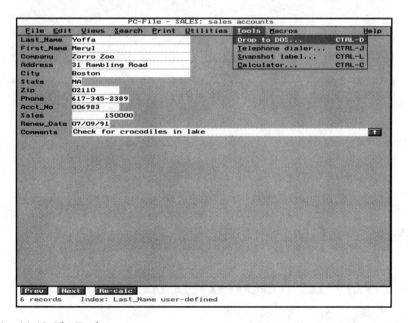

Fig. 11.18. The Tools menu.

3. Select Snapshot Label from the Tools menu or press Ctrl-L to start the print job. PC-File prints the snapshot labels immediately. If you have more than one snapshot label assigned to a database, PC-File prompts you to select the snapshot label you want to use (see figure 11.19).

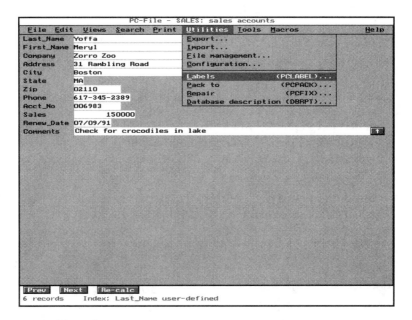

Fig. 11.19. The Utilities menu.

If you want to print the snapshot labels directly to the printer, be sure the printer is properly connected to your computer and turned on. PC-File prints the snapshot labels.

If you want to produce a mass mailing and print many names and addresses on sheets of computer labels, PC-File provides a special program called PC-Label, as explained in the next section.

Printing Mailing Labels with PC-Label

In PC-File, you can print hundreds of labels at a time on multiple column mailing labels. To do this, you use PC-File's mailing label program called

PC-Label. This special mailing label program lets you print three or four labels across a standard sheet of computer labels.

Creating labels in the program PC-Label requires four basic procedures:

1. Start the PC-Label program.

2. Define a template for a label format.

3. Print the labels.

4. Save the label format.

These procedures are explained in the next few sections.

> You cannot use the mouse in PC-Label. You use the keyboard to make selections and move around the screen.

Starting PC-Label

To start the PC-Label program, follow these steps:

1. Use the File Open command to open the database for which you want to create mailing labels. PC-File displays the first record of the database in the window.

2. Select Utilities from the menu bar. PC-File displays the Utilities menu.

3. Select Labels from the Utilities menu. PC-File displays the PC-Label Main menu (see figure 11.20).

Now define a template as covered in the next section.

Defining a Template

The second procedure for printing labels with PC-Label is to define a template for a label format. The most important parameter settings that you specify when creating a template for a label format are Label Source Type, Label Source Location, Label Sheet Definition, and Label Layout. The instructions on defining these settings are described in the next few steps. The other definitions contain the most commonly used settings for defining a label. You easily can change these default settings by following the Help screens on the right side of the screen that PC-File provides as you move to each definition.

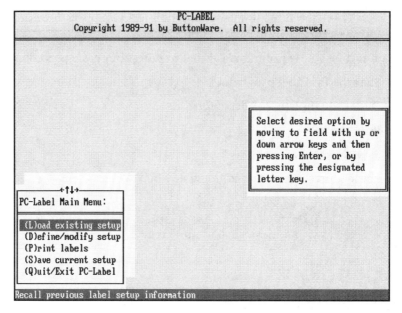

Fig. 11.20. The PC-Label Main menu.

To define a template for a label format, follow these steps:

1. Select Define Label Setup from the PC-Label Main menu. PC-Label displays the label Setup screen (see figure 11.21).

   The Setup screen has three areas. The first column contains parameters for each PC-Label setting. The second column shows the default settings for each parameter. A help window is displayed on the right. As you select each setting, PC-Label displays information in the Help window to assist you in defining the template.

2. The Label Source Type is the first setting and it displays PC-File 6.0.

3. If PC-File 6.0 is not displayed, keep pressing Enter to cycle through the source types until PC-File 6.0 appears on the screen.

   There are six source types available: PC-File 6.0, PC-Calc+, Comma-delimited, ASCII-L, ASCII-C, and PC-File+. The source types are described in the Help window on the right.

4. Press the down-arrow key to move to the second setting, Label Source Location, and press Enter to highlight it. This is where you enter the database and directory for which you want to define a template. For example, type *c:\pcfile* and press Enter.

   PC-Label prompts you to select a database file.

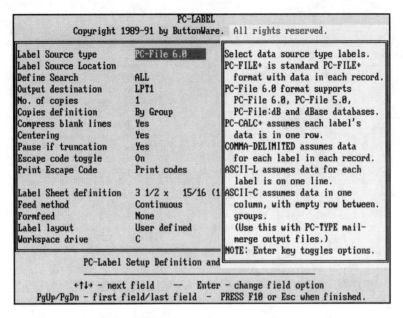

PC-LABEL
Copyright 1989-91 by ButtonWare.

Label Source type	PC-File 6.0	Select data source type labels.
Label Source Location		PC-FILE+ is standard PC-FILE+
Define Search	ALL	format with data in each record.
Output destination	LPT1	PC-File 6.0 format supports
No. of copies	1	PC-File 6.0, PC-File 5.0,
Copies definition	By Group	PC-File:dB and dBase databases.
Compress blank lines	Yes	PC-CALC+ assumes each label's
Centering	Yes	data is in one row.
Pause if truncation	Yes	COMMA-DELIMITED assumes data
Escape code toggle	On	for each label in each record.
Print Escape Code	Print codes	ASCII-L assumes data for each
		label is on one line.
Label Sheet definition	3 1/2 x 15/16 (1	ASCII-C assumes data in one
Feed method	Continuous	column, with empty row between.
Formfeed	None	groups.
Label layout	User defined	(Use this with PC-TYPE mail-
Workspace drive	C	merge output files.)
		NOTE: Enter key toggles options.

PC-Label Setup Definition and

↑↓ - next field   —   Enter - change field option
PgUp/PgDn - first field/last field - PRESS F10 or Esc when finished.

Fig. 11.21. *The PC-Label Setup screen.*

5. Use the arrow keys to highlight the file and press Enter. The path is displayed in the Label Source Location field, for example, c:\pcfile\sales.

6. Press the down-arrow key to move to the Label Sheet Definition setting at the bottom of the setup screen. Then press Enter. The default is the 3 1/2 x 15/16 (1-up) label format.

   PC-Label gives you 14 predefined templates to choose from in the Label Sheet Definition window (see figure 11.22). The label dimensions and number of labels to a sheet appear in the window.

7. Select the template that matches your label stock. If you cannot find one that matches, you can design your own layout with the User-defined Label Sheet Definition feature. For more information on setting up a user-defined Label Sheet Definition, refer to your PC-File documentation.

   For example, the 3 1/2 by 15/16 (1-up) label is the most commonly used label. These are the single column computer labels on continuous form paper. Use the arrow keys to move to the label stock you want and press Enter. You are returned to the Setup screen.

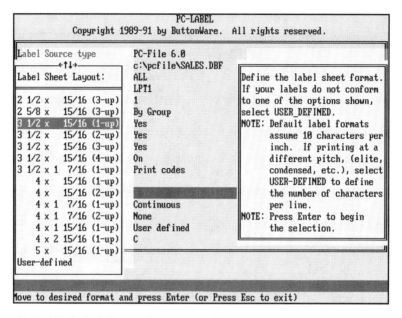

Fig. 11.22. *The Label Sheet Definition window.*

8. Press the down-arrow key to move to the Label Layout setting at the bottom of the Setup screen. Then press Enter. PC-Label displays the Label Layout screen (see figure 11.23). This is where you design the layout of the label.

   You can define four areas in the Label Layout screen: locate the fields, add text, define the borders, and format the characters. The field names and numbers as well as the system fields (as explained in Chapter 10, "Generating Reports") appear at the top of the Label Layout screen. The edit window appears in the middle of the screen. This is where you enter the label layout information. The character format markers appear at the bottom of the screen.

9. Move to the row where you want to start the label. For example, use the down-arrow key to move the cursor to Row 2 in the edit window. Notice the row and column indicator in the bottom right corner of the edit window.

   Starting the address on line 2 leaves a blank line at the top of the label. Enter the at (@) sign before each field or the text you enter. This fixes the data so that it starts in the same location each time you print. If you want to slide the data to the left until it encounters other data and remove the trailing spaces, enter a question mark (?) before the field or text you enter.

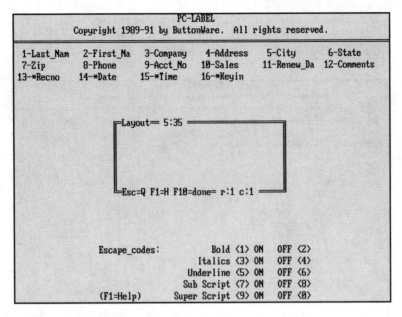

Fig. 11.23. The Label Layout screen.

10. Type @ (at) followed by a field number to specify the field you want in the label. The field names appear at the top of the screen. PC-File assigns a number to each field. The number appears to the left of a field name.

    Using the sample SALES database, on Row 2 type *@2?* to specify the FIRST_NAME field. The question mark (?) removes any trailing spaces in the first name when it encounters the last name. Then press the Spacebar to leave space between the first and last name. Type *?1* to specify the LAST_NAME field. Press Enter to move the cursor to Row 3.

11. Type *@3* to specify the COMPANY field. Press Enter to move the cursor to Row 4.

12. Type *@4* to specify the ADDRESS field. Press Enter to move the cursor to Row 5.

13. Type *@5?* to specify the CITY field. Then press the Spacebar. Type *?6?* to specify the STATE field. Press the Spacebar twice. Type *?7* to specify the ZIP code field.

The question marks (?) remove any trailing spaces in the CITY, STATE, and ZIP code fields. Figure 11.24 shows the sample fields in the label layout.

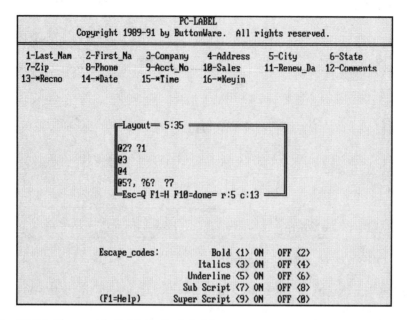

Fig. 11.24. *The sample fields in the label layout.*

14. Press F10. You are returned to the Setup screen.

15. Press F10 again to exit the Setup screen. You are returned to the PC-Label Main menu.

Printing Labels

You can print labels to a printer or to a file by using PC-Label. For the purposes of this lesson, you print the labels directly to a printer. If you do not have the label stock, you can print the labels on plain white paper and then photocopy those labels to label paper.

To print the labels, follow these steps:

1. Select Print labels from the PC-Label Main menu. PC-Label prompts you to put the label stock in your printer.

2. Put your label sheet or continuous form paper in the printer.

3. If you are not sure about the placement of the label stock in the printer, select Yes. PC-Label steps you through a series of screens that help you position the first sheet in the printer properly. If you know how to place the label stock in the printer, select No.

4. If you select Yes in Step 3, PC-Label prompts you to align the label stock again. If you want to test the alignment again, select Yes. If you know the alignment is correct, select No. PC-Label displays the first label and asks you if you want to print it.

5. If you want to print the label, select Yes. If you do not want to print the current label and want to continue to the next label, select No. If you want PC-Label to print all the labels without previewing on the screen, select X, Yes & don't ask. PC-Label prints the labels on the label stock.

Saving the Label Format

After you define the label setup, save it for future use. PC-Label lets you save the label format before or after you print the labels. Make sure you save the label format before you exit PC-Label; otherwise, the label setup is lost.

To save the label format, follow these steps:

1. Select Save Current Setup from the PC-Label Main menu. PC-Label prompts you to enter the drive and directory where you want the file to be stored. At this point, do not enter the file name. The current directory displays in the text box.

2. Press Enter to accept the current directory or enter a different drive and directory. PC-Label displays the Save Setup Options dialog box (see figure 11.25).

3. Select New File.LBL. PC-Label prompts you to enter a file name.

4. Type the file name for the label setup; for example, type *MKTLABEL*. PC-Label automatically assigns the file extension LBL when you enter the file name and save the label format.

5. Press any key to exit the Save Current Setup screen.

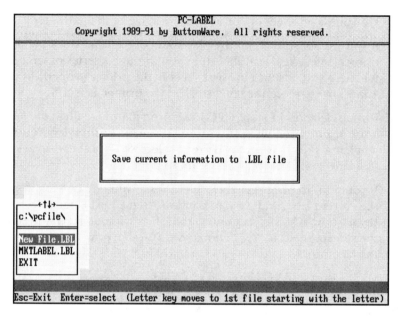

Fig. 11.25. The Save Setup Options dialog box.

Exiting PC-Label

When you finish using the PC-Label program, press Q or select Quit/Exit PC-Label from the PC-Label Main menu. You are returned to the Utilities menu in PC-File.

Summary

In this chapter, you learned how to produce form letters using PC-File's letter-writing feature. You also found out how you can print mailing labels quickly using PC-File's snapshot label feature. You learned how to use the PC-Label program to print labels on label stock.

The capability to generate reports, form letters, and labels is a powerful and sophisticated feature of PC-File. A special capability you can explore that is not usually found in a database program is PC-File's graphing feature. The graphing feature which lets you create pie charts, bar graphs, line graphs, and scatter graphs is explained in the next chapter.

12

Creating Graphs

P C-File's unique graphing feature allows you to create a variety of graphs from your database for presentations.

This chapter introduces you to the various graph types such as line graphs, bar graphs, pie charts, cumulative bar and line graphs, and scatter graphs. You learn how to define a graph by using only numeric entries. You find out how to summarize graph data with subtotals and totals, accumulating values (the actual numeric data in the database) or counts (the number of records in the database), and adding titles. You find out how to choose the graph type as well as save your graphs. You examine how to enhance and view your graphs on the screen before you print them. You learn how to edit and print your graphs.

Graphing Databases

In PC-File, you can create presentation-quality graphs that represent the information in a database. With a few keystrokes, you can turn large amounts of data from a database into a graph, revealing a picture not immediately apparent in a list or report format.

A graph is a visual representation of data. As you can see in Figure 12.1, graphs offer a different perspective on the data stored in your databases. They say "a picture is worth a thousand words"; in some cases, a graph can uncover a trouble spot or pinpoint the beginning of a new pattern. You can analyze past or present data and forecast situations by graphing data. Just as you can set up a database to create what-if scenarios, you can use graphs to help foresee future directions.

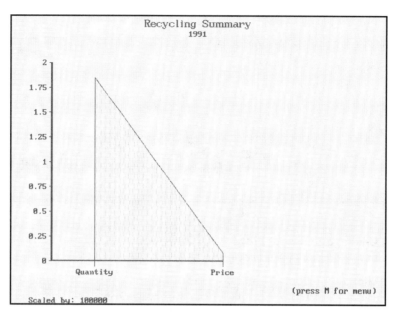

Fig. 12.1. *A graph created by PC-File.*

PC-File lets you create a wide variety of pie charts, line, and bar charts. For a detailed list of graph types, refer to the next section.

You create a graph using the commands in Print Graphs menu. You can view your graph at any time as you are building it. PC-File lets you add a grid to your graph to make it easier to read. You can calculate and display an average and smooth averages. When you are satisfied with the way the graph looks, you can print it on a printer or plotter, or save it in a file on disk for future use.

Checking System Requirements

There are several system requirements that you should check to see if your monitor can display graphs and if your printer can print graphs. To find out what type of monitor you have, refer to your monitor documentation.

You can display PC-File graphs on the following monitors: Hercules or Hercules-compatible monochrome, CGA, EGA, or VGA. You can print your graphs on the following dot-matrix printers: Epson FX, Epson MX, IBM, and Okidata. You also can print your graphs on two laser printers: HP Laserjet and PostScript.

If you have a printer other than the printers mentioned, you might be able to use the DOS GRAPHICS command to print graphs as they appear on the screen. For information on this command, refer to your DOS documentation.

Examining Graph Types

With PC-File, you can create four basic types of graphs: pie charts, bar graphs, line graphs, and scatter graphs. You can enhance these basic graphs to create horizontal or vertical bar charts, overlapped bar charts, and cumulative bar and line graphs. Once you complete a graph, you can switch from one graph type to another to find the one that best represents your data.

For information on each graph type, refer to the next few sections.

Pie Charts

A pie chart is used to illustrate the relation between two or more values by representing the values as parts to a whole. Pie charts are useful for showing total expenses, total sales, and percentages of the whole for a particular period of time. Figure 12.2 shows a pie chart created by PC-File.

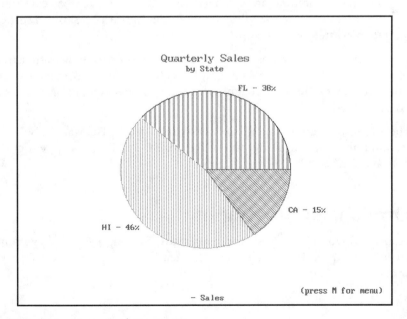

Fig. 12.2. *A pie chart created by PC-File.*

Each set of values is shown as a slice of the pie. Only two sets of data may be plotted at onc time. The first set of data represents the labels on the pie chart; the second set of data contains the values for the slices of the pie.

Bar Graphs

A bar graph represents a change over a few time periods. It shows a relationship between two data series over a few time periods or shows trends over many time periods. Bar graphs are useful for comparing yearly sales for each region over a period of years. A bar graph can illustrate numerical amounts such as dollars, time, and mileage.

A bar graph uses vertical or horizontal bars either extending upward, or from left to right from the x-axis, to indicate magnitude. Each bar represents a value in a set of data. PC-File determines the height of each bar according to its value and the scale specified on the y-axis.

You can plot more than one set of data. The bars for each set of data appear side by side. PC-File assigns each set of data a different fill pattern or color. PC-File also determines the width of each bar according to the number of values plotted. The more values plotted, the narrower the bars.

There are two types of bar graphs in PC-File: vertical and horizontal. Selecting the type of bar graph is a matter of preference. The traditional bar graph contains bars that are arranged vertically, with each bar extending upward from the x-axis to indicate magnitude. Figure 12.3 shows a vertical bar graph created by PC-File.

The bars in a horizontal bar graph are arranged horizontally, rather than vertically as in the traditional bar graph. Each bar extends from left to right from the x-axis to indicate magnitude. Figure 12.4 shows a horizontal bar graph created by PC-File.

The x-axis labels appear on the left side of the graph. The y-axis labels and scale numbers appear at the top of the graph. The legends appear at the bottom of the graph.

Overlapped Bar Graphs

An overlapped bar graph is a more attractive bar graph. The bars within a group overlap each other. Figure 12.5 shows an overlapped bar graph created by PC-File.

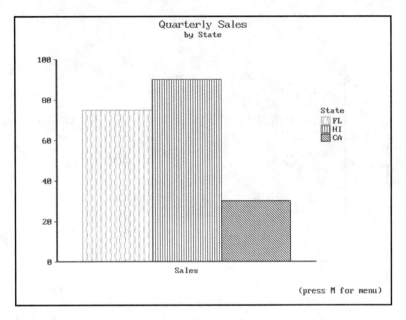

Fig. 12.3. *A vertical bar graph created by PC-File.*

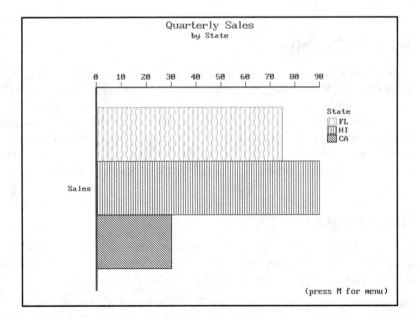

Fig. 12.4. *A horizontal bar graph created by PC-File.*

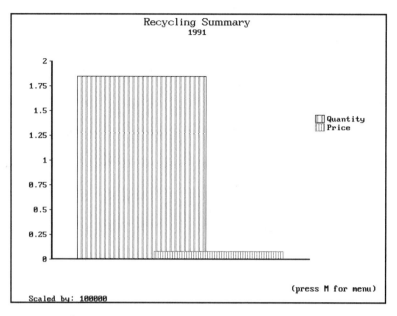

Fig. 12.5. *An overlapped bar graph created by PC-File.*

Scatter Graphs

A line graph and a scatter graph are similar except that a scatter graph does not contain the lines between the points. Only the points show on the graph. Scatter graphs are useful for plotting a large number of points. As a rule, if you want to plot more than 20 points, use a scatter graph or line graph as they show a clearer visual summary of your information than other graph types. You can also show an average of the points plotted by drawing a line on the scatter graph. Figure 12.6 shows a scatter graph created by PC-File.

Line Graphs

A line graph shows change over a few or many time periods. You can use a line graph to show a relationship between two series of data over periods of time. A line graph also can show statistical trends over time.

Line graphs are useful for identifying dips and rises in a set of numbers. For example, a line graph can show monthly sales totals for a particular year, illustrating low winter sales and a rising trend. You also can use a line graph to plot engineering and scientific data. For example, you can show how ocean tides in one coastal line vary over several months or how a heart rate changes as physical activity increases. Figure 12.7 shows a line graph created by PC-File.

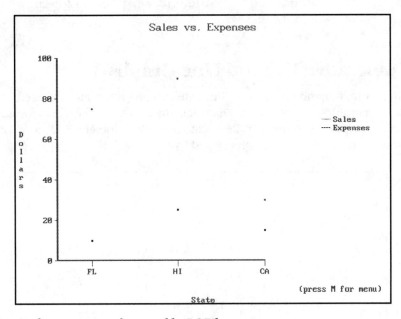

Fig. 12.6. *A scatter graph created by PC-File.*

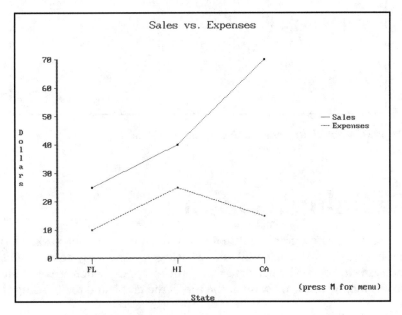

Fig. 12.7. *A line graph created by PC-File.*

A line graph connects each piece of data in a series with a line. If you have more than one series of data, PC-File displays a separate line for each. A line graph plots the data from left to right, the order that the data appears within fields and records in the database.

Cumulative Bar and Line Graphs

Cumulative bar and line graphs illustrate running totals and are useful for plotting multiple variables. PC-File totals the points on the y-axis for each group at a given position on the x-axis to produce the graph. Figure 12.8 shows a cumulative line graph created by PC-File.

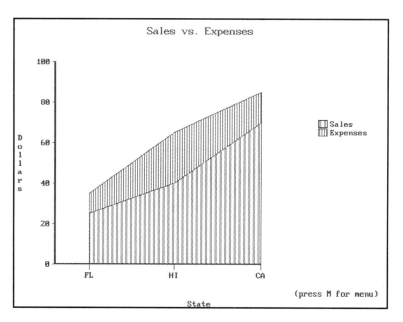

Fig. 12.8. *A cumulative line graph created by PC-File.*

Defining a Graph

Before you create a graph in PC-File, you might find it easier to sketch the graph on paper first. You could draw a basic graph and indicate which fields you want to use and what data you want to appear when it is graphed. Determine the titles you want at the top of the graph and the headings for labeling the axes. Once you determine what the graph will look like, you can create the PC-File graph in only one or two minutes.

When you name a graph, PC-File automatically adds the file extension .GR to the graph file.

Before you decide on the type of graph you want, think about the following four questions:

- Which fields do you want to graph?

- Are you graphing subtotals or totals?

- If you are graphing subtotals, which field or fields will define the subtotal break?

- Are you using values, which represent the actual numeric data, or counts, which represent the number of records?

To define a graph, follow these steps:

1. Select Print from the menu bar. PC-File displays the Print menu.

2. Select Graphs from the Print menu. PC-File displays the File Selection dialog box (see figure 12.9).

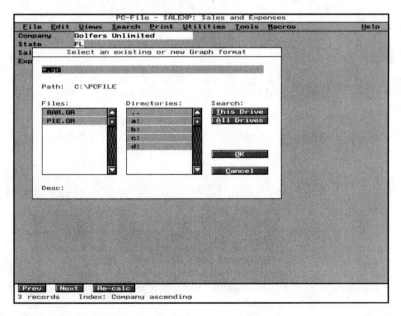

Fig. 12.9. The File Selection dialog box.

3. Enter a file name for your graph in the text box. For example, type *salespie*. PC-File automatically adds the file extension .GR for the graph file.

4. Click the OK button. PC-File asks you how you want to summarize the data (see figure 12.10).

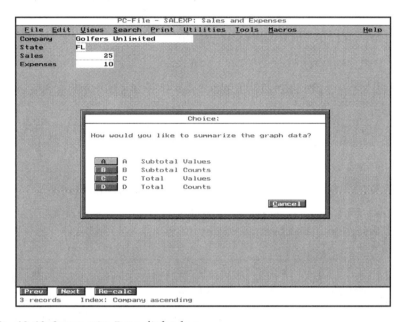

Fig. 12.10. Summarize Data dialog box.

For information on using subtotals and totals, using subtotal breaks, accumulating values or counts, and adding titles, refer to the next few sections.

5. Select a Summarize Data option. For example, if you want to graph totals instead of subtotals, and counts instead of values, select Total Counts. PC-File displays a Field Selection dialog box.

6. Select the fields you want to graph in the order you want them to appear on the graph. The data displays in the graph from left to right.

For instance, if you had a sales database and you wanted to track sales by state, you would select the SALES field. When you have selected the fields for graphing, PC-File displays the Titles and Headings dialog box (see figure 12.11).

Fig. 12.11. *Titles and Headings dialog box.*

7. Enter the main graph title, the subtitle, and the headings in the appropriate text boxes. If you want to skip a title, press Enter to move to the next text box. When you finish entering the titles, click the OK button.

8. Select the graph type. For example, select vertical bar. PC-File prompts you to save the graph.

9. If you want to save the graph, select Yes. If you want to use the graph only once, select No.

   If you select Yes in Step 8, PC-File prompts you to enter an optional description for the graph.

10. Type a description or leave it blank and select OK.

    If you select subtotals in Step 5, PC-File displays a Field Selection dialog box.

11. Specify the field you want for the subtotal break. For instance, select the STATE field to categorize sales by state. PC-File prompts you to select which records you want to graph.

12. If you want to graph all of the records, select All. If you want to graph some of the records, select Some.

13. If you select Some records in Step 12, PC-File prompts you to perform a search and enter search criteria, as described in Chapter 6, "Searching and Retrieving Records." PC-File displays the first record and the Output dialog box.

14. If you want to graph the current record and display the next record, select Yes. If you want to skip the current record and display the next record, select No. If you want to graph all of the selected records without further prompting, select All.

PC-File displays the graph on the screen. At this point, you can use the graph menu commands to enhance the graph and then print it, as explained later in this chapter.

Using Subtotals and Totals

When you define a graph, PC-File asks you if you want to use subtotals and totals in your graph. If you want to graph the data within one or more fields, use subtotals. The subtotals show the subtotals for one or more fields. For example, in the sample SALES database used earlier in this chapter, the STATE field is specified for the subtotal break, and therefore PC-File shows each state either in legends on the right side or along the horizontal axis at the bottom of the graph to describe what each bar or line represents. A subtotal is not a field that shows actual data inside the graph; a subtotal further defines the graph.

If you want to compare the totals of two or more fields, use totals. The totals show the summation of all the records from several fields. For example, in the sample SALES database, the STATE and EXPENSES fields can be specified as the fields you want to use for totals. PC-File adds the data for all of the records from each field and displays their totals for sales and expenses in the graph.

If you select subtotals, PC-File prompts you to define a subtotal break. A subtotal break is a field that you can use to group data, or it can be a calculation. This is similar to the subtotal break in a PC-File report.

Typically, the subtotal break is the field that you plot along the horizontal axis of the graph. It is based on the category heading you specify, as explained later in this chapter, and is usually not the field that you are graphing. For example, if you want to graph sales by month, the subtotal break field is MONTH. If you want to graph sales by region, the subtotal break field is REGION.

Accumulating Values or Counts

When you define a PC-File graph, you are prompted to select accumulating values or counts. Values represent the actual data in the database that you want to graph. Counts represents the number of records you want to graph.

Values always represent numeric data. In most situations, you want to select values. For example, if you want to graph sales commissions by each salesperson, class attendance by week, or increases in recycling bottles by year, select accumulating values.

Counts represent a record count or data that is not numeric. In some situations, you want to select counts. For instance, you can count the number of sales made by each salesperson, instead of adding the sales amounts. In this case, you would graph the number of records, each record representing a sale, instead of graphing the sales data.

In another example of using counts for non-numeric data, you can graph the number of employees that work in each field office by counting the records by field office.

You must select one way to summarize the data. In this case, you could select Subtotal Values, or Subtotal Counts, or Total Values, or Total Counts.

Adding Titles

PC-File provides four titles for a graph. They include the main graph title, a subtitle, a category heading, and a variable heading.

The main graph title and subtitle appear above the graph. They are the same as the report title and subtitle in a PC-File report.

The category heading appears along the horizontal axis of a graph. It usually describes the contents of the field that you select for the subtotal break, as explained earlier in this chapter. For instance, if you want to graph sales by month, the field called MONTH is the field on which you categorize the data. Thus, MONTH is the category heading.

The variable heading usually appears on the vertical axis of the graph. It describes the data of the fields you want to graph. For instance, if you want to graph sales by month, SALES is the variable heading.

There are a few exceptions for adding titles to graphs. In horizontal bar graphs, the headings are reversed; the category heading appears along the vertical axis, and the variable heading appears along the horizontal axis of the graph. In pie charts, the variable heading appears below the chart, and the category heading appears with a legend on the side of the chart. A legend further describes the wedges of the pie.

When you enter a title, you can use upper or lowercase letters, numbers, or both. The titles are case sensitive and display exactly the way you enter them. All titles are optional; press Enter to skip a title.

Enhancing and Printing Graphs

Once you display a graph on the screen, you can use the Graph menu commands to perform any of the following actions:

- Add one or more of the optional graph features

- Switch to a different graph

- Print the graph

With the graph displayed on the screen, press M to display the Graph menu (see figure 12.12).

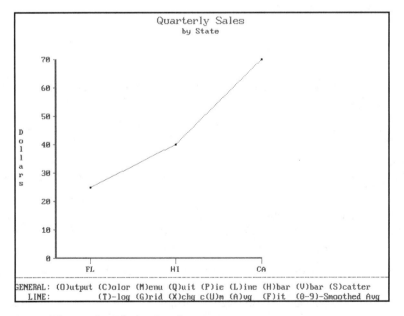

Fig. 12.12. The graph with the Graph menu.

The Graph menu consists of two menu lines. The General menu contains options on the top line and remains the same for every graph type you display. The Type menu contains options on the bottom line and changes depending on the type of graph you display. The name of the menu also varies depending on the type of graph you display. For example, if you display a pie chart, the name of the menu is called Pie.

To select options from the menus, press the appropriate letter enclosed in parentheses. If the menu is not displayed, you can still select options by pressing the appropriate letter. You cannot use the mouse in the graph menus; you must use the keys to select menu options.

There are nine options in the General menu. The first three options— Output, Color, and Menu—are used for printing the graph, displaying the graph in color on the screen, and switching to another menu, as explained later in this section. The last five options—Pie, Line, Horizontal bar, Vertical bar, and Scatter—are used to switch graph types. The Quit option is used to exit the graphing utility and return to the PC-File menu bar.

You can turn the menu display on and off using the Menu option. If you turn off the menu, PC-File displays the message Press M for Menu in the lower right corner of the screen. To remove this message, press Shift-F1.

Enhancing Graphs

Type menu options are used to enhance your graph. You can add a grid, display a calculated average and smooth averages, and change the scale for your graph.

PC-File provides 14 enhancement options. These options vary depending on the type of graph you display. The options that appear on the second line in the Type menu change depending on the graph type.

The following section lists the Type menu options and describes each option:

The Bound option: Changes the scale of a graph and lets you specify the minimum and maximum value for the scale on the x- and y-axes. To use the Bound option, edit the graph file, for example, SALESBAR.GR, by using any text editor or word processor. Insert the BOUND command before the first title line in the file. For example, BOUND:0,0,200,1,0,1000 sets the y-axis scale to a minimum value of 1, a maximum value of 200, and a maximum cumulative value of 1000. The BOUND command appears in the Type menu so that you can use the customized scale for the graph at any time.

The Log option: Changes the scale along the vertical axis to a logarithmic scale. The default Scale type is set to a linear scale where the increments are 10, 20, 30, and so on. For example, a logarithmic scale contains increments of magnitude such as 10, 100, 1000, 10000, 100000, and so on. This scale is generally used for the y-axis only, as shown in figure 12.13. Press T to select Log. Press T again to return to the normal scale. Use with bar, line, and scatter graphs.

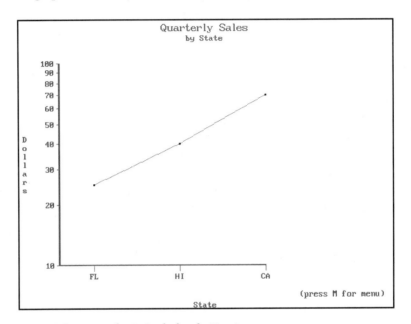

Fig. 12.13. *The Logarithmic Scale for the Y-axis.*

The Grid option: Adds grid lines to your graph, as shown in figure 12.14. Press G to select Grid. Select Grid again to remove the grid. Use with bar, line, and scatter graphs.

The Xchg option: Switches the way the multiple data elements are displayed. Press X to select Xchg. Select Xchg again to return to the original graph. Use with all graph types. For example, Xchg switches the order of the lines in a line graph or bars in a bar graph. If you have two sets of bars and one set represents sales for three states and the other set represents expenses for the same three states, PC-File displays three sales bars on the left and three expenses bars on the right in a vertical bar graph.

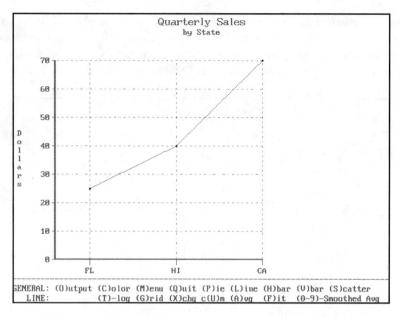

Fig. 12.14. *The grid lines in a graph.*

If you press X, PC-File displays a sales bar and an expenses bar adjacent to each other for each state, as shown in figure 12.15.

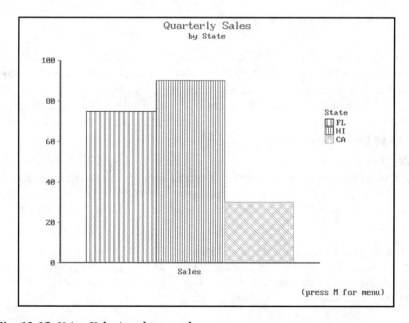

Fig. 12.15. *Using Xchg in a bar graph.*

The Cum option: Generates cumulative line and bar graphs and stacks bars or lines on top of each other. Press U to select Cum. Select U again to return to the original graph. Use with bar and line graphs. Figure 12.16 shows a cumulative bar graph, and figure 12.17 shows a cumulative line graph.

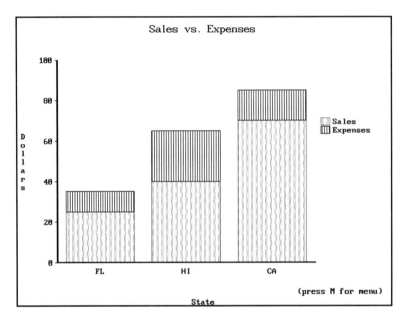

Fig. 12.16. *A cumulative bar graph.*

The Avg option: Draws a line across a graph showing the average or mean of all the data. Press A to insert the line. Select the graph type again to remove the line. Use with bar, line, and scatter graphs. Avg allows you to see which points are above and below the average. For example, in a bar graph, press A to insert the average lines across the bars, and select V(bar) to remove the lines (see figure 12.18).

The Overlap option: Produces a more attractive bar graph by allowing the bars within a group to overlap each other. Press E to overlap the bars as shown in figure 12.19. Select Overlap again to return to the original graph. Use this option with bar graphs, but do not use with it with cumulative bar graphs.

The Fit option: Displays the trend of your data by drawing a line in your graph. Select Fit to insert the line. Select the graph type again to remove the line. Figure 12.20 illustrates a Fit line showing trends in a scatter graph. Use FIT with line and scatter graphs.

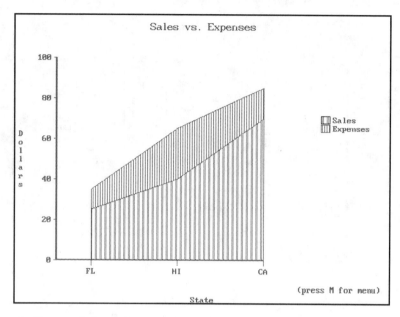

Fig. 12.17. *A cumulative line graph.*

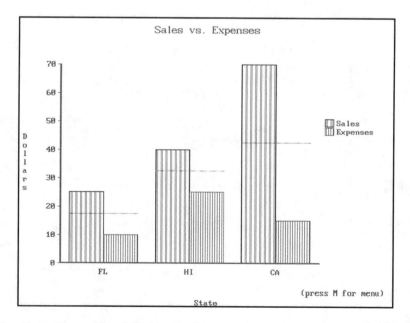

Fig. 12.18. *The average line in a bar graph.*

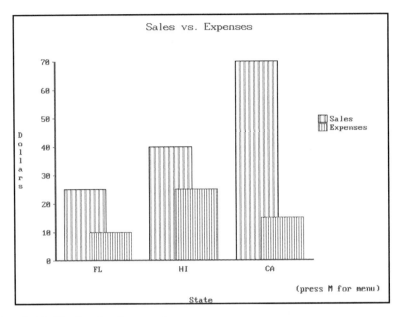

Fig. 12.19. The Overlap bar graph.

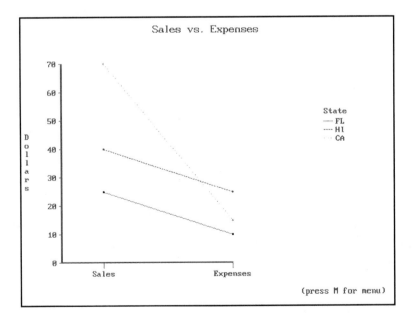

Fig. 12.20. A Fit line showing trends in a scatter chart.

The (0-9)Smoothed Avg option: Shows trends of large amounts of data that vary considerably. To do this, the option calculates an average for each point on the graph based on the values of a specified number of data points to the left and right of that point. To remove the lines, select the graph type again. Use this option with line and scatter graphs.

To smooth the average, you select a number from 0 to 9 to control the amount of smoothing you want. The number represents the number of points to the left and right of the point used in the smoothed average. For example, if you select 3, the average for each plotted point includes 3 points to the left and 3 points to the right of the current point. The higher the number you select, the more smoothing occurs.

The Aspect option: Makes pie charts round on the screen and printout by adjusting the aspect ratio of height to width of the circle. In the Pie type menu, press A to select Aspect to display a circle enclosed in a box. Press P for Portrait or L for Landscape to select the print mode. Use the arrow keys to adjust the dimensions of the circle until it appears round and the box appears square (see figure 12.21). Then press P to produce a test printout of the graph. Select the printer. PC-File prints the graph. Press Q to exit the Aspect screens. If your pie charts appear elliptical instead of round, adjust the height and width with Aspect.

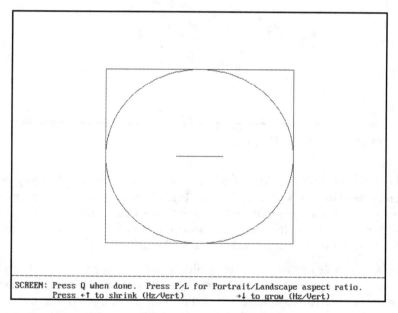

Fig. 12.21. *Using Aspect to make a pie chart round.*

The Wedge option: Emphasizes or explodes specific slices of a pie chart by pulling wedges of the pie away from the center. To explode a pie, press W to select Wedge. PC-File displays a small version of the pie on the left side of the screen. The slice that is made up of solid color is the curent slice that you can explode. To detach the slice, press D. If you change your mind, you can press A to attach it. To skip to the next slice counter clockwise, press S to skip. PC-File changes the next slice to a solid color. You can detach, attach, or skip a slicc by pressing D, A, and S, respectively. If you want to return all slices to the pie at once, press N. When you finish exploding the pie, press Q to return to the full-size display of the pie, as shown in figure 12.22.

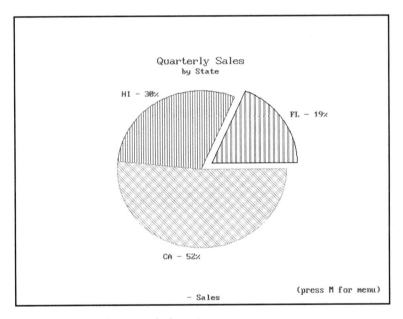

Fig. 12.22. Using Wedge to explode a pie.

The Disp option: Unclutters a pie chart by moving the heading and percentage labels to a separate legend. Press D to create a legend and move the heading labels next to it, as shown in figure 12.23. Press D again to add the percent labels to the legend, as shown in figure 12.24. Press D a third time to remove the legend and return to the original pie chart.

The (1-2)#pies option: Displays multiple fields on separate pie charts by displaying two pie charts on the screen simultaneously. Before you use this option, be sure you have selected two fields for the graph. Press 2 to display two pies side by side, as shown in figure 12.25. Press 1 to display one pie.

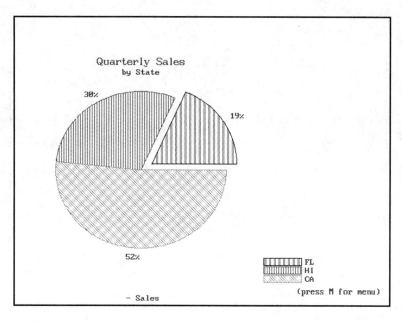

Fig. 12.23. *Using Disp to show legend and heading labels in a pie chart.*

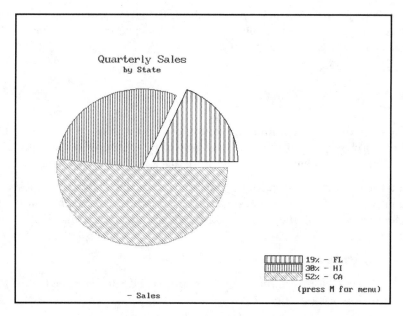

Fig. 12.24. *Using Disp to show legend and heading label with percents.*

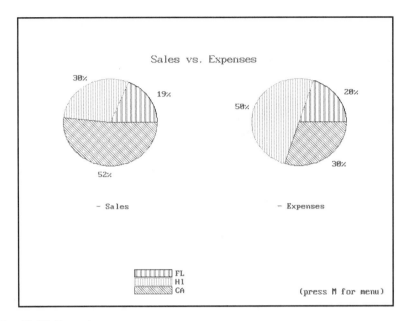

Fig. 12.25. *Two pies.*

The Next group option: Displays multiple fields on separate pie charts and lets you cycle through the pies. Press N to select Next group and cycle the pies either one or two at a time.

Adjusting Colors

If you are using a color monitor, you might find that some colors may not show up clearly on your screen. If you have a monochrome or CGA monitor, the Color option has no effect on these black and white screens.

You can use the Color option to select the colors that show up the best and select the foreground and background colors on the screen. The colors you select are saved to a file called PCG2.ASP, and you can use this file in future graphing operations.

To change colors, follow these steps:

1. Select Color from the General menu. PC-File displays the Color dialog box (see fig. 12.26).

2. Change the foreground and background colors until you see the color combination you want. To adjust the foreground colors,

press F repeatedly to cycle through the foreground colors. To change the background colors, press B repeatedly to cycle through the background colors.

You can turn off any of the detail colors. To do this, first press the number that appears to the left of the respective color bar. PC-File displays N to the right of the bar when the color is turned off. Press the number again to turn it back on.

If you want to see the colors on the screen, press Q at any time. Press C to return to the color screen.

3. When you finish selecting colors, press Q to exit the color screen.

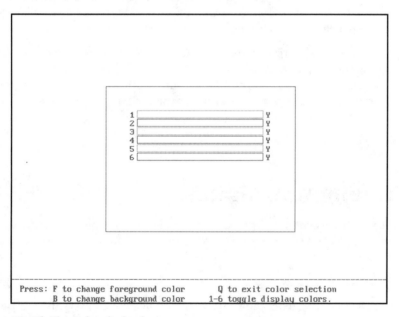

Fig. 12.26. The Color dialog box.

Switching Graphs

PC-File lets you switch to a different graph type at any time. When you have created a graph, you can switch to a different graph type by selecting a graph from the Type menu. For example, select Line to switch to a line graph. Keep changing the graph type until you see the graph that best represents your data.

Viewing a Graph

After you create a graph, PC-File automatically displays the graph on your screen. You can view a graph at any time by completing the following steps:

1. Select Print from the PC-File menu bar.

2. Select Graphs from the Print menu and PC-File displays the File Selection dialog box.

3. Select the file you want to view.

4. Select the records you want to include in the graph. If you want to include all records, select All. If you want to select some records, select Some to perform a search on the records. PC-File displays the Output Records dialog box.

5. Select Yes to output one record at a time. Select No to skip outputting the record. Select All to output all the records. Select Quit to cancel viewing the graph. PC-File outputs the records, displays the Information box, and tells you that the output procedure is completed.

6. Select OK and PC-File displays the graph.

Printing Your Graph

If you want to print your graph, select Output from the General menu. When the graph prints, PC-File removes the menu bar from the screen and does not print it.

To print a graph, follow these steps:

1. Select Output from the General menu. PC-File displays the Output menu.

2. If you want to print the graph upright on the page, select Portrait. If you want to rotate the graph 90 degrees and print a large image of the graph, select Landscape. The landscape option is useful for overhead transparencies. If you want to produce a graphics file that you can import into documents created in most word processing or desktop publishing programs, select GIF. GIF files are stored in the current directory.

   If you select Portrait or Landscape in Step 2, PC-File prompts you to select the output printer.

3. If you want to send the graph to an Epson FX or LQ printer, select Epson. To print on an IBM, Epson MX, or Okidata printer, select IBM. For all HP Laserjets and compatibles, select Laserjet. For PostScript printers and compatibles, select PostScript. PostScript produces the highest quality graph printout.

4. If you select PostScript in Step 4, PC-File displays a menu. Select a PostScript option from the menu.

   PC-File prompts you to print to a file or to a printer.

5. Select File if you want to print the graph later. Select Printer if you want to print the graph immediately. PC-File prompts you to select the fill pattern.

6. If you want to produce various patterns in the bars of bar charts and the wedges of pie charts, select Pattern fill. If you want to fill those same areas in shades of gray, select Gray fill. The Gray fill option prints the graph faster.

As PC-File prints your graphs, the colors on the screen change to show the progress of the printing process. If you are printing your graph on a PostScript printer, PC-File redraws the graph on the screen twice. When the printing process is complete, PC-File redraws the graph on the screen and displays the menu again.

Editing Graphs

A PC-File graph is linked to the data in the database. If you change an entry in the database, PC-File automatically creates two files: the .GR graph file and the GRAPH.ME file. The graph you created is automatically assigned the file extension GR. For example, SALESPIE.GR represents a pie chart in the SALES database. The GR file contains the settings you selected to create the graph. The GRAPH.ME file contains the data for the current graph. There is only one GRAPH.ME file, and it is updated every time you run a graph.

You edit a graph by making changes to the GR file by using the Report Modify command in PC-File. You can edit the GRAPH.ME file with any text editor or word processor. But the only time you might want to edit the GRAPH.ME file is to insert the BOUND command to change the graph's scale, as explained earlier in this chapter.

If you selected the wrong field for the subtotal break or if you selected the wrong records, you could either edit the GR file or simply create the graph again. Because it takes only a minute or two to create a graph in PC-File, it might be easier to recreate the graph and delete the old graph with the File Management Delete command, as explained in Chapter 9, "Changing the Design of a Database."

To edit a graph, follow these steps:

1. Change the .GR extension to .REP by using the DOS RENAME command at the DOS prompt. For example, type RENAME SALESPRE.GR SALESPIE.REP

2. Return to PC-File and select Print from the menu bar.

3. Select Reports from the Print menu. PC-File displays the Reports Operations dialog box.

4. Select Modify from the Reports Operations dialog box. PC-File displays the Report Format dialog box.

5. Select the Language report format. PC-File displays the File Selection dialog box.

6. Select the graph file you want to edit.

7. Change the graph file the same way you would change a report. Refer to your PC-File documentation for information on using the Language format.

8. Return to the DOS prompt and change the file extension back to .GR with the DOS RENAME command.

9. Return to PC-File and view the graph.

Summary

This chapter gave you a foundation for creating various graph types such as line graphs, bar graphs, pie charts, cumulative bar and line graphs, and scatter graphs. You learned how to define a graph by using subtotals and totals, accumulating values or counts, and adding titles. You examined how to enhance your graphs and view your graphs on the screen before you print them. You learned how to edit and print your graphs.

In the next chapter, you can learn about working with other PC-File features such as the telephone dialer, the calculator, and macros.

13

Using Other PC-File Features

In this chapter you learn more ways to make your work easier with PC-File. You learn how to save space on your disk by packing your database to remove deleted records.

The PC-Fix feature lets you repair a damaged database. PC-Fix handles some of the problems that prevent you from accessing your database.

With PC-File's telephone autodialing feature, you can store frequently used phone numbers and place phone calls. Autodialing saves you time and keystrokes.

Another PC-File time-saving feature is the calculator. With the calculator you can perform arithmetic calculations and store the answer. Then you can transfer the answer to a field in your database.

With PC-File's flexible and powerful macros feature, you learn how to save frequently used text and commands. Recording keystrokes and playing them back saves repetitive typing. You are shown how to assign these keystrokes to a key so that you can then recall the series of keystrokes any time by just pressing one key.

Packing Databases

When you use the Edit Delete or Edit Global Delete command to delete one or more records (as explained in Chapter 7, "Modifying Records"), you can change your mind about records you have deleted. After you delete records, you can undelete them with the Edit Undelete command.

PC-File can recover your deleted records because it does not actually erase the records when you delete them. It just removes them from the screen so that you no longer see them.

If want to get rid of the deleted records altogether, you can pack the database and PC-File will erase the deleted records from your database. Once the database is packed, however, those records are gone. There is no unpack command.

At times, packing a database is very useful. If you want to get rid of all records in a database and start over again, you can use the Utilities Pack command to do just that.

Deleted records take up space on your disk, space that is used again when you add records. If you add new records to your database, PC-File replaces the deleted records with the new records. Therefore, those records that have been written over cannot be recovered.

Deleting more records than you add can create wasted space on your disk. If you do not add a lot of new records, you should pack your database to remove the deleted records. But if you add more records than you delete and you do not rewrite your memo fields, you should not have to pack the database.

Editing a memo field may be another occasion for packing a database. Sometimes, when you make changes to a memo, PC-File writes the memo to a new place in the memo file. If you pack your database, you can recover any lost memo space.

If you have a large or complex database, packing the database can take some time. For example, if your database contains more than 20,000 records, packing it can take several hours.

Before you pack a database, follow these three procedures:

1. Make a backup copy of your database just in case the packing procedure causes problems. Usually the packing procedure does not cause problems, but caution is always a good idea. For information on backing up a database, refer to Chapter 9, "Changing the Design of a Database."

2. Check the amount of space on your hard disk to make sure there is enough space to complete the packing operation. You should have enough space to store two databases the size of the database you want to pack, less the deleted files. This is the same amount of space as the database you are packing.

   Use the DOS directory command to check the amount of space on your disk. First, change to the directory in which your database is stored. For example, type *cd\pcfile* and press Enter. Then type *DIR* at the DOS prompt. DOS displays a list of the database files. Add up the number of bytes for all the database files, DBF, DBT, and HDB. Make sure the sum is less than the number of bytes available, which appears at the end of the directory list.

   If you don't have enough space on your disk, delete files you no longer need. Be sure to back up the files before you delete them. Keep deleting files and checking the amount of space on your disk until you have enough space to pack the database.

3. When you pack a database, PC-File creates a new database and removes the deleted records in the new file. When PC-File is finished, you must either rename the new database or move it to a different directory to maintain the same file name. Decide on a new name for the database, or keep the current name by selecting the different drive and directory to which you want to move the new database.

To pack a database, follow these steps:

1. Use the File Open command to open the database you want to pack. If you do not open a database, PC-File prompts you to select the path and database you want to pack when you select the Utilities Pack to command.

2. Select Utilities from the menu bar. PC-File displays the Utilities menu, as shown in figure 13.1.

3. Select Pack to from the Utilities menu. PC-File displays warning information and prompts you to proceed with packing (see figure 13.2). PC-File prompts you to enter the path and database for the new database. For example, type *c:\pcfile\client2*.

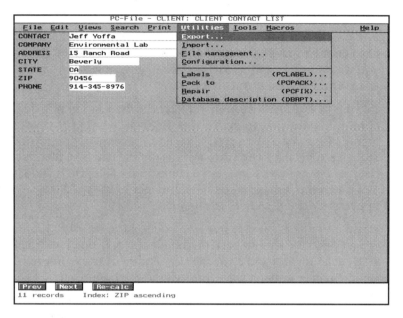

Fig. 13.1. *The Utilities menu.*

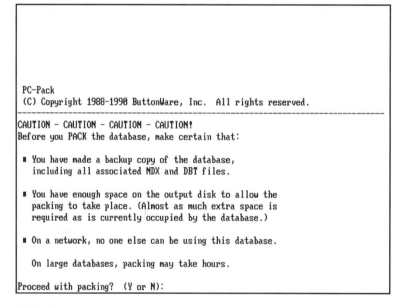

Fig. 13.2. *The pack database screen.*

4. Press *Y* to continue with the packing operation or press *N* to cancel the packing operation. If you want to use the same name for the current database, enter the new directory and the same file name to move the database to a different directory.

   PC-File packs the database and displays how many records it found.

5. Use the File Open command to open the new database. PC-File prompts you to rebuild the indexes.

6. Follow the instructions on the screen to rebuild the indexes. For information on rebuilding indexes, refer to Chapter 8, "Indexing Records."

7. Check the new database to find out if it was correctly packed. To do this, browse through the records in Table View by selecting Views Table view from the menu bar. To take a closer look at the records use Record View, as explained in Chapter 7, "Modifying Records."

8. Use the Utilities File Management Delete command in PC-File (as explained in Chapter 9, "Changing the Design of a Database") or the DOS DELETE command to delete the original database. For information on the DOS DELETE command, refer to your DOS documentation.

Repairing Databases

Suppose a power interruption, such as a blackout or power surge, occurs, or suppose you turn off the computer without exiting PC-File properly, or suppose you kick the power cord from the outlet—and, as a result, you cannot access your database. If you access your database and the data is incorrect or scrambled, you can use PC-File's PC-Fix feature to repair the database.

With the PC-Fix feature, you can repair a database and fix some of the problems that have occurred. If more serious problems such as lost clusters (as explained in your DOS documentation) are present, you might want to use the dBASE File Recovery or dBASE dSalvage program designed specifically for recovering damaged databases.

If you cannot access your database or the data looks scrambled, follow these procedures before using PC-Fix to repair your database:

1. Rebuild all indexes for the database. For information on rebuilding indexes, refer to Chapter 8, "Indexing Records."

2. Make a backup copy of your database. Be sure you do not erase or overwrite any existing backup copies of your database (as explained in Chapter 9, "Changing the Design of a Database"). This way, you can at least have the original backup copies if something else goes wrong. PC-Fix attempts to rebuild a database in place. In some cases, the resulting database can be damaged more than it was before the repair was attempted.

3. Use the DOS CHKDSK command to check for any file errors. Be sure to exit from PC-File, Microsoft Windows, and any other program first. At the DOS prompt, type *chkdsk/f* and press Enter. DOS lists the files and file errors on your hard disk. If there are any errors, correct them in DOS. For information on the DOS CHKDSK command and correcting errors, refer to your DOS documentation.

   Make sure you do not use the database until the errors are corrected. You also can use a disk repair program to check for errors and correct them on your hard disk.

Do not use the Drop to DOS command to exit PC-File when you want to use the DOS CHKDSK command. This procedure can damage your File Allocation Table and your hard disk. Also, do not use the Drop to DOS command to run the CHKDSK/F command. If you are running Windows, make sure you exit from Windows and return to the DOS prompt before running the command.

4. Use the DOS CHKDSK command to check the amount of space on your disk. First change to the directory in which your database is stored. For example, type *cd\pcfile* and press Enter. Then type *CHKDSK* at the DOS prompt. DOS displays a list of files and the space available on your hard disk. If the disk is full, you must delete files that you no longer need on the disk or move files to another disk to free up space.

5. If the problem still exists, use the PC-Fix feature to repair the database.

To repair a database using PC-Fix, follow these steps:

1. Use the File Open command to open the database you want to repair. If you do not open a database, PC-File prompts you to select the path and database you want to repair when you select the Utilities Repair command.

2. Select Utilities from the menu bar. PC-File displays the Utilities menu.

3. Select Repair from the Utilities menu. PC-File displays the PC-Fix screen, as shown in figure 13.3. Press Enter to continue. PC-File prompts you to enter the path and database for the database you want to repair. For example, type *c:\pcfile\client*.

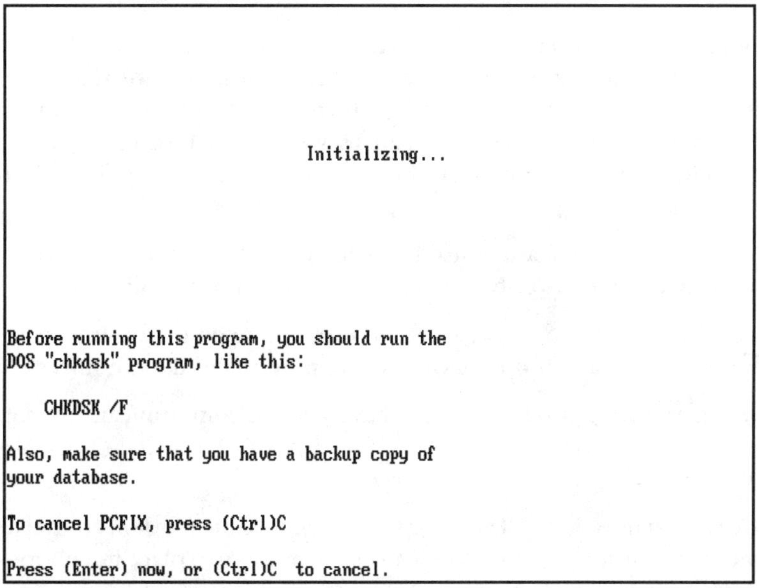

```
                          Initializing...




Before running this program, you should run the
DOS "chkdsk" program, like this:

    CHKDSK /F

Also, make sure that you have a backup copy of
your database.

To cancel PCFIX, press (Ctrl)C

Press (Enter) now, or (Ctrl)C  to cancel.
```

Fig. 13.3. The PC-Fix screen.

PC-File checks the .HDB header file for information about the database and then creates a new .DBF file in a different area on the disk for repairing the database. PC-File prompts you to clean up bad data in the file.

4. Select Yes to clean up bad data in the file. The PC-Fix program runs and attempts to repair your database. PC-File prompts you to rebuild the indexes.

5. Follow the instructions on the screen to rebuild the indexes. For information on rebuilding indexes refer to Chapter 8, "Indexing Records."

6. Check the database to find out if it was corrected. To do this, browse through the records in Table View by selecting Views Table View from the menu bar. To take a closer look at the records use Record view, as explained in Chapter 7, "Modifying Records."

Using the Telephone Dialer Feature

An important and fun feature in PC-File is autodialing. To use this feature you must have a modem. You can display records in your database that contain a phone number and use PC-File to dial the phone. Thus, you can talk to another person, or listen to an answering machine or to voice mail. You cannot, however, talk to another computer such as a bulletin board or fax machine.

PC-File's autodialing feature also lets you keep a log of the phone calls you make so that you can verify the charges on your phone bill.

If you want to use the autodialing feature, you need to confirm that your equipment and data fit the following equipment and data requirements:

Communications port: You must have a serial communications port on your computer. For example, look for either COM1, COM2, COM3, or COM4.

Modem: You must have a Hayes or Hayes-compatible modem connected to your communications port. PC-File uses the modem to place the phone call. After PC-File dials the phone number, the modem is no longer needed. PC-File bypasses the modem so that you can talk on your handset, as explained in the next requirement.

Handset: The handset is the actual telephone. You can use either a dial-pulse phone or touch-tone phone. PC-File assumes you have a dial phone unless otherwise specified. To specify a touch tone phone, change the modem dialing command in your configuration profile, as explained in Appendix A, "Installing and Configuring PC-File."

You must plug the telephone into the modem. Usually, the word "phone" or "handset" appears on the modem's connector.

Database: You must have phone numbers in your database that PC-File can use to place the call. The phone numbers must be stored in a field called phone or a field that contains the word phone as part of the field name in your database. You also can have multiple phone fields in a database. If there is more than one phone field, PC-File prompts you to enter the phone field you want to use.

Preparing a Database for Autodialing

There are several important steps involved in preparing a database for autodialing. First you need to make sure that the modem port and dialer settings are correct in your configuration profile, as explained in Appendix A, "Installing and Configuring PC-File." The following guidelines must be followed when you are defining your database:

The PHONE field: Be sure to use the word *phone* in the phone field; for example, you can use phone, telephone, phone#, phone no. You can have multiple phone fields in a database.

The phone number: Be sure to use numeric digits for a phone number. Define the field as a character-type field; do not use letters in a phone number. For example, enter (800)528-8866 instead of (800)J-BUTTON. You can enter spaces, parentheses, or hyphens, but they are not necessary.

Embedded Commands: You can enter Hayes modem commands in the phone number field. This is optional. For example, ATD is a command that alerts the modem that you want to use it. For information on modem commands, refer to your modem documentation.

Comments: You can enter comments in the phone number field. A comment is information in a phone field that is not sent to the modem. You must precede the comment with a semicolon; for example, *622-2888;ask for Sam.*

Long distance codes: Be sure to include the area code for long distance numbers. Do not include the 1, the long distance access code, with these phone numbers because PC-File automatically adds the 1 for all phone numbers that are 10 digits or longer. If the long distance number is within your area code, however, be sure to include the 1. If the number starts with a 0, for phone numbers outside the U.S. and Canada, PC-File does not add the 1 to the phone number.

Table 13.1 lists some examples of valid phone numbers and describes each phone number.

Table 13.1
Valid Phone Numbers

Phone Number	Description
622-2888	Local call, using hyphen for clarity
1-622-2888	Long distance call within the area code, using hyphens for clarity
1 622 2888	Long distance call within the area code, using spaces for clarity
(305)622-2888	Long distance call to a different area code, using parentheses and hyphens for clarity
305-622-2888	Long distance call to a different area code, using hyphens for clarity
011-634-244-1	Foreign call, using hyphens for clarity

Placing a Call

Before you place a call, make sure the following items are in place:

- Modem is hooked up correctly.
- Telephone is hooked up correctly.
- Port codes are properly configured in the PC-File configuration file.
- Access codes are properly configured in the PC-File configuration file.

To place a call using autodialing, follow these steps:

1. Display the record that contains the phone number you want to call in Record View or Table View, as explained in Chapter 7, "Modifying Records."

   If you select Table View, highlight the record that contains the phone number you want to call. You do not have to highlight the phone number itself.

You can place a call only from a record in a database. You cannot place a call from a letter or report that contains phone numbers.

2. Select Tools from the menu bar. PC-File displays the Tools menu, as shown in figure 13.4.

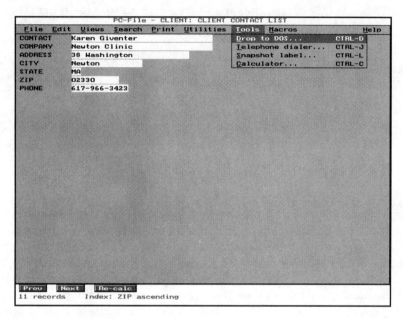

Fig. 13.4. The Tools Menu.

3. Select Telephone Dialer from the Tools menu. Instead of Steps 2 and 3, you can press Ctrl-J. J stands for Jingle.

4. Select the phone number you want to call. If there is more than one phone field in the record, PC-File prompts you to select the phone field you want to use.

5. Wait while the modem dials the number. You can hear the modem dialing and the rings or the busy signal. At this point, PC-File provides instructions on the screen.

6. Pick up the handset and press Enter. Picking up the handset releases the modem from the phone line. Then you can have a phone conversation. Pressing Enter starts the timer that records the length of the call. The timing message appears on the screen.

If you pick up the handset before the modem is finished dialing the number, you interrupt the dialing process.

7. When you finish the call, press Enter again to stop the timer. Then put the handset back on the telephone cradle.

If you want to use your computer while you are talking on the phone, you can stop the timer whenever you want. The timing message disappears from the screen. Then you can continue the phone conversation. The entry in your phone log reflects a shorter call duration because the timer stopped earlier in the call.

Keeping a Phone Log

PC-File keeps a phone log for each database. Each phone call you make is added to the end of the current database phone log. The phone log file name contains the name of the database and the file extension .CDS; for example, CLIENT.CDS. An entry in a phone log contains the current date, phone number dialed, starting time, call duration, and the port to which the modem is connected. The phone log entry also can contain information from fields that include these characters: name, company, city, state, country.

The phone log is in ASCII character format. You can display or print the phone log with any text editor or word processing program that reads ASCII files. The following is a sample phone log created in PC-File.

-09-17 09:10:33 001 PC-File

    COM port 4

    Voice connection

    Connected with Joshua

    Phone number (201)339-4532

    Comment: call placed to New Jersey

-09-17 09:12:33 009 PC-File

    COM port 4

    Comment: 2.0 minutes duration

-09-17 09:13:30 002 PC-File

    COM port 4

    Voice connection

    Connected with Marissa

    Phone number (305)339-4532

    Comment: call placed to Florida

-09-17 09:16:30 009 PC-File

    COM port 4

    Comment: 3.0 minutes duration

> If you have to change the .CDS file extension when displaying or printing the phone log file in a word processing program, be sure to save it as a text file. This way, you can continue adding phone calls to it in PC-File.

You also can use the DOS PRINT command to print the log directly from DOS. To do this, at the DOS prompt change to the directory that contains the phone log file. Then type *print CLIENT.CDS*, for example, and press Enter. DOS prints the phone log to the default printer. For more information on the DOS PRINT command, refer to your DOS documentation.

If you want to delete a phone log you no longer need, you can use the DOS DELETE or ERASE command. First change to the directory that contains the phone log file you want to delete. At the DOS prompt, type *DEL CLIENT.CDS*, for example, and press Enter.

The next time you make a call using the autodialing feature, PC-File creates a new log for the current database.

If the phone doesn't dial, you can check three areas: the phone access commands in the database PRO file, the cable connections, and the modem. The phone access commands normally are added to the PC-File PRO file, but these commands may not be included in the database PRO file. If you open a database for which you want to use auctorial, and the database PRO file doesn't contain the phone access commands, PC-File blanks out the phone access commands in the PC-File Pro file. To fix this problem, select Utilities Configuration, change the phone options, and save the file with the same database name. Making these changes should allow you to dial successfully. Otherwise, check to make sure the cable connections are seated properly or that your modem is operating properly.

Using the Calculator

Instead of using a desktop or pocket calculator, you can use the Calculator feature in PC-File. It lets you perform arithmetic calculations and stores the answer in a buffer. Then you can transfer the answer to a field in your database.

To use the calculator, follow these steps:

1. Select Tools from the menu bar. PC-File displays the Tools menu.

2. Select Calculator from the Tools menu. PC-File displays the Calculator text box. Instead of Step 1 and 2, you can press Ctrl-C to access the calculator.

3. Type the calculation in the text box (see figure 13.5). For example, type *25*89+1*.

4. Click the OK button. PC-File displays the Answer dialog box.

5. If you want to erase the answer, click the OK button. If you want to save the answer to a buffer, click the Memorize button, as shown in figure 13.6.

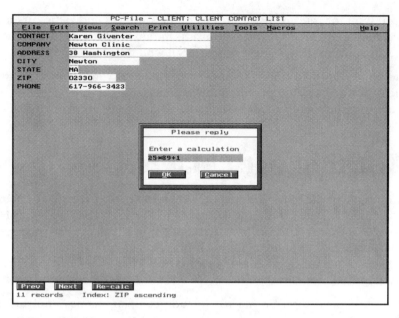

Fig. 13.5. *A calculation in the Calculator text box.*

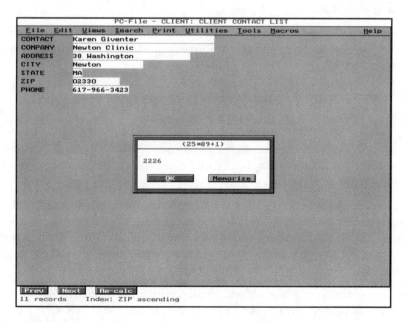

Fig. 13.6. *The Answer dialog box.*

If you want to write an answer from a buffer to a field, move the cursor to the field and press Shift-Ins. PC-File inserts the answer in the field. If the field already contains data, PC-File overwrites it with the answer.

The buffer can hold only one answer at a time. If you perform another calculation and save the answer, PC-File replaces the previous answer in the buffer with the second answer. The buffer is cleared when you exit PC-File.

Working with Macros

Often you type the same information or enter a series of commands. It can be tedious to enter the same keystrokes over and over again. PC-File provides a macro recording feature to remedy this. You can store information and a series of commands to disk for repeated use. This eliminates the need for repetitive typing, and there is less chance for making typing mistakes.

Common items stored in macros include company names, individual's names, cities, ZIP codes, and so on. You also can store a series of commands, such as opening a database, creating and printing a weekly report, and closing a database.

To create a macro, you record the keystrokes and then play them back. Continue reading the next section "Recording a Macro" to create your own macro.

Recording a Macro

Recording a macro saves keystrokes and commands for later use during a PC-File session. You can play back those keystrokes and commands later by pressing only one key.

Keystrokes can be stored with the record function, which acts much like a tape recorder. When the record function is turned on, all keystrokes entered are recorded. Then you can assign a key on your keyboard to the recorded sequence of keystrokes so that you can recall them all with a single keystroke, as explained later in this chapter.

You can use only the keyboard when you record a macro. PC-File ignores the mouse commands during the recording operation and skips over them when you execute the macro.

Before you record a macro in PC-File, it's a good idea to test the steps for the macro. Perform the keystrokes and write them down on a piece of paper. That way, you can record the macro easily by using your notes as a guide.

To record a macro, follow these steps:

1. Select Macros from the menu bar. PC-File displays the Macros menu (see figure 13.7).

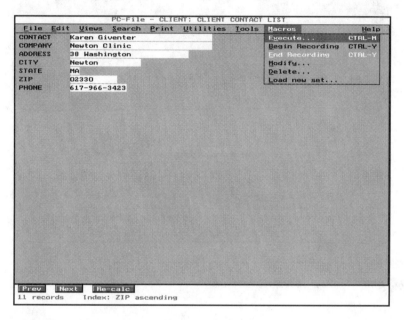

Fig. 13.7. *The Macros menu.*

2. Select Begin recording from the Macros menu.

    PC-File displays the Macro Message window, as shown in figure 13.8.

3. Press Enter to remove the Macro Message window and begin recording. PC-File displays the message, "Recording macro," in the lower right corner of the screen. Every time you press a key, PC-File beeps to remind you that you are recording the keystrokes.

4. Enter the keystrokes and commands you want to store in a macro. The commands perform their normal functions as you record them. For example, select File Close from the menu bar to record the commands for closing a database file.

If you make a mistake, you can correct it while you are recording the macro. As a result, the mistake and the correction are stored in the macro. You must edit the macro as described later in this chapter.

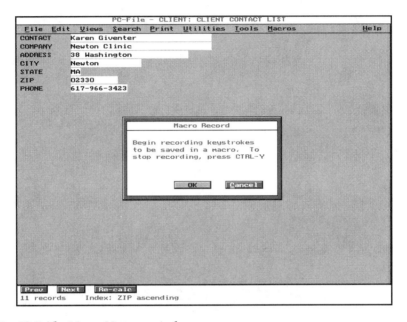

Fig. 13.8. The Macro Message window.

5. When you are finished entering the sequence of keystrokes you want to record, press Select End recording from the Macros menu or press Ctrl-Y again.

   PC-File prompts you to identify the macro and displays the letters a to z in the window, as shown in figure 13.9.

6. Select a letter from the window. For example, *c* is appropriate for identifying the File Close macro. PC-File prompts you to enter a description of the macro. The description is optional; however, you ought to describe the macro so that when you edit the macro, you can clearly identify its contents.

7. Enter a description of the macro; for example, type *closes a database*. A macro description can have a maximum of 30 characters. PC-File displays the macro contents, as shown in figure 13.10.

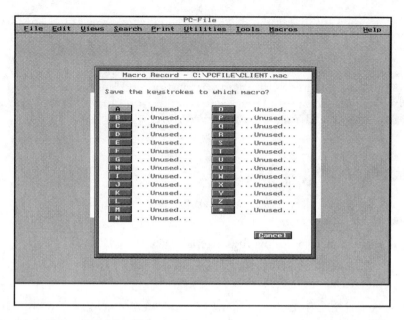

Fig. 13.9. *The macro identifiers.*

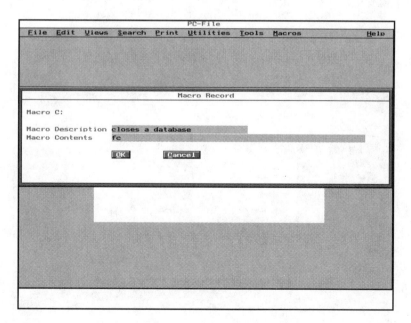

Fig. 13.10. *The macro description and contents.*

8. If you want to edit the macro, you can do so at this point. For information on modifying a macro, refer to your PC-File documentation.

9. When you finish, click the OK button.

PC-File also provides a shortcut for starting and ending the recording function. Instead of using the Macros menus, you can press Ctrl-Y to start recording and Ctrl-Y again to stop recording.

Executing a Macro

Once you record keystrokes, you can execute them to save yourself time and keystrokes.

To execute a macro, follow these steps.

1. Position the cursor where you want to play back the sequence of keystrokes in PC-File.

2. Select Macros from the menu bar and then select Execute from the Macros menu. A shortcut for executing a macro is pressing Ctrl-M. PC-File displays the Macro window, as shown in figure 13.11. The Macro window contains the macro identifier letters.

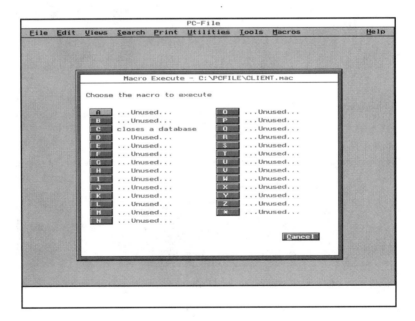

Fig. 13.11. *The Macro Execute window.*

3. Select the letter that represents the macro you want to execute. For example, select *o* to run the File Open macro. You can use the arrow keys to highlight the letter and press Enter, or click with the mouse on the letter.

PC-File executes the macro and plays back the keystrokes you recorded. You can replay the same keystrokes as many times as necessary during the current PC-File session.

To stop executing a macro, press Esc.

Editing a Macro

PC-File lets you edit a macro by modifying the macro keystrokes you recorded in the macro file. Both the macro description and definition can be changed. Macro definitions consist of names enclosed in braces. For example, when you press Enter and record the macro, PC-File enters the macro definition {ENTER} in the macro file. Macro definitions appear in uppercase, but you can use both upper- and lowercase letters when you modify a macro.

To edit a macro, follow these steps:

1. Select Macros from the PC-File menu bar.

2. Select Modify from the macros menu. PC-File displays a list of macro files.

3. Select the macro you want to edit.

4. Make your changes by using the arrow keys to move around the macro contents text box. Use the Insert key to add characters, the DEL key to delete characters, and type over existing characters with new characters. Figure 13.12 shows the Macro dialog box.

5. When you finish making changes, select OK.

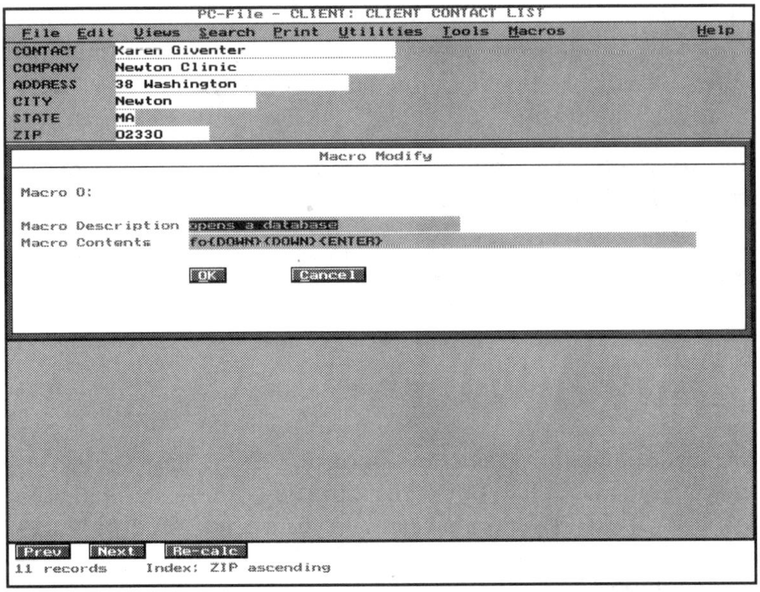

Fig. 13.12. The Macro dialog box.

Creating a Pause Macro

In PC-File, you can create a pause macro that causes the macro to stop and wait for you to enter data from the keyboard. The pause macro is useful when you enter a new title for a report each time you run the report or when you want to enter specific criteria in a formula search.

To create a pause macro, enter the Macro command {INPUT} where you want to prompt the user to enter data from the keyboard. Using the example of entering a new title for a report each time you run the report, your macro entry would look like this:

{TAB} {INPUT} {ENTER}

This simple pause macro inserts a tab and causes the macro to stop. You type the title, press Enter from the keyboard, and the macro resumes by processing the Enter command to move to the next field in the report.

PC-File beeps twice when it encounters an {INPUT} macro command to remind you to enter data from the keyboard. The message "Pausing" displays on your screen also.

Creating a Startup Macro

A startup macro is executed automatically each time you start PC-File or open a database. You cannot invoke a startup macro from the keyboard.

To create a startup macro, you identify the macro with an asterisk (*). For example, you create the macro you want and when PC-File prompts you to select the macro identifier, you select * instead of a letter. Startup macros are handy when you want to make sure that a particular index is the current index when you open the database or when you print a daily report.

You can create one startup macro per database and one startup macro to execute automatically when you start PC-File. If you print a particular daily report every time you start PC-File, you can set up a startup macro to print the report every time you start the file.

Summary

This chapter showed you important features in PC-File that demonstrate the power and sophistication of the program. You learned how to pack a database and how to repair a damaged database. You also learned how to use the Calculator feature. You found out how to use the autodialing feature to place phone calls automatically. Finally, you were shown how easy it is to store and recall keystrokes and commands with macros.

Installing and Configuring PC-File

I n this appendix you review the hardware and software requirements for installing PC-File. You look at the steps for installing PC-File on a hard disk system, and you learn how to configure your system using PC-File's Utilities Configuration command.

Meeting System Requirements

Before you install PC-File, make sure that you have the right hardware and an acceptable version of DOS. You must have the following equipment:

- IBM PC/XT, PC/AT, PS/2, or an IBM-compatible.

- A hard drive with at least 1.5M available, or a minimum of 720K available on a single floppy disk.

- At least 450K available RAM; more RAM is recommended.

- MS-DOS or PC DOS Version 3.0 or later.

- Any of the following monitors: color graphics adapter (CGA), enhanced graphics adapter (EGA), video graphics adapter (VGA), Hercules adapter.

- One of the many printers PC-File supports, including the Hewlett-Packard LaserJet and PostScript printers, cartridges, and soft fonts.

The following equipment is optional:

- Microsoft Windows Version 3.0.
- A Microsoft or Microsoft-compatible mouse.
- A Hayes or Hayes-compatible modem.

Installing PC-File

Installing PC-File takes about 5 minutes. Be sure that you have the time to finish before you start the installation. If you turn off your computer during installation, you will experience difficulty installing the program.

Buttonware has labeled the three 5 1/4-inch disks for ease of reference as Disk One, Disk Two, and Disk Three.

The two 3 1/2-inch disks supplied by Buttonware are labeled for ease of reference as Disk One and Disk Two.

To install PC-File on a hard disk system, follow these steps:

1. Insert the PC-File Disk One in Drive A.

2. At the C> prompt, type *A:* and press Enter to change to the A> prompt.

3. At the A> prompt, type *install* and press Enter.

   The installation program begins. You can exit the program at any time by pressing Ctrl-X. PC-File displays the installation screen.

4. Press any key to continue installing PC-File. You are prompted to select the files you want to install.

5. Use the arrow keys to move the cursor to the files you want and press Enter. For example, to install PC-File for the first time, select Install PC-File 6.0 program and application files. If you want to re-install only the program files, select Install PC-File 6.0 program files only. If you want to install the PC-File 6.0 program and application files to floppy disks, select Install PC-File 6.0 to floppy disks.

   PC-File prompts you to select the drive to which you want to install the files. The amount of space available appears next to the disk drive letter.

6. Select the drive you want to which you want to install PC-File. Use the arrow keys to move the cursor to the drive letter you want and press Enter.

PC-File prompts you to enter the directory to which you want to install the files. The default directory is \pcfile.

7. Accept the default directory PCFILE or change the directory if you want. If you leave the directory text box blank, PC-File creates the default directory called PCFILE automatically.

   Then the install program copies the program files. PC-File displays two status boxes on the screen. The top status box shows you the status of the current file that PC-File is copying. The bottom status box shows you the status of the entire installation procedure.

   When appropriate, PC-File prompts you to insert Disk Two and Disk Three.

8. Remove the disk in the drive and insert the next disk.

   After the program files are installed, PC-File asks you to enter the directory to which you want to install the sample files. These files contain sample databases that you can use with the PC-File tutorial. The default directory for sample files is called PCFILE\SAMPLE.

9. Press Enter to accept the default directory. PC-File asks you if you want changes made to the CONFIG.SYS file.

10. If you want to let PC-File update the number of buffers and files in the CONFIG.SYS file, select the option that lets PC-File make the changes to your CONFIG.SYS file and press Enter. Otherwise, select No to prevent PC-File from making the changes to the CONFIG.SYS file.

11. When you finish installing PC-File, remove the disk from Drive A and put the original disks in a safe place.

Now you are ready to start PC-File (see Chapter 1).

Configuring PC-File

When you have installed PC-File, the next step is to check the configuration parameters in the Configuration profile to see if it suits your needs. For example, you can change the screen colors, set a default database to open when you start the program, or change the printer defaults. Table A.1 lists the configuration parameters and describes each parameter.

Table A.1
Configuration Parameters

Parameter	Description
Mode of operation	Turns graphics mode on and off. VGA, EGA, or Hercules-compatible monochrome is the default for graphics mode. CGA is the default for character mode.
Palette	Specifies screen colors. Blue is the default for VGA, EGA, and CGA. Gray is the default for monochrome.
Default view	Specifies Record View or Table View when you open a database. Record View is the default view.
Case sensitivity	Specifies whether PC-File distinguishes between upper- and lowercase letters during sorts and searches. The default for case-sensitive searches is off. The default for case-sensitive indexes is off.
Database default	Specifies the database you want PC-File to open automatically when you start the program.
Printer defaults	Specifies the printer port, printer, and page length. LPT1 is the default printer port. The default page length is 66 lines.
Dialing	Sets the modem port and enters dialing codes and prefixes for autodialing. COM1 is the default modem port. The default long distance code is 1. ATD is the default modem dialing mode.
Snapshot	Defines the mailing label formats and printer port for generating snapshot labels.
Passwords	Defines passwords for securing a database.

To change a configuration parameter, follow these steps:

1. Select Utilities from the menu bar. PC-File displays the Utilities menu.

2. Select Configuration from the Utilities menu. PC-File displays the Configuration window, as shown in figure A.1.

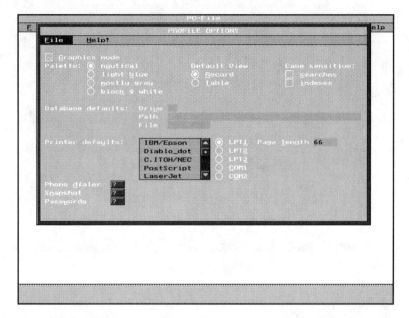

Fig. A.1. The Configuration window.

PC-File also displays a menu bar at the top of the window that contains two options: File and Help. The File command is explained later in this section. The Help command displays a Help window that contains information on the configuration parameters, as shown in figure A.2.

3. Use the arrow keys to move to a parameter you want to change. Select an option button or type the appropriate information to make the changes you want. You can use the keys or the mouse to do this.

4. When you finish changing the parameters, select File from the menu bar. PC-File displays the File menu, as shown in figure A.3.

5. Select Save as from the File menu. PC-File displays a list of configuration files.

6. To save the current profile, type the name in the text box or select the name from the list. Then press Enter. PC-File prompts you to overwrite the current profile with the changes.

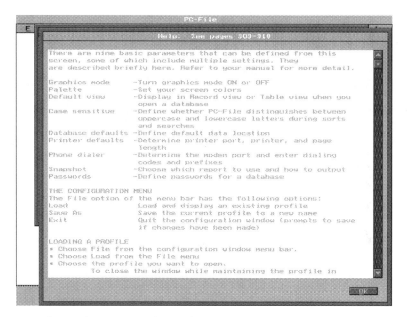

Fig. A.2. *The Configuration Help window.*

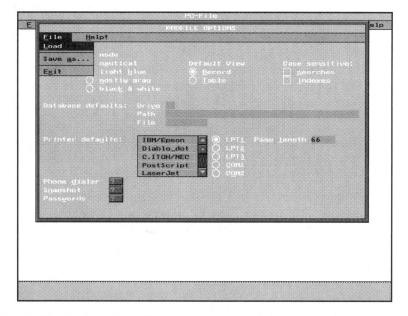

Fig. A.3. *The Configuration File menu.*

7. Select Yes. PC-File updates the configuration file. You can create as many configuration files as you need and switch between them. For example, if you want to change the colors of the screen, create a configuration file and name it GRAY.PRO. When you want to change the screen color to gray, load the GRAY.PRO configuration file.

8. To exit the Configuration window, select File Exit from the menu bar. You are returned to the PC-File menu bar.

B

Quick Reference

Hot Keys

Key	Function
Ctrl-A	Recalculate field data
Ctrl-B	Blank from cursor to end of field or line
Ctrl-C	Access the calculator
Ctrl-D	Drop to DOS
Ctrl-E	Expand memo field to a window
Ctrl-F	Duplicate field from previously viewed record
Ctrl-H	Set insert mode
Ctrl-I	Switch to another index
Ctrl-J	Dial phone number
Ctrl-L	Print snapshot label
Ctrl-M	Display macros menu to execute macro
Ctrl-N	Display next record in Record view
Ctrl-O	Flip data in the current field
Ctrl-P	Display previous record in Record view
Ctrl-R	Duplicate previously viewed record
Ctrl-S	Continue search

Key	Function
Ctrl-T	Switch between Table view and Record view
Ctrl-U	Undo editing in current record
Ctrl-V	View memo window
Ctrl-W	Display current cursor location for letters, Free Form, and language reports
Ctrl-X	Toggle index locking
Ctrl-Y	Begin and end macro recording
Alt-O	Select OK button in dialog boxes and windows
Alt-C	Select Cancel button in dialog boxes and windows
Alt-F7	Use with arrow keys to move dialog boxes and windows
Alt-F8	Use with arrow keys to resize memo window
Alt-F1O	Resize memo window to full screen
Alt-Backspace	Undo editing in the current field
Shift-Del	Delete selected text and copy to buffer
Ctrl-Ins	Copy selected text to buffer
Shift-Ins	Paste selected text from buffer

Index

Q-R

Que Helps You Get The Most From Windows!

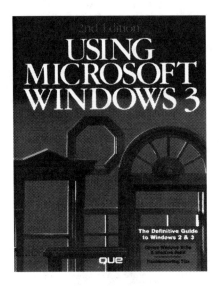

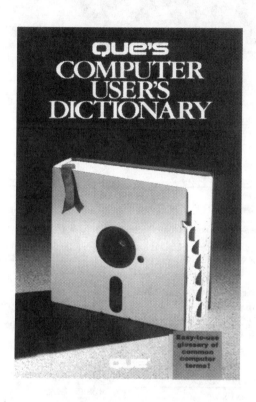

Find It Fast With Que's Quick References!

Que's Quick References are the compact, easy-to-use guides to essential application information. Written for all users, Quick References include vital command information under easy-to-find alphabetical listings. Quick References are a must for anyone who needs command information fast!

Teach Yourself
With QuickStarts From Que!

The ideal tutorials for beginners, Que's QuickStart books use graphic illustrations and step-by-step instructions to get you up and running fast. Packed with examples, QuickStarts are the perfect beginner's guides to your favorite software applications.

1-2-3 for DOS Release 2.3 QuickStart
Release 2.3
$19.95 USA
0-88022-716-8, 500 pp., 7 3/8 x 9 1/4

1-2-3 for Windows QuickStart
1-2-3 for Windows
$19.95 USA
0-88022-723-0, 500 pp., 7 3/8 x 9 1/4

1-2-3 Release 3.1 + QuickStart, 2nd Edition
Releases 3 & 3.1
$19.95 USA
0-88022-613-7, 569 pp., 7 3/8 x 9 1/4

dBASE IV 1.1 QuickStart,
Through Version 1.1
$19.95 USA
0-88022-614-5, 400 pp., 7 3/8 x 9 1/4

Excel 3 for Windows QuickStart
Version 3 fo rWindows
$19.95 USA
0-88022-762-1, 500 pp., 7 3/8 x 9 1/4

MS-DOS QuickStart, 2nd Edition
Version 3.X & 4.X
$19.95 USA
0-88022-611-0, 420 pp., 7 3/8 x 9 1/4

Q&A 4 QuickStart
Versions 3 & 4
$19.95 USA
0-88022-653-6, 400 pp., 7 3/8 x 9 1/4

Quattro Pro 3 QuickStart
Through Version 3.0
$19.95 USA
0-88022-693-5, 450 pp., 7 3/8 x 9 1/4

WordPerfect 5.1 QuickStart
WordPerfect 5.1
$19.95 USA
0-88022-558-0, 427 pp., 7 3/8 x 9 1/4

Windows 3 QuickStart
Ron Person & Karen Rose

This graphics-based text teaches Windows beginners how to use the feature-packed Windows environment. Emphasizes such software applications as Excel, Word, and PageMaker and shows how to master Windows' mouse, menus, and screen elements.

Version 3
$19.95 USA
0-88022-610-2, 440 pp., 7 3/8 x 9 1/4

MS-DOS 5 QuickStart
Que Development Group

This is the easy-to-use graphic approach to learning MS-DOS 5. The combination of step-by-step instruction, examples, and graphics make this book ideal for all DOS beginners.

DOS 5
$19.95 USA
0-88022-681-1, 420 pp., 7 3/8 x 9 1/4

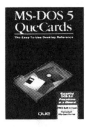
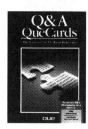

BUSINESS REPLY MAIL

First Class Permit No. 9918   Indianapolis, IN

Postage will be paid by addressee

11711 N. College
Carmel, IN 46032

BUSINESS REPLY MAIL

First Class Permit No. 9918   Indianapolis, IN

Postage will be paid by addressee

11711 N. College
Carmel, IN 46032